Pray With Me

365 DAYS OF INTERCESSORY PRAYER

A *Journey To Joy* Book

Jamila Jackson

Copyright © 2024 jamiladanielle designworks

Jamila Jackson

Pray With Me: 365 Days of Intercessory Prayer

All rights reserved. No part of this publication may be reproduced, stored in a retrieval system, or transmitted in any form or by any means, electronic, mechanical, photocopying, recording, or otherwise without the prior written permission of the author and publisher.

Published in the United States by loved+blessed®, an imprint of jamiladanielle designworks publishing, a division of jamiladanielle designworks.

loved+blessed® is a registered trademark of jamiladanielle designworks.

www.lovedandblessed.com

Cover Design by: Jamila Jackson

Author Photograph by: Christopher L. Malcolm Photography

ISBN: 978-1-7372395-2-9

2024 – First Edition

DEDICATION

To the God of all creation, who designed me with a purpose and assigned me the task of writing this book. I pray that it reaches the prayer warriors that You selected before the foundation of the earth to pray with me.

To my husband, Micah, who challenged me to pray out loud and expanded my understanding of the power of praying with others.

To my Mom, who modeled the importance of kneeling nightly before God. To my Dad, who showed me that worship is prayer.

To my friend Paula, who encouraged me to finish this assignment by reminding me that God has someone waiting on this book.

And to you, my fellow prayer warrior. Someone needs to be lifted up and covered by the prayers we will pray together. Let's get started.

Hey You,

Thank you for opening this book. Thank you for joining me in prayer. The Holy Spirit inspired me to write a book of intercessory prayers. He was very specific in His instruction. Jamila, don't write prayers for others to speak over themselves, help them be less self-focused and lift up others. He started with me y'all. He challenged me to find a balance between praying for myself and my loved ones and praying for those I don't know and will never meet. He challenged me to pray for people I think "deserve" my prayers and people who I can't stand. His Word tells us to pray without ceasing, to pray for our enemies, and to pray in all circumstances. So, this is my effort to be obedient to His instruction. It started with daily prayer prompts that I post inside of the lovedandblessed.com community and now has expanded to this book.

I ask for your grace in advance, because if you know me, you know I write the same way I speak….in long run-on, sometimes stream of consciousness sentences. I also throw commas and other punctuation around and leave them wherever they fall. I apologize to my Mom and those who will notice the many grammatical errors in this page and the pages that follow. I've chosen to leave each prayer written exactly how I prayed it, run-on sentences and all. I hope this won't distract you. Instead, I hope that my genuine unedited prayers will encourage you to be free and kneel before God as you are. The one true God isn't checking our grammar, He is checking our hearts. He hears every silent prayer and the ones spoken aloud too. He understands and answers the ones that are perfectly formatted, the ones that are incomplete sentences, and the ones that come out as groans.

Thank you for praying on behalf of others and going on this journey of intercessory prayer with me. I hope it will transform your prayer life as it has transformed mine.

Hugs,

jamila

DAY 1

FOR THOSE STRUGGLING WITH A DECISION THEY MADE

Father God, Today I pray for those who are struggling with a decision they made. Their struggle is a blessing because it means they are aware that there may be something left undone or something that needs to change about their decision. Thank You Father for convicting their heart. I don't know how they came to their decision or if they sought You as they were making it, but I do know that You say in Your Word that You will never leave or forsake us. I pray they are seeking You as they wrestle with the consequences they are experiencing or know will come. If their decision was in disobedience to what You told them to do, then I pray they seek Your forgiveness. I pray they seek Your guidance of how to proceed forward as they surrender to Your Will for whatever comes next. Let them know that there is nothing they can do to separate them from Your love even if they have made a terrible mistake. Humble them and strengthen them to give themselves grace as You have already done. Give them the humility and courage to make right whatever they have done wrong in Your eyes. If this involves apologizing to someone, please give the recipient of the apology a heart of kindness and mind to be understanding and accepting. If this involves breaking a promise they should not have made to someone, please prepare that person's heart and help them see why even if they are disappointed, this change is what is best. In the course of correcting the original decision, help everyone involved see Your hand in the situation. In the name of Jesus. Amen.

DAY 2

FOR PRAYER WARRIORS

Father God, thank you first for the ability to pray. I can't imagine not being able to communicate with You. I am so grateful. It can be hard to maintain a consistent prayer life that includes thanksgiving and praise and requests for not only me and those I love, but also for others too. It is also tough to pray without ceasing when what we see does not line up with our hopes in regards to how You will answer our prayers. So today I pray for the prayer warriors. Your children who never give up. The ones who have been praying for me that I don't even know. The ones who consistently constantly pray for others, asking nothing for themselves in return. I pray that You always hear them. I pray that they pray in accordance with Your Word and in alignment with Your Will. I pray You would continually fill them with hope so that they never give up seeking You for help. Oh, Father thank You for hearing all the prayers, no matter how many they pray. Thank You for hearing every voice that is directed towards You and being faithful to answer every time. Thank you for the prayer warriors. In Jesus' name, Amen.

DAY 3

FOR CHILDREN EXPERIENCING HOMELESSNESS

Oh Father, for the children from birth to teenage years who don't have a permanent roof over their heads, I pray. Give them a sense of safety and security in You, even if they don't have a home. For those living in a car, on the street, in a hotel or couch surfing, please send them a special dose of care. Protect them from being taken advantage of. Protect them from feeling discouraged and give them hope that things will get better. Help them to stay clean physically and also not turn to drugs, alcohol or crime in desperation. Provide food and clean water. If they are with their family, please make a way for their parents to find consistent employment way above the poverty line so that they are able to provide a home for these children and cover the expenses of life. May any medical needs they have be tended to, give them access to care. And please make a way for education to be available to them. Give them the foundation they need to not fall behind their peers. If these children are alone, Father I pray Your Holy Spirit would guide them into safe shelters where they can get the support and resources they need to persevere and get access to what they need so that they can build a life for themselves. I thank You in advance for how You will make a way out of no way for them and give them a testimony of strength, perseverance and praise to share with others. May they always know there is a better future for them even when they can't see how they are going to get there. In the name of Jesus, Amen and Amen.

DAY 4

FOR THOSE CURRENTLY AFFECTED BY A FIRE

Father God, I come before you thanking You for Your mercy that is new every morning, but also asking for your protection for those currently effected by fires. For those whose homes have already been lost. Lord, I ask You to comfort those who are grieving the loss of all their possessions. I know that they are "things" but it is not easy to accept that all you own, all you've worked for, the mementos and gifts you've been given are gone. Please give them shelter Lord, see that their needs are met as they cope with this unexpected loss. Father, I pray Your protection over those who may still be in harm's way, those who have not been evacuated. For the firefighters and safety personnel who are managing this situation, please give them the strength and strategies to put out the flames. Father I just ask Your mercy upon these people. Father whatever the cause of the fire, we know You are still in control and can put out the flames. In Jesus' name, Amen.

DAY 5

FOR THOSE STARTING COLLEGE

Father, I come before You today praying for those who are starting college in this season. It is an exciting and scary time. Such a big life change and yet change is the norm in life. I pray for protection for those staying local and those going far from home. No matter where they are that You would put Your hedge of protection around them and comfort their families by removing any worry. Father, I ask that You help them to focus on their studies and not get distracted by all the newness of the experience and the craziness of college life. Help them to make good friends that will last a lifetime. Help them to enjoy this season of their life and may it prepare them for what You have planned for their future. Thank You for allowing them the opportunity to go to college. Not everyone gets that chance so we don't take that for granted and I pray they will be good stewards of this opportunity. In the name of Jesus. Amen.

DAY 6

FOR THOSE HAVING A HARD TIME PRAYING

Father, Son, and Holy Spirit, I come before you on behalf of those who are having a hard time praying. They have a desire to pray and want to feel connected to You yet they feel distant at the same time. Help them to not allow everything that is going on around them to consume too much of their time and focus. May Your Holy Spirit fill their mind, clearing out anything that is distracting them from You. Pull them into Your light if they have retreated into darkness, and help them be determined to make their way out with You. Help them not to focus their eyes on earth but on Heaven. Help them to lift their eyes to You, the Maker of heaven and earth because You will not let them slip and be distracted by the world's chaos. Give them confidence that You are listening and that they don't need the perfect words in order to bring their prayers to You. Help them to feel Your peace and let their thoughts and words flow freely to You. Let them know that You hear them and that their prayers do not go into a void. May Your peace be upon them forevermore. Amen.

DAY 7

FOR FAMILIES STRUGGLING TO SPEND QUALITY TIME TOGETHER

Father, in this world full of things that can distract our attention, so many families are having a hard time prioritizing spending quality time together. Or when we do all get together, we still find things to distract us like watching sports or a movie or going to an amusement park, which are all good, but we so rarely just sit down, hang out, and chat. With our immediate families and extended families – with the families You bless us with by blood and the families we have made for ourselves. Father, I come before you to ask that You would help families around the world to get free of the busyness and drama and seize opportunities to get together more to just catch up and listen and talk about what is going on in their lives. May these be times to laugh and enjoy each other's company in meaningful ways. In the name of Jesus. Amen.

DAY 8

FOR THOSE WHO HAVE HAD THEIR IDENTITY STOLEN

Father, this is such a frightening feeling. Some experience this violation from strangers and others through the betrayal of someone they know. No matter the situation, it is hard emotionally and financially. It has become so common in this fallen world. Please help those who are in this situation to stop the fraud that is being perpetrated on them. Remove any financial debt that has been caused. Remove all access that the thieves have to their personal information and finances. Give the person experiencing this relief from anxiety and worry as they deal with getting things straightened out. Whether someone has stolen their credit card or bank details or someone has stolen their social security number or even image and social profile online, give them peace and patience as they work through everything, they have to do to get control of their identity back. However, they are being violated please give them strength and let them know that it will all be cleared up and they will have victory. May Your judgment be upon the perpetrators and may they be prevented from doing this to others. In the mighty name of Jesus, Amen.

DAY 9

FOR THOSE WHO HAVE LOST A MOTHER

Father, Son, and Holy Spirit having a mom or woman in your life who fills that role is a blessing beyond description. Mothers are special and Your Word calls them blessed. I thank You for every mother today and for those who have passed away. The pain of losing a mom can feel unbearable and the grieving can go on for what seems like forever, BUT GOD, we know You are our Comforter, You are a mother to the motherless, so we ask You to comfort those who have lost a mom. Fill their minds with loving memories that make them laugh and smile. May Your Spirit surround them like a mother's hug so they know they are not alone. Be with them as they grieve and please turn their mourning to joy as they give thanks for the mother You blessed them with here on this earth and that I pray is now rejoicing with You in heaven. In Jesus' name, Amen.

DAY 10

FOR TAXI AND RIDE-SHARE DRIVERS

Father, I pray for those who provide transportation for others, specifically for taxi and ride-share drivers. For those who use a company-provided car or their own vehicle to take people where they want or need to go. I pray for their protection and safety as they drive. Not only protection from any car accidents or incidents but also protection from any danger that a passenger might pose. I pray that every person who enters their car will have a spirit of peace and gratitude for the service that is being provided. I pray for the safety of the passengers as well. Father, give the drivers the rest they need to be alert, the discernment to make good decisions in the routes that they take, and a joy in their hearts that is felt by every person who gets into their car. In the name of Jesus, Amen.

DAY 11

FOR THOSE WHO DON'T HAVE HEALTH INSURANCE

Oh, Father how some take for granted sometimes that they can go to the doctor without fear of having to pay the bills. How some take it for granted so much that we put off scheduling routine appointments that are completely financially covered when there are so many who struggle to be able to get a routine physical exam, to see a dentist or eye doctor even for the basic care needed to function in life. Father, for those without health insurance, I pray You would make a way for them to get the medical wellness care they need and mental wellness care they need without going into debt. I pray You would provide access in ways that they don't expect. And that they would actually get full coverage for themselves and their families. And a special prayer for those who are already struggling under the weight of medical bills that are were not covered by insurance, Father, please give them relief. Clear their debt so they would not feel the mental anxiety that they feel. Make a way for payment plans or complete debt forgiveness. Please do not let money get in the way of any serious lifesaving procedures that are needed for anyone. In the name of Jesus. Amen.

DAY 12

FOR BELIEVERS TO HAVE AN OPEN HEART

Father, as believers we are always in a season of learning. Learning about you, ourselves, others, and the world. I pray we would be open to everything You have to teach us. That we would be listening for the Holy Spirit moment by moment. That we would learn through studying the scriptures, personal reflection and the insights of others that You have given wisdom to. Help us to discern who to listen to and learn from. Help us to not miss any lesson You are teaching us, no matter how hard it may be. Open our hearts and minds to humbly hear You. Give all believers an open heart, not closed off by hurt, anger or pain. Open hearts towards you and others. Open minds towards all people, seeing them as worthy of love and respect as part of Your creation. Challenge believers to live in the world and not close our hearts off from it. Remind us that we can't do Your work and shine Your light if we do not confront darkness. Like the Bible says, may all believers turn to You with an open heart so that the veil is lifted and we can truly see. And may our openness bring us into a deeper understanding and relationship with You. Amen.

DAY 13

FOR RECONCILIATION BETWEEN ESTRANGED FAMILY MEMBERS

Oh, Father, I come before you on behalf of those who need reconciliation in their family. I ask that You would touch the hearts of those who are estranged. Help them see beyond what has happened in the past, help everyone in this situation to heal, help everyone to forgive, help everyone to see each other through Your loving and merciful eyes. May the reconciliation be a testimony of their family's love of You. May that testimony be an example to the younger generations who will remember it as they grow up and one day have families of their own. May the landscape of the deep valley estranged family members are experiencing begin to rise up and up and lift the whole family to a place of joy and peace. In the name of Jesus. Amen.

DAY 14

FOR THOSE WHO SERVE IN THE ARMED FORCES

Father, I come before you praying for those who serve in our armed forces. I pray thanksgiving for their willingness to serve! I ask for their physical protection and the protection of those they will serve alongside. For their emotional protection, that the Holy Spirit would help them to process the things they will see and experience throughout their service. For their mental acuity to help them learn, train and grow, and perform their duties to the utmost ability that You would give them Oh Lord. For wisdom and guidance in all their decisions. That they would always know how much their family and friends love them. That they would feel the support of their country. For comfort in any moments of homesickness or loneliness. For courage in moments of fear. That they would hear words of encouragement and hope as whispers from Your Holy Spirit in moments of doubt. That they would stay in great health and physical shape. That they would make lifelong friends whom they can talk to and feel like someone understands what they go through. That they would serve with honor and be appreciated for all they accomplish. And that their service would bring You glory and fulfill the unique and special purpose that You have for their life. In the name of Jesus, Amen.

DAY 15

FOR CONSTRUCTION WORKERS

Thank You Lord for those with the talent and skill to build! Those who have the physical strength to work construction and the knowledge to know how to do things properly so that buildings are functional, beautiful, and safe! May we never take for granted the hands that built the structures we walk into or pass by. We ask for Your protection upon them as they do their work. Keep them safe from danger or harm. Please provide the equipment and resources and training they need to do their jobs with excellence. May they be proud of what they have built. Bless the labor of their hands. Also, give them rest and relief from their aches and pains from physical labor. May they have the health insurance they need to take care of their bodies. May they be paid a fair wage for their work and be able to provide for themselves and their families. Thank You for these amazing men and women who work in the field of construction Lord! Amen.

DAY 16

FOR SENSELESS TRAGEDIES

Father God, somewhere in the world Your people are heartbroken that a tragedy has occurred today. I pray for everyone effected, especially the families of anyone who lost their lives. I pray their loved ones are now rejoicing with You. For those who are left to grieve Father, I pray for Your comfort now. That Your Spirit would speak to their hearts and help them through their time of mourning. Father, for the surrounding community I pray they would be strengthened and come together to love on one another. Father this world has experienced tragedy before and we know in this fallen world, more tragedy will come, but Father we will not fear. We will remain strong because we know You are still in control. We may not understand why these senseless things are allowed to happen, but we do know You Lord and I have faith in You. I pray that these tragedies will ultimately draw us closer together as people and closer to You. Father please heal those who are heartbroken please encourage those who are in despair. In Jesus' name I pray. Amen.

DAY 17

FOR THOSE WHO HAVE LIED

Father, first I acknowledge that I have lied. I repent for any lies I have not already confessed and ask Your forgiveness now. Please hear my prayer. I know lying grieves You. So, I come before You to pray for those who have lied. No matter what the lie is about, I know there are no big or small lies. Lying is a sin. Please help those who have lied to acknowledge and repent, so that they may represent You well in all they do. Help them be a good reflection of You with their choices, showing that the truth is always the right answer. For those who have lied thinking that they are protecting someone else, help them instead to speak the truth with love and compassion even in difficult situations. Help them to navigate conflict that may come from the truth. Even as I pray for liars now, knowing that as Paul said, I am chief among them, I praise You for how You have used those sins in my past for Your glory. How my repentance has often been met with undeserved blessings. So, Father, I pray You would do the same for others. Convict their spirits of the lies they have told and help them to be an example of humility to others. Use it to help them grow in character and to testify that we are all sinners and that it is only by Your grace that we are saved. Deepen their faith and grow their desire to walk by the Spirit in all that they do and ay. Father, for those who are caught in the midst of a lie right now, I pray they will lay the situation at your feet and rest because they know You will work it all out for good. Help us all accept that there are consequences to our actions and praise You for how You use everything as a part of Your plan. In Jesus' name, I pray. Amen.

DAY 18

FOR WRITERS

Father God, for those with the desire to write please help them to use their words for Your glory. To educate, entertain, and positively encourage the world. Not to cause division or pain. May the words that You created be used for good and not evil. Help them have clearness of mind and discern what you want them to say. Let them know that their voice matters. Give them confidence that they have something important to say. Renew their determination when they want to give up. Remove distractions that cause writer's block and fears to cloud their minds. Provide the tools they need to write, whether that be a computer, a typewriter a pencil, or a pen. Thank You for the talent You've given them to express their thoughts and tell a story. Thank you for the courage of those who will share their testimony to encourage others and remind them they are not alone. Thank You for those who will write educational material of any kind and help others expand their knowledge. Thank You for fiction and non-fiction writers. Thank You for the secular and religious content You inspire them to create. Whatever You have called them to write may it be received by its intended audience in celebration of what they have co-written with You. In the name of Jesus, Amen.

DAY 19

FOR PEACE ON EARTH

God the Father, the Son and the Holy Spirit, let there be peace on Earth. Let us all show goodwill towards each other. Not just during holiday seasons, but every single day. May Your peace live in our hearts and minds. May we treat each other the way that we hope to be treated. May we see each other as brothers and sisters first, as Your children always, no matter our differences or hurts we've caused each other. May there be peace within each individual heart, within families, within communities, within churches, within businesses, within schools, within governments, between cities, states and countries. May Your peace that surpasses all understanding rain down upon us and reign throughout the Earth. Amen.

DAY 20

FOR POLITICIANS

Father, I pray fervently for all those in politics here in the country where I live and around the world. Give them wisdom and discernment in their decisions. Convict them of things they are doing that are not for the good of those they represent. Give them a sense of compassion for others and a desire to fully understand the challenges they are leading the way to fixing. Help them to listen to each other with respect. Give them clarity of when to stand their ground and when to seek compromise that is for the good of Your people. Direct their hearts and minds and humble them to know that they have no power without You. Remind them that their role is to serve and give them a servant's heart. Protect them and keep them safe from harm and danger. Encourage them to not give up on fighting for what is right and defending those who do not have the power or voice to defend themselves. Thank you, Lord, for those politicians who serve others and are not self-seeking. Encourage them when they feel like the obstacles they face are insurmountable. Remind them that nothing is impossible with You. Lift them up and help them to do great things in this world for Your Glory! In Jesus mighty name, Amen.

DAY 21

FOR THOSE WHO DON'T HAVE ACCESS TO THE INTERNET

Oh, how we can take the internet for granted! There are people all over the world and even here in the country where I live, that don't have access to the internet. We use the internet for so many things today. How disenfranchised people who cannot access it are. We use it to stream entertainment and things like social media, yes, but it has also become an important part of daily life, helping us with so many basic needs. It is the place where so much information is stored. It has become our encyclopedia for knowledge on demand. It is the tool that we use to share urgent news quickly of emergencies, impending natural disasters and so much more. It is essential for access to education, jobs, banking, medical services, and mental health resources. It is used to connect devices in our homes like phones, televisions, and even security alarms. Some even have internet access in their cars, for navigation or emergency SOS services. For those who do not have access to the internet, please let it not be an obstacle to the plans You have for their life. Whether it is not available in their area or they cannot afford it, I pray that You would help them gain access to everything they need through other resources. Help them stay connected to others through offline modes of communication. If it's Your Will Father, I pray that You would give them access so that they can choose to use it if they want to. Father, thank You for the ways that the internet makes our lives easier and I pray that everyone around the world would be able to have internet access as a tool. In Jesus' name, Amen.

DAY 22

FOR THOSE WHO TURN TO FOOD

Father, thank You for all the delicious food we can experience here on Earth! What delicacies You allow us to enjoy! Yet, there are times when we turn to food not for enjoyment or nourishment, but to soothe our pain or relieve our anxiety. Father, for those who turn to food instead of You, I ask You to give them self-control. Direct them to healthier ways of processing what they feel. Help them find outlets that support their mental and physical wellness. Father, let them not feel shame for turning to food, but convict their spirits to turn to You instead. Help them with their specific need. You know why they turn to food. You know every detail and emotion they feel. Give them victory over anything that is unhealthy in their relationship to food. Let them taste and see that You O Lord, You are good and sufficient to fulfill all their needs. Let those around them be a support and encouragement, reinforcing that they have the strength to resist any temptation. Whatever their battle – overeating, bulimia, anorexia, binge eating, yo-yo dieting, addictions to caffeine, sugar, salt – anything that we do that is an attempt to use food in an unhealthy way please break this addiction. For those who use it to feel a sense of control, I pray that You would help them surrender their control to You. For those who use it to calm anxiety, I pray that You would help them to cast their cares on You. For those who use it to mask or ease their pain, I pray that You would help them to overcome and find relief. Amen and Amen.

DAY 23

FOR THOSE WHO WILL BE IN A CAR ACCIDENT TODAY

Father, we never expect to be in an accident but we know that You already know what car accidents will occur today, tomorrow, and in this coming week. I ask in advance that you protect all those who will find themselves in this situation and that they will not be hurt physically or mentally by this experience. That no bystanders will be injured. That no one who sees the accident will be emotionally scarred. That the vehicles involved would be strong and protect the occupants from harm. That the vehicles would not be damaged beyond repair. That You would make a way for them to be repaired and operable so that they still have transportation. May everyone involved remain calm no matter who is at fault and work to resolve things justly. May they all be wearing their seatbelts and if there are any young kids may their car seats be secured properly and keep them safe. May any animals also be properly harnessed or in a carrier that protects them from injury. If it is Your Will to allow someone involved to physically be hurt today, may they get the medical help they need quickly and recover to full strength. I pray for the strength, willingness, and compassion of anyone who stops to help and of the emergency or law enforcement personnel who are called to any scene. In the name of Jesus. Amen.

DAY 24

FOR THOSE RECOVERING FROM BACK SURGERY

Father, You are the Healer and great physician. You designed our bodies with such detail and care. What imagination to design our spines and back muscles with such intricacy. For those who are recovering from back surgery in this season of their lives, please encourage them throughout the process. When they have to push through the pain and when they feel like their recovery isn't going as quickly as they want. Give them patience coupled with perseverance to follow through on everything they need to do to regain their ability again. May the doctors, nurses, physical therapists, and others who are involved in their care give them good guidance on what to do, how active to be, and when they need to rest. May they show compassion at all times. May the family or support system of those recovering also practice patience and compassion as they help their loved one recover. May they cheer them on when they feel discouraged. For those recovering Lord, please give them a vision of their future self to cling onto in moments when they have to push through the pain and discomfort that is a normal part of the recovery process. May their full recovery be their testimony for others they will meet who will go through a similar experience in the future. I thank You in advance for their healing and continued strength. In Jesus' Name, Amen.

DAY 25

FOR THOSE IN A SEASON OF CHANGE

Change is exciting, but sometimes fear of the unknown and anxiety accompanies it. When that fear creeps in we can't let it derail us from enjoying the journey and putting our trust in You. Father, thank you for change. Thank you for keeping our lives moving forward in the direction You have planned. We know that Your plans are for our good (Jeremiah 29:11) and we should not lose heart in our momentary struggles (2 Corinthians 4:16-17) There is a season for everything and for Your reasons this is the season You have allowed us to be in right now. (Ecclesiastes 3:1) So we will not despair or let our fear derail us from following the path You are revealing before us. We will be strong and courageous (Deuteronomy 31:6) encouraged in knowing that even in this time of change for us, You are always the same. (Hebrews 13:8) So we trust this new thing You are doing in our lives (Isaiah 43:19) and will not be anxious (Philippians 4:6-7). Thank you, Father. In Your Son, Jesus' Name, Amen.

DAY 26

FOR POLICE OFFICERS WHO HAVE BEEN SHOT

I thank You God for the willingness of police officers to protect and serve their fellow man. I thank You for the courage You give them to run toward danger when most of us would run away. I pray You would guide and give wisdom to every officer, to help them handle every situation they find themselves in with Your love, grace, and sense of justice. And especially today for those who have been shot in the line of duty, I pray for their complete healing. Physically and mentally. That they would not experience any lasting physical challenges or mental trauma from their experience. That You would completely restore. In the name of Jesus. Amen.

DAY 27

FOR THOSE WHO WORK IN THE AIRLINE INDUSTRY

What a marvelous thing it is that we can travel by air! Thank you for allowing the invention of airplanes and the whole industry that air travel has now become. Today I pray for those who work in the airline industry. For pilots, please give them adequate rest, so that they are alert and able to fly planes safely through any turbulence they may encounter. Help them remember their training and guide their hands with skill as they take off and land. For flight attendants, who are responsible for getting passengers safely onto and off of the plane, making sure everyone is aware of what to do in an emergency, and ensuring everyone has a pleasant flight, please give them joy in their hearts and the ability to deal with kind and unkind passengers in their care. May they be treated with respect and not taken for granted, harassed, or hurt in any way. For air traffic controllers, the ground crew, and anyone else who participates in guiding the planes on runways, tarmacs, at the gate, and along their flight paths, please give them alertness and eyes to see and the words to communicate to keep everyone safe and avert any accidents. For air marshals, help them to protect those in flight and give them discernment to know when to step in and how to handle each situation they face. For security agents, TSA agents, and airport police, please help them do their jobs to the utmost ability you would give them to ensure the safety of all who pass through the airport and who board a plane. For those who make or load food that will be consumed by passengers in the airport or on the planes, thank You. For those who keep the airports and planes clean, thank You. For baggage handlers and gate agents, thank You. For the mechanics who ensure the planes operate properly and are maintained, thank You! There are so many people and roles that I know nothing about, so I ask that You cover anyone I have left out of this prayer, because I know that You know them all. In Jesus' name, Amen.

DAY 28

FOR ACTORS

Jesus, I lift up to you actors. Those just starting out and those who have a long list of credits to their name. Those who act in stage plays, T.V. shows, movies or any form of entertainment. Father, I thank You for allowing them to participate in their passion, regardless of whether it is the way they make their living or something they do for fun. Through their acting may they gain a deeper understanding of the human condition. As they prepare for each role, may it be a tool You use to open their eyes to the lived experience of others, as they play characters that are different from themselves. May they find fulfillment through their work and may it have a positive impact on the audience that sees it. For actors who are feeling discouraged in their careers, please give them hope and direction to know what the next step You want them to take is in their career. For actors who are feeling encouraged, may they share some of their joy with others in their industry who struggle. For all actors, give them discernment in the roles You want them to audition for and accept. Give them eyes to see beyond the compensation or the glitz and glamour of a project and to understand the impact it will have on the world. Help them to know that if they pass on a role that You have told them not to accept, that You have something better planned for them in the future. Please help actors continue to improve at their craft and bless them for the entertainment that they provide to the world. In the name of Jesus, Amen.

DAY 29

FOR PEOPLE WHO WON'T EAT TODAY

Not everyone will eat today. Many around the world will go hungry. Some may even be right next door. Father, You are The Provider. I pray that someone who is hungry will be blessed with a meal today. I pray that all who hunger would be nourished by You and that You would provide food for their belly and comfort for their souls. No having enough food to eat can affect our mental well-being Lord, so I pray that You would also give them the strength to make it through the hunger pains and frustration of not being able to eat. If I cross paths today with someone who is hungry Lord, please convict my heart and mind to be the one who blesses them with something to eat. Even if it means giving them something I planned to eat myself. Use me Lord. And put this same conviction into the hearts of others who will encounter someone who is hungry. Let us not take for granted how important that food is and do what we can to help meet the basic needs of others. We often think of those who are living on the streets, but I recognize that there are also people in their homes right now Lord, who can't afford to buy food or who are skipping meals so that others in their family can be fed. In all circumstances, I pray that everyone, around the world, has at least one meal today. In the name of Your precious Son Jesus I pray, Amen.

DAY 30

FOR MEMBERS OF A HATE GROUP

Oh Father, please I beg You to cleanse the minds of those who are a part of any group that has hatred in their heart for others. Your greatest commands tell us to love - to love You and love others as ourselves. Open their eyes to see that they don't love You or themselves when they hate others. No matter the reasons that they believe their hate is warranted, whatever pain the enemy tapped into to fill their minds with hate, I pray those shackles would be broken! In the name of Jesus, that they would be snapped out of the lies that they live by and realize that the group they are in is evil and toxic. Convict their hearts that You are not proud of their behavior and increase in them a desire to seek Your Truth. Especially for those in hate groups that claim to know You Lord. Oh, Father, they do not represent Your love, they do not represent Your righteousness - open their eyes to see You, to see Your Truth - to actually understand Your Word is for every person on this earth and that they are not superior to anyone else. Humble them in Your presence Lord. May their knees bow and may they repent of their wicked and evil ways. May their minds be cleansed. May whatever wounds and hurts caused them to be open to hateful beliefs be healed. May these groups break up as member after member sees the light and walks towards their future with love for You and others in their hearts. In the mighty matchless name of Jesus and Abba Father with Your Holy Spirit who can do above what we can imagine or think! Amen.

DAY 31

FOR THOSE WHO ARE LEARNING ANOTHER LANGUAGE

Father, there are so many languages in the world. Not being able to fluently communicate with each other can cause confusion, so I pray today for those around the world who are trying to learn another language. I marvel at Your creativity in all the different languages that are spoken and even the uniqueness within languages like Spanish which is spoken differently in different parts of the world! It's amazing! And yet it can be hard to learn a new language. So please give perseverance to those who are trying. Help them understand and recall and speak with clear pronunciation. Help them learn to speak and read and write. The more of us who can understand each other the better! The more people who can communicate, the more unity we can have. The more empathy and understanding. So oday, Lord, please help those who are learning a new language no matter their reason why, no matter their age, no matter the language. Help those who are learning a spoken language and those who are learning sign language. Help them stay dedicated to learning until they are fluent. Help them to practice and not feel nervous when they communicate. May those who already speak the language respond with compassion when mistakes are made because they appreciate that the other person is trying. Thank You for the beauty of all languages and help us to all appreciate them more. Amen.

DAY 32

FOR THOSE IN PRISON

Father, first please forgive me for any judgment or assumptions in my heart about how or why someone is in prison. I know prisons around the world are filled with those who are truly guilty and those who are not. The Bible, through the life of Paul, is proof that You allow innocent people to be imprisoned for Your purpose. So today I pray without reservation or judgment for those who are in prison for whatever reason. May they have the mental and emotional strength to make it through. May no physical harm fall upon them. May they receive the nourishment they need to survive with the food that is provided. May they have access to and take advantage of the resources like therapy or educational or work programs. May these either set them up for a successful return into society if that is Your Will. Or may these resources help them to live a life that has meaning and contributes positively to others from inside the prison walls if Your Will is for them to remain there. I pray that those who may need psychiatric care receive it. Those who have health issues would receive treatment. That those who work in, run, and manage the prison would do their jobs with excellence, remembering that the prisoners are fellow human beings. May the guards be kept safe and treated with respect. Oh, Father, I can't imagine what it's like being locked behind bars. May those who are guilty truly repent and ask Your forgiveness for what they have done. May they come to know You in the pardon of their sins. And may they become a light in what can be a very dark place. In the name of Jesus. Amen.

DAY 33

FOR THOSE IN THE PATH OF A STORM

Holy Spirit, I come before you on behalf of those who are right now in the path of a storm. There may be storms I am aware of, but I know there are also storms happening all around the world that I may never hear about but that still impact people's lives. So, I pray to You today, because You know everything that is going on everywhere. Please cover and protect those who have no protection – those without shelter or warmth – without shoes or a jacket – without socks or even underwear. Give them shelter that is safe and strong enough to withstand the storm. Protect them from rain, wind, lightning, thunder, and whatever else the storm may bring. For those who are living on the streets or in their cars or in inadequate or unsafe housing with leaks or flimsy walls. For those with no heat or electricity or access to the internet or telephone lines for communication. For those with housing but who are caught out on the roads or stuck at work, and for those going through this storm while staying in a hospital or rehabilitation center, or nursing home. Whatever the situation, please protect them through this storm. And Holy Spirit, please give courage and protection to those who have to be out in the storm in order to help others. All emergency responders that have to go into the storm to rescue others and get them out, including the medical personnel who risk their lives to save the lives of others. For the workers who clear the roads so that emergency teams can get in and out and the utility workers who sometimes go in while the storm is still raging to help fix communication lines so that emergency systems can operate. For those in the path of any storm today, please protect them, please comfort them and please bring them through safely. In the name of Jesus, Amen.

DAY 34

FOR TRYING TO ADOPT

Jesus, I thank You for those whom You have given a heart to adopt and are trying to provide a family for a child. Thank You for placing that desire in their heart to adopt someone into their family. I think of how that models Your love for us and am so thankful that I have been adopted into Your family. So, for those trying to adopt, please give them wisdom and discernment throughout the process. Guide them to the right agencies, people, and resources they need to adopt the child or children You have already ordained to be a part of their family. They may not even know yet who the child is, but You already know and I ask that You prepare their heart to accept this child when they meet them. May they feel a sense of immediate peace, like what they have been searching for has been found, so that there is no doubt that this is their child. May that confidence remain steadfast throughout the adoption process. It may be long and tedious, and there may be moments of doubt or obstacles they have to navigate around, but may that God-confidence always remind them that You will make a way because this child is meant to be loved and cared for by them. During the wait, Lord challenge them to do everything they can to prepare space in their heart, lives, and home for this child or these children. Bless them financially to be able to provide, bless them in the work of their hands so that there is stability for the future, and make room for this child that they can call their own in the home. Prepare the home for the adjustment. For the person or people who are adopting, please give them compassion empathy, and patience to extend to this child as they adjust to their new life. Prepare them in advance with access to any resources or support they may need. I thank You again, Lord, for giving them a heart to adopt and pray blessings on their home. In Your Name, I pray, Amen.

DAY 35

PRAYER PROMPT
FOR A FRIEND

Ask the Holy Spirit to bring a specific friend to mind. Use this space to note who you prayed for or to write your prayer for them.

DAY 36

FOR THOSE IN THE ENTERTAINMENT INDUSTRY

Father, Your creativity in all things never ceases to amaze me. How You inspire people to use their talents to create so many forms of entertainment that we can enjoy. Today I pray for all those who work in the entertainment industry in any capacity. For those that are writing, directing, producing; for those who are in front of the camera and behind; for those who create costumes and lighting and sound; for those who create special effects or edit; for those who are agents or lawyers or managers; for those who provide food, craft services or other services on set or behind the scenes. For all these people and people in roles I've never heard of, Father I ask You to guide them to do their jobs with a level of excellence only You can inspire. In television, movies, streaming channels, and content available through websites or apps, I pray that in all mediums of entertainment, ou would not only change what is being created and presented to bring You glory but also that you would change our hearts and minds as those who consume content. That people would feel compelled to not watch those things in which You are not glorified. Not watch those things that bring evil and sin and hate and idolatry and ungodly behavior or violence towards others into our minds. May we choose to turn the channel, not click on the stream, not buy the ticket, not watch, not read, not share, not partake in entertainment that You have not designed for Your good. May all forms of entertainment be used in some way to shine a light on You. In the name of the Father, the Son, and the Holy Spirit. Amen.

DAY 37

FOR FACTORY WORKERS

How we can take for granted the people all over the world who make the things we use. Today I pray for factory workers. I am grateful for the people who make the clothes I wear, the shoes on my feet, the furniture I sit on, the appliances I cook with and use for personal care, the car I drive, or the cars I've been driven around in. For the people who make the computers and mobile phones, I've used, the counters, shelves, and check-out machines in stores. The workers who made the boxes and bags that are used to deliver packages to my home. Father God, there are so many people working in factories that I've never thought of or considered, but You know them all and You know how hard they work to make things that many of us take for granted. We can take for granted the time and effort that went into making the zipper on our jacket or the shoelace in our sneakers, but there is a person who was a part of that process that You used to create those things so that I could use them. So, today I thank You for them. I pray You would continue to increase their talent in their craft, and that they would learn new techniques in their field. I pray You would ensure they are paid a fair wage and blessed financially in ways that ensure their household is taken care of. I pray that as the world changes and technology is integrated more and more into how factories operate and how things are made, that every worker remains employed, either by being given the opportunity to train in new areas of the factory or manage the technology that is being used. I pray that rather than replacing them, that technology would make their work physically easier. And Father, I pray that much of the innovation of how technology can be used in different types of factories around the world is invented by factory workers themselves who know best how it could be applied to the benefit of the industry. That these workers would patent and license their inventions and that would provide for them a financially secure future they might not have imagined for themselves. Please bless the work of their hands, expand the knowledge in their minds, and may those of us who use the things they build and manufacture not forget the people behind the things we use every day. In Jesus' name, Amen.

DAY 38

FOR THOSE PLANNING AN ACT OF TERRORISM

Father, Son and Holy Spirit, it is so hard to pray for people who are planning on hurting others BUT You tell us to pray for our enemies. I pray urgently now for changed hearts and convicted minds of those who plan and plot to do harm. For those who are planning an act of terrorism right now or in the future, please arrest their thoughts and destroy their plans. Remove the evil spirit that has overtaken their sense of love for their neighbors. Prevent them from harming anyone else or themselves. Prevent them from damaging property, no matter the value of it, because their goal is destruction that causes terror and fear to rise up in others regardless of the cost. Turn them from the evil path they are on and like Paul on the road to Damascus stop them in their tracks and turn their hearts towards You. Blind their ability to see a way to bring their evil plan to fruition. Foil their attempts at every turn. If there are those in their sphere of influence who can speak truth and conviction and peace into their hearts on Your behalf, I ask that You embolden them right now to say whatever needs to be said to stop this evil from happening and get this person the mental help that they need to see the error of their thoughts. Give those peacemakers the courage to call in law enforcement and others who can prevent this person or group of people from the terrorism they are plotting. Father, I pray for Your protection over the people and places that are being targeted. Jesus, I pray You would open the eyes and hearts of those who plot evil to see how they have let the enemy into their spirit. And Holy Spirit, I pray You would overwhelm their mind with Your self-control, peace, and love so that they would repent and lose all desire to follow through with their evil plans. Amen.

DAY 39

PRAYER PROMPT
FOR SOMEONE WHO'S ETHNIC HERITAGE IS DIFFERENT FROM YOURS

Ask the Holy Spirit to bring to mind someone to pray for who is of a different cultural background than you. Use this space to make a note of their name or write a prayer for them.

DAY 40

FOR THOSE WHO HAVE LOST A FAMILY MEMBER IN A MASS SHOOTING

Father, Son and Holy Spirit, where do I begin? It is overwhelming to think of the pain and agony experienced by those who have lost a family member in a mass shooting. The anger and grief that must be bubbling up in their spirit! When will these horrific shootings stop? Why do You allow them to happen? How are they supposed to move past this pain? I know the answer is far beyond my understanding. I know You do allow bad things to happen to everyone. But I have to admit that it doesn't always make it easy to accept. I know the answer is Your comfort. The comfort only You can give. I know You are able to comfort everyone in every situation, so Lord, I ask today that You would speak to their hearts and comfort their brokenness, their agony, their despair. Their anger is righteous Lord, yet I know Your Word tells us to forgive our enemies. So, I ask that You would help them to find a path to forgiveness through You. Give them reassurance that You are in control even now. Reassure them that their loved one's life had meaning and that You knew long ago that this day would come. May this reassurance help them to grieve not like those who do not believe. May this reassurance help them to guard their hearts against hardening. Comfort them as they grieve Father. Please bring comforters alongside them to walk with them through this season and in moments throughout the rest of their life when this tragedy comes to mind. Give them your unexplainable joy even in this midst of this sorrow, like no one but You can. In Jesus' name, Amen.

DAY 41

FOR THOSE WHO TURN TO SHOPPING

Father, some of us use shopping to soothe our pain. When we are feeling low, discouraged, depressed, anxious, etc., we turn to new things to make us feel better. No matter what it is, or what it costs, we know deep down that these things are only temporary, short-term bandages on the voids we are trying to fill. Father, for those who turn to shopping, help them instead turn to You. Help them to gain a clear understanding of their emotions and to discern when they are shopping to fill an emotional need. Father, please help them to be good stewards of the financial means You have blessed them with. Let them not accumulate debt or waste their money on things that will not sustain the joy they seek. Whisper to their hearts when they go to make that unnecessary purchase and give them the conviction to leave their cart empty and instead ask You for what they truly need. You O Lord can fill any void. You O Lord can soothe any pain. And the comfort You provide does not wear off. It is everlasting. I pray for those who are addicted to shopping in any form. Please give them the will-power to resist and the desire to seek help to resolve whatever has caused them to turn to material things instead of to You. In the name of Your Son Jesus, I pray. Amen.

DAY 42

FOR CHILDREN WHO DON'T HAVE A COMPUTER TO DO THEIR SCHOOLWORK

Computers are so essential to education in our world today Father. I pray for children who do not have a computer or access to one to do their schoolwork. I pray You would make a way for them to get access to one so that this would not be a stumbling block to their education or the opportunities they have in life. Without access to a computer, many children don't have access to the internet, which has become our encyclopedia and the most effective tool for research. Without access to a computer, many children will not be able to learn the skills of navigating technology, which will place them at a disadvantage for employment in the future, limiting their options and their dreams. For children in countries or communities where they can't physically get to or go to school for any reason, please provide a way for them to attend virtually. I know that a computer is seen by some as a luxury, but in this fast-advancing world, a computer seems like a necessity. Yet, if it is not Your Will to provide one to a child or one to their family, I pray that You would provide a way for them to have access to one, at school, through a library, by the generosity of sharing extended by a neighbor, a friend or their local church. Father, whatever Your Will, I just pray that children who don't have a computer to do their schoolwork would be able to overcome any disadvantage this causes in their lives. In the name of Jesus, Amen.

DAY 43

FOR NATIONAL PARKS

Father, how beautiful are the parks, the parts of Your creation that we preserve and set aside to protect land and wildlife. First, I thank You for these beautiful spaces, these landscapes preserved in their natural state where so many people go to relax and enjoy. For many of us, it's the closest glimpse of what the Garden of Eden may have been like before the Fall. What beauty and peace can be found in these areas. For the parks and those who work to take care of them, thank You. I pray for their continued preservation, that for the national parks in the United States of America and those in other countries around the world, all people would recognize their beauty and value. That the animals, insects, and other creatures that live there would be at peace, healthy, and thrive. That those who visit would be respectful of Your Creation and take care to not destroy anything or leave trash behind. That those who work to preserve them with their hands would be blessed with the physical strength and energy they need. That those who protect them would be blessed with the discernment to know what to do, and how to enforce the rules and guidelines that have been established. For those who manage these areas or set laws regarding them, may they be led by Your Spirit to do what is best for Your Creation and what allows all people equal access to enjoy and experience it. For national parks around the world, may we preserve them and never take them for granted. Amen.

DAY 44

FOR THOSE SEARCHING FOR GOD

God the Father, God the Son, and God the Holy Spirit, I come before You today on behalf of those who are searching for You. Those who don't realize that You are right there with them need only ask You to come into their life. For those who are searching for You in the wrong places, people, or things, please wake them up to the reality of who You are and that the place they are going to, the people they are listening to, or the things they are idolizing are not You. For those who know who You are but are blind to You in their life, open their eyes so that they search no more, realizing that there is nowhere that they are that You are not. You say that those who seek You will find You, so I thank You for that truth and that promise and pray for all those who are searching for You. May they find You right where You have always been, waiting for them to ask You to come into their life. Hallelujah and Amen.

DAY 45

FOR DAUGHTERS

For daughters of every age, Father, I come before You in prayer. How special to be a daughter. A daughter of the King and a daughter in an earthly family. For daughters, I ask that You show them Your love, directly and through their parents. Let them know that You are proud of them and that they are valued and worthy. Give them inspiration based on women of the Bible that You have great assignments for them and that they were created for a purpose. In that right timing Lord, please illuminate Your plans for their life and give them the determination to walk in the path that will bring those plans into reality. Protect daughters from emotional harm. May the words spoken over them and to them be those that uplift and don't tear down. Protect them from physical harm. May they know their bodies are Your temple and may others be prevented from hurting them. May they also be prevented from hurting themselves. May they have women in their lives, mothers or others, who mentor and teach them with godly wisdom and love. Protect your daughters Oh Lord. Thank You for loving Your daughters Oh Lord. In every age and stage of life, I pray for Your daughters Lord. Amen and Amen.

DAY 46

FOR THOSE STRUGGLING TO MAKE THEIR CAR PAYMENT

Father, thank You for cars and the transportation they provide to get us to places we need to go and places we want to go! Right now, someone is struggling to make their car payment Lord. I don't know why and the reason is not my concern. My concern is that this can be such a hard situation to be in and create so much anxiety and worry. Please make a way for them to get caught up financially and continue to have access to transportation. If they are in a situation where they have a car that they cannot afford, help them to either increase their income or reduce their expenses so that the stress of the car payment is no longer something they have to carry every month. If Your Will is for them to get a less expensive car or to sell the car and use public transportation, please help them to put their trust in You and make this decision. However, You resolve this situation in their life Lord, I just hope that they will see Your hand at work in it and give You the glory when this anxiety is relieved. In Jesus' name, Amen.

DAY 47

FOR THOSE WHO MOURN

Holy Spirit, for those who mourn, may they be comforted through their grief until their joy is restored. The grief and sorrow of death can be debilitating, even for those of us who know that for believers, death means eternal life. Remind those who mourn of that Lord, that there is still joy even in their sorrow. Give them peace even though they may feel like they are in a valley of despair. And for those who have lost a lot of loved ones in this season and it just seems like it's too much to bear, please give them strength. Bring others alongside them to comfort them and lift their spirits when they can't encourage themselves. May You bring their mind to the Bible often where they can find words of comfort and peace. May they give themselves time and grace to heal emotionally without allowing themselves to get stuck in a place of sorrow. I pray today for those who mourn and stand on Your Word that says they will be comforted. In the name of Jesus, please be their comfort, Amen.

DAY 48

FOR THOSE BATTLING ALCOHOL OR DRUGS

What a struggle those battling drugs and alcohol face! Father God, I come before You on behalf of those who find themselves addicted to a substance. Father, You know how this happened. You know all the details. I don't know the cause of their pain or the situation that has created in them this seemingly uncontrollable desire for the relief or escape that comes from the substance they are now addicted to. But You God, You know their heart and their mind. And with You it is possible for them to have victory over this addiction. So, Father, I ask that You would perform a miracle in their life right now Lord! That they would have no desire for this substance anymore. I pray it would be immediate, but God, if it is Your Will that they go through a process over time to overcome this substance, then I trust Your Will and pray that You would give them the support, determination, emotional and physical strength to persevere. Please not only give them victory over this substance, but also help them to find relief from whatever caused this addiction in the first place. Every day, please give them the strength to choose not to partake in this substance. Remove every craving. Heal the pathways in their brain that could make them susceptible to relapse. Give them strength to choose to resist no matter the temptation. Thank You in advance for their daily victory! In the mighty name of Jesus! Amen.

DAY 49

FOR AREAS OF THE WORLD EXPERIENCING A PANDEMIC OR OUTBREAK OF DISEASE

Father, I come before you now because You are The Healer. The Author of our faith and the Creator of our lives. You designed our bodies in such marvelous and magnificent ways that we can never fully understand. As much as we know, we are still learning day-by-day new things about how You designed the human form. How far above our thoughts are Yours! How awesome is Your creativity. Father, there are areas of the world battling pandemics and outbreaks of diseases. Battling viruses and illnesses that we know very little about. So much research has been done around the world about different diseases and pandemics of the past that can inform those who are currently facing an outbreak. We thank You for the insights we have been able to learn and pray You will guide the minds and hands of the scientists and the researchers and reveal to them how to eradicate current outbreaks of disease. We thank You for the medical professionals and healthcare workers and others around the world, who are selflessly doing everything they can to keep others healthy. We acknowledge that outbreaks of disease affect all of Your children. Not just us here in the country I live in, but around the world. So I pray for the world, not just my nation. I pray for areas around the world wo are experiencing a pandemic or outbreak of disease. And Father, I don't want to neglect to lift up those who are battling other illnesses and diseases too. Those whose care may be being affected, neglected or ignored during this time. With so much focus on one battle, I don't want to forget to ask You to intercede for those who are sick with other health issues on top of the outbreak their area is experiencing. Father, touch all those who are sick. Please heal them of their afflictions. Physical and mental. Ensure medicines reach those in need. Ensure treatments and medical care remain accessible to everyone. Please touch them Father from the top of their heads to the soles of their feet and give them comfort and Your peace. Father, I pray for the complete and total healing of everyone who is sick. I know Father that Your ways are too vast for me to totally understand, so if Your Will is that some have to suffer with their afflictions for a while, I ask that You would give them Christ's perseverance and like the woman with the issue of blood, that they would eventually be made well. But that in the meantime they would feel close to You. That they would not feel forgotten or forsaken, but that their trust and faith would grow. And that those of us who are not experiencing illness would not take that for granted but that they would find ways to help, care for and encourage others as they wait on You. For current outbreaks of disease around the world and for future ones that You allow to come, I pray these things in the name of Your Son, Jesus Christ. Amen and Amen.

DAY 50

FOR MARRIAGES

Father God, I pray today for marriages to reflect Your love for us. For those who have been married for years, for newlyweds, for those who are engaged and those who one day hope to be engaged and for those who fear the possibility of divorce. Marriage like everything in life is a journey, a process that we can only get through with You. I pray you would prepare the hearts of those who are single to be ready for the spouse You are preparing for them. I pray you would encourage them to not lose hope. I pray You would strengthen the marriages You have already ordained and be the cord that binds them together. May married couples be an encouragement and support system to other married couples. May their transparency with each other give them perspective in all situations and remind them that they are not alone. May this fellowship give them couple friends that cheer them on and celebrate every anniversary. Save those marriages that are struggling Lord. In the midst of trials help them to see each with Your eyes and show each other love and respect no matter what. That at whatever stage a courtship or marriage might be at, Lord please help them not forget that their relationship reflects to the world Your deep love for us. So, let husbands and wives love each other deeply and honor You with how they treat each other. Let their joys and the struggles they overcome together, be a testimony of Your goodness to the world. In Jesus' Name, Amen.

DAY 51

FOR CHILDREN WHO DON'T KNOW CHRIST YET

Jesus Christ, my Savior, I know Your timing is always right and I can trust in it. I come before You hopeful that those children who don't yet know You as Savior, will come to know You very soon. What a blessing it is to know You and trust You from a young age. I hope for that for the children of today. I pray they would know who You are, how You love them, and the teachings of Your Way to help them navigate this life. If they have questions or concerns about You, I pray they will go to someone in their life who loves You, that can help them grow in their knowledge and understanding of Your Word. I pray they would come to know Your sacrifice and what that means for them and their relationship with the Father and the Holy Spirit. I pray that every child would come to know You in the pardon of their sins and accept You as Lord, Savior, and friend. In Your Name, The name Jesus. The name above all names, I pray. Amen.

DAY 52

FOR FRIENDSHIPS THAT ARE GROWING APART

Jesus, it is hard when a friendship grows apart. You have been a friend to me, so I come before You today asking that You would be with those in a friendship that is experiencing a growing separation. Jesus, I pray You would be with each person and give them awareness of the situation and insight into what You would have them do. Give them clarity on if this is the natural plan for the friendship and if they are meant to move on in this season or if there is something that needs to be nurtured between them and their friend to reconnect. I accept that some friendships are not meant to remain the same forever. Like any relationship they have their ebbs and flows. Even in my relationship with You, I can see that. Please help those who aren't sure what to do, to know what words to speak and what actions to take. For friends who are meant to continue being in each other's lives, please encourage them to talk to each other and express their concern for the distance they are starting to feel. Guide them in how to correct the path of division they are on. Strengthen their communication and may their friendship grow stronger and bloom. And for friends who are meant to grow apart and either not be as close as they once were, or are meant to break and go their separate ways, give each person discernment and clarity as to why. May there be no hard feelings or anger, but instead understanding and appreciation for what the friends have been to each other in the past. Give them each the courage to move on if that is Your Will and create new bonds of friendship with the people You have for them in this new season of their life. And for all of them, remind them that they are never alone and always have a friend in You Jesus. Thank You for being a friend to me too, Amen.

DAY 53

FOR SURROGATES

Thank You Lord for women who are willing to carry a child for someone else. Please protect the baby in their womb and may it grow healthy and strong. Please protect the surrogate's health physically and mentally also. Prepare them for the birth and the moment when the baby will be given to the parent or parents that they are carrying the child for. Father, these situations can be complicated. The reasons for surrogacy, the complications of who's egg and sperm created the embryo, the legal considerations and so much more are all things that can make for a stressful situation for the surrogate and everyone involved. You know every situation Lord, You know every heart, You even know everything about that baby who has yet to be introduced to the world, so I put my trust in You and pray that the surrogate does as well. I pray they know You or maybe through this process, come to know You and knows how much You care for them and the life they are helping to birth. I pray that You would help her to deal with the emotions that come from handing a child she gave birth to to someone else. I pray that whatever the situation, if she is going to remain in contact with the child or not, that You would help her to process all that she feels. I pray that the child is loved and well cared for always and I praise You because I'm guessing that this child is the answer to its parent's prayers. I hope there will always be a good relationship between the surrogate and the parent or parents and that they would always treat each other with love, compassion and respect for the role they have played in the life of the child. Thank You Lord for the miracle of surrogacy and the blessings it has brought to so many lives. Amen.

DAY 54

FOR COWORKERS WHO ARE IN INTERPERSONAL CONFLICT

Father God, Today I pray for coworkers, for those who work for the same company and who should be working collaboratively to achieve the company's goals, but instead are at odds because of interpersonal conflict. I pray that they will be able to resolve the conflict themselves or that someone else will step in to help facilitate a resolution that will allow them to work harmoniously going forward. If apologies are needed, I pray that they would humble themselves and willingly speak words to each other that will help diffuse the situation, heal hurt feelings, and allow them to let go of the issues that caused the conflict in the first place. Give them the right words to speak to show grace to their coworker during any difficult conversations. May their pride not get in the way of letting go of anger. May they not gossip about their coworker to others. May they not sabotage them or plot anything that would cause them harm or damage their reputation. May they recognize that ongoing conflict at work causes unwanted stress and can get in the way of their own productivity and career goals. Father, I pray that all interpersonal conflicts between coworkers will be resolved today! In the name of Jesus, I pray. Please bring peace to their offices and these coworker relationships, Amen.

DAY 55

FOR THOSE WHO ARE CLOSING A BUSINESS

Today, I come before You Lord in prayer for those who are in the midst of closing businesses small and large, sole-proprietorships to corporations, new businesses to those who have been around for years and years. No matter the stage, oh how hard it is to close a business! Give the business owners discernment and wisdom on if this is the right thing to do and how to go about it. Help them handle all the details of letting go of any employees, notifying clients or customers, selling or storage of equipment and inventory, closing an office, retail space, warehouse, etc. There is so much to do Lord. I pray You would bring helping hands to make sure that everything gets done. I pray that whatever the reason is for the closure, You would help them to process what is happening and learn something from both their successes and failures in the business. I pray they will treat the employees they have to let go with kindness and compassion and pay them any wages owed. If possible, that they would even be able to offer severance to help them as they look for another job. I pray that those who are closing a business will be able to recover financially from any negative impact that the closure may cause. I pray the closure would not impact their ability to start another business in the future if that is their desire. Help them to pay any outstanding debts, fulfill any outstanding orders, and maintain positive relationships with vendors and customers. Father, I don't know why their business has to close, but You do. May they understand what happened and maintain a right perspective. Lord, please send someone into their life to encourage them during this season by reminding them that even if their business failed, they are not a failure. In the name of Jesus, Amen.

DAY 56

PRAYER PROMPT
FOR A CELEBRITY

Ask the Holy Spirit to bring to mind a celebrity that could use your prayers. Use this space to make a note of their name or write a prayer for them.

DAY 57

FOR CAREGIVERS

Holy Spirit, please lift the spirits of caregivers, those who care for others. For those taking care of family members or for those who have been hired to care for someone else, I pray for them all. Thank You for the servant's heart You gave them and the compassion they show. Please give them the physical strength they need to help. Give them rest when they are physically weary and please protect their bodies from injury. Please give them mental strength, so that they can make good decisions, be patient and show love to those in their care. Help them to not become frustrated or weary. May they have support from others that they can ask to help when they need a break. May they feel supported and not alone. May they make time to take care of themselves emotionally and physically, so that they can always be at their best. May they not feel burnt out. And may they know how much they are appreciated! I pray they have good relationships with the person or people in their care and that they hear often that they are doing a good job and that they are not taken for granted. It is so easy for caregivers to give so much that they have nothing else to give. I pray that before any of them get to that point, they will take a break and renew their mind, body, and spirit. I pray that they know You and how much You care for them. Holy Spirit, may Your fruit of love, peace, joy, patience, kindness, gentleness, faithfulness, goodness, and self-control be evident in their life. May others feel it whenever they are around them. May they be a ray of sunshine in the lives of those they care for and point them to You. Amen.

DAY 58

FOR THE COAST GUARD

Today I pray for the coast guards of the United States and those serving their country around the world. For the officers in training, for those on active duty, for the reserve, the volunteers and the civilians that support them. Their mission is to search and rescue, to protect people and property, homeland security and so much more. Thank You for their service and dedication to their responsibilities. May their vessels be well-maintained and safely carry them wherever You would have them go. May their equipment operate properly and be an asset to their work. Give them physical and mental strength and health as they perform their duties. Give them eyes to see danger and the wisdom to handle it. Guide them in situations of search and rescue and give them the focus and determination to persevere even when their effort might seem hopeless. Give them hearts that value human life and show compassion as they respond to natural disasters and emergencies. May they have access to the healthcare they need physically and mentally as they recover from the stress and strain of their work. Keep them safe when they are called upon to respond to chemical, oil, and other dangerous spills in the ocean. And may they know they are not taken for granted but appreciated for the work they do. In the name of Jesus, Amen.

DAY 59

FOR SONS

Jesus, today I pray for sons. You can relate to what they experience, so I ask You to be a friend to them. That the pressures of their responsibilities to their family would not be overwhelming. That they would always feel loved and supported as they mature in age and wisdom. Encourage them to never stop dreaming about the future and open their eyes to the good things You and the Father have planned for them. I pray every son would know that they have a Father in Heaven that loves them and wants a relationship with them regardless of if they have a relationship with their earthly father. I pray they have good male role models in their life that encourage and challenge them with godly insights. I pray they have friendships that are strong and genuine. That they can have open and honest conversations about their feelings and their needs. Lord Jesus, for sons, I pray You would give them direction and make clear the assignments the Father has for their life. And that they would accept them, as You did in the garden of Gethsemane. Give them courage to do the Father's Will, even if it's hard. And at the end of it all, may they hear "well done". Amen.

DAY 60

FOR THOSE WHO WANT FINANCIAL SECURITY

Financial security is a blessing that not everyone in this world has. Financial uncertainty can cause so much worry, anxiety and fear. For those who desire financial security Father, I pray You would be their provider. Help them to increase their income with new job opportunities, side hustles, or other means. Help them to plan for the future and give them clarity of what being secure financially means to them. With this clarity, help them to budget and save. Give them discernment of how and when to spend and what sacrifices they may have to make to reach their financial goals. When unexpected expenses arise, may they not be discouraged. Please make a way for them to cover them. May family and friends be supportive and not be a stumbling block to their financial goals. Give them self-control to stay the course even when they really want to spend money on something that they don't need. Reward their good stewardship over their finances by spoiling them in unexpected ways and may they know that is You blessing them and encouraging them to stay the course. I pray they would reach their financial goals and give You glory and praise. In the name of Jesus, Amen.

DAY 61

FOR THOSE WHO ARE EXPERIENCING A HEALTH ISSUE AND DON'T HAVE A CLEAR DIAGNOSIS

Father, You know how frustrating it is for us when we know that something is wrong with our bodies, but the medical professionals we have seen cannot determine what is going on. You in Your infinite wisdom know exactly what is happening, but for whatever reason You are not allowing a diagnosis to be made clear. I pray for those who find themselves in the midst of this type of situation. They feel pain, but no one can figure out why. They can tell that their body isn't functioning normally, yet no one can identify what's wrong. They are having a hard time describing their symptoms or they are describing them perfectly, but no one believes them. Please give them peace in the midst of confusion and let their answer be You Lord. Don't let them despair. Even if the doctors are not able to give them answers let their hope and peace come from You. Embolden their trust in You Father as they go through seeing different doctors and different tests. As they wait on results, be their patience. When results come back negative, help them navigate the complicated feelings of both relief and disappointment that can coexist. Help them be grateful and praise You that they don't have what they feared and help them accept that they still don't have an answer. Father, I pray that You would give their doctors wisdom and clarity to discern exactly what is going on and then the ability to treat it. But in the meantime, I pray Your peace on those who are waiting for a diagnosis. In the name of Jesus, Amen.

DAY 62

FOR CHILDREN WHO ARE IN JUVENILE DETENTION

Regardless of what they may have done or why they ended up there, I pray for those who are in juvenile detention. Father, may it be a safe non-violent place for them to live temporarily while they await their court date. May those who run it show kindness, care and compassion regardless of their belief in the youth's innocence or guilt. May the facility be kept clean and well maintained with areas for the youth to be able to go outdoors and get exercise. May they have access to medical and mental health care and education. May they have reputable legal counsel that gives them good advice. If they are guilty Lord, I pray You would convict them to confess and repent and accept the consequences of what they have done. If they are found guilty and moved to a correctional facility, may Your protection follow them there and may they use their time of incarceration to prepare to be a productive member of society if released in the future. If they are innocent Lord, I pray that their stay in juvenile detention would be brief and that the truth would quickly come to light. That they would not be emotionally scarred or traumatized by the experience. In the name of Jesus, Amen.

DAY 63

PRAYER PROMPT
FOR YOUR CHURCH

Pray for the church you attend. For the Pastor, the ministry leaders, the current members, visitors, and future members yet to come. Use this space to make notes or write out your prayer.

DAY 64

FOR THE RENEWAL OF NATURE AND NATURAL RESOURCES

Creator of the Universe and this planet we call Earth, I pray today for the renewal of Your creation. For nature and the natural resources, we use, abuse and sometimes take for granted. Your Word says that the world is wasting away. We know it will never again be like it was in the beginning. Yet, I pray that You would help us identify ways for natural resources around the world that have been depleted by our usage and consumption to be reproduced in enough quantity to support humankind. That the resources we need from nature can be preserved in ways that meet human needs. I pray there would be a spirit of charity among nations to share what they have and not horde from those suffering and in need. Give the leaders of the world discernment and wisdom and inspire them to work together in collaboration because resources like air, the waters of the ocean and the rays of the sun have no border and affect us all. In the name of the Father, the Son and the Holy Spirit I pray, Amen.

DAY 65

FOR SCHOOLS

For schools today, I pray Oh Lord. May they be places of education based on factual information and truth. May Your Spirit fill the halls and classrooms, the outdoor spaces and gyms. May there be unity of the administrators, faculty, students, parents, and community surrounding the school. May diversity of thought be encouraged in a way that helps students develop the critical thinking they will need to navigate the world outside the classroom walls. I pray for the protection of every campus and the courage of those whose job it is to protect it to rise to the occasion if there is ever a need. For the staff who keep the campus and its facilities operating smoothly, clean, and well maintained, please help them to do their job with excellence and know they are appreciated and not taken for granted. May each school building be kept up to code for the safety and well-being of all who go inside. May the equipment that is needed in classrooms or for extra-curricular activities be available and suitable for use. May students respect their teachers and teachers respect their students. May parents and teachers work together to make the best decisions for the student's education. May every school have counseling services available to support students who are struggling and need guidance or support. May every school have the funding it needs to meet its mission and set its students up for success. For schools around the world who don't have the building or access to resources that they need, I pray You would perform a miracle and make a way and remedy whatever situation the face. In the name of Jesus, Amen.

DAY 66

FOR ATHEISTS

Father for those who don't believe You exist, I pray that they would come to know You before it is too late. You know their heart and mind and what has made them come to this conclusion. I pray You would bring people and situations into their life that would challenge them to question how certain things could happen if there isn't a God. Open their eyes to Your Glory. Confront them with who You are. I thank You that You allow us the free will to choose if we will love You and accept Your Son, Jesus Christ. The fact that You don't force us to love you is proof that You love us unconditionally. Help atheists to recognize this. Help them to see that there is no way to explain life without You. Bring someone into their life who can answer their questions with kindness and understanding and guide them in Your Word. May they come to know Your character and how it is reflected in the world around them. May they seek You and find You right where You have always been, waiting for them to acknowledge You. I pray today that atheists would accept Jesus Christ as Lord and Savior. Amen.

DAY 67

FOR THOSE WHO HAVE FALLEN INTO IDOLATRY

Father, Your Word tells us not to create or worship idols. We are to put nothing before You. We are not to ascribe Your power to anything or anyone but You. Today I come before You on behalf of those who have fallen into idolatry. Those who have a strong interest in spirituality but don't know Jesus. Draw them away from any idolatry, ungodly practices or belief in the power of inanimate objects, like crystals. May they know that You created the universe and that it has no power on its own. May they worship the Creator and not the creation. Draw them to You, to Your Holy Spirit, the One True Living God. Convict Christians who are worshipping anything or anyone other than You. Give them ears to hear how the enemy may be using Christian language to disguise his schemes. We know that the devil knows Your Holy Word and tries to twist it to deceive. For those Christians who think they are speaking for You but instead are promoting the schemes of the enemy, I pray Your Holy Spirit would help them to see the error of their ways in Jesus' name. Bring their thoughts and words into obedience with The Truth. Amen.

DAY 68

FOR THOSE WHO ARE CARING FOR THEIR PARENTS

Father God, thank You for those whose parents are alive. Thank You for all the years of life they have experienced and all those that are yet to come. How hard it is for children to take on the role of caregiver to their parents. First, I thank You for their willingness to give of their time and energy in this way. I pray for those who have had a good relationship with their parents as well as for those who now find themselves taking care of a parent who didn't take care of them. I pray for those who feel unappreciated, that they would know that You are proud of how they obey Your Word by honoring their parents. I pray for those who feel their lives have taken a detour or their dreams are on hold. Help them to find ways to continue to move forward along the path of the assignments You have for their life. Please don't let them become discouraged or give up on their own dreams. Bring helpers to relieve them and give them time to rest and take care of themselves. May they not feel guilt for prioritizing their self-care when necessary. Give them breaks from their responsibilities so they can renew their spirit and their joy can overflow to their parents. Give them peace and patience when conflict arises. Give them the courage and discernment to make decisions that are right for their parents and the ability to navigate difficult conversations if their parents don't agree with the decisions they have made. Father, for those who are caring for their parents and all the challenges that come with it I pray today. Amen.

DAY 69

FOR THOSE WHO ARE SAVING FOR THEIR DREAMS

Thank You for the ability to dream! Father, for those who have dreams that require financial resources, I pray You would help them to reach their goals. Help them have a realistic idea of how much money they need and how long it will take to save it. Open their eyes to ways they can create streams of income, find a second job, sell items through garage sales or online, create a successful crowd-funding campaign, or re-work their budget to save more from the income they already have. Whatever the means, give them clarity on the best path to save what they need. Give them focus, determination, wisdom, and perseverance. Don't let them fall into any get-rich-quick schemes or risky investments. Give them the patience to follow a plan that You lay out before them. Keep them encouraged along the way when speedbumps get in the way. Help them to keep the faith and concentrate on their end goal without distraction. Whatever the dream, when they have the funds to make it happen, I pray that they testify to everyone that they were able to save because You are able! In the name of Jesus, Amen.

DAY 70

FOR THOSE WHO HAVE LOST A FATHER

Heavenly Father, for those whose fathers have passed away, today I lift them up to You. The relationship between father and child is such a special one. And the grieving process is so unique for each person based on the type of relationship they had with their dad. May they have sweet memories that bring a smile to their face. May they cherish the lessons they learned from their dad and his example. May they honor his life by living by those life lessons, passing them on to their children, or sharing them with others. For those who had a difficult relationship with their father, may they find peace regarding any lingering hurts or unresolved pain. Holy Spirit, comfort them and give them confidence that their father loved them even if he had a hard time expressing it. May all who have lost a father still have someone in their life that they can go to when they need "fatherly advice". And may their relationship with You Father God, grow stronger and deeper in the years ahead. In the name of Your Son Jesus Christ, I pray. Amen.

DAY 71

FOR THOSE WITH BIPOLAR DISORDER

Father, Son and Holy Spirit, today I come before You on behalf of those with bipolar disorder, those who live with manic depression. There are so many things we don't completely understand about the human mind and Your intricate design. We don't fully understand how our genetics; our environment and our emotions interact. We don't know why You allow some to have a mind that works differently than others. Only You know why the things we call "disorders" exist. Specifically, today I pray for those with diagnosed and undiagnosed bipolar disorder. Those who are not able to control periods of their lives that swing from manic, high energy to the depths of depression that can cause them to lose touch with reality and even have suicidal thoughts. Holy Spirit, touch their minds and help them to move through these periods with Your guidance. Guide their words, their choices, and their behavior. Protect them from harm or from unintentionally causing harm to others. You know their hearts and that this disorder can impact their ability to think clearly. Father, please bring help and support into their lives, through family, friends, and medical professionals who can provide the medication or therapeutic services that they need to manage this disorder and live happy and productive lives. Jesus, please walk beside them, and may they not feel ashamed of this disorder that they cannot control. May they seek You and know that no matter their mood, they are not alone. Help them see clearly that You are there on their good days and their bad ones and that You will never leave their side. In the name of the Father, the Son, and the Holy Spirit, Amen.

DAY 72

FOR THOSE WHO FEEL LIKE GIVING UP

Father, we all experience moments where we feel like giving up. Life can be hard. Sometimes we feel like giving up on our dreams, sometimes we feel like giving up on our job, sometimes we feel like giving up on a goal we've set for our life, sometimes we feel like giving up on believing in others, trusting others, forgiving others, and sometimes we feel like giving up on ourselves. And for some they experience moments when they are so discouraged that they feel like giving up on trusting You. Today I ask that You would give an extra dose of perseverance and determination to those who feel like giving up. Renew their energy and strength. May they experience a fresh dose of hope and clarity on the next steps they should take. Remind them of Christ's perseverance and that they can do all things through Jesus Christ. If they don't know Him, may this situation be the one that drives them to seek to know Him and what a friend He is to those who are weary. Amen.

DAY 73

FOR THOSE IN ABUSIVE RELATIONSHIPS

I pray urgently today for those in abusive relationships. For their physical and emotional protection. Lord Jesus, please make a way, right now, today for them to get to safety, away from the abuse. May they easily find support and the resources they need to stay away from their abuser and not ever feel the desire to go back. If they need medical care, may they receive it. If they need mental health care, may they receive it. May their abuser never be able to contact them or find their location. May they be provided with safe shelter and a way to survive financially while they establish a new life for themselves. Help them to know their worth, the value You put on their life and wellbeing. Help them to maintain perspective on the situation and boldly proclaim that they will not allow anyone to treat them that way ever again. Give them strength even if they feel weak. Give them courage even if they feel discouraged. Give them joy even if they feel sorrow. Give them hope even if they feel hopeless. May others who have their best interest at heart, come alongside them and help them in any way they need. May they never experience an abusive relationship again and may their story be a testimony of triumph that they share to inspire others to do the same. In the name of Jesus, Amen.

DAY 74

FOR THOSE FEELING UNCERTAIN ABOUT THE DAYS AHEAD

Father, I thank You for today and pray for those feeling uncertain about the days ahead. I thank You in advance, not knowing what their days hold, but knowing You are in control. I pray they will trust You with their whole heart. I hope that God-confidence will fill their minds. If they have been experiencing some rough days lately and battling the spirits of fear and anxiety, I ask You to reassure them that those don't come from You. Give them the inner strength that comes from knowing they can overcome anything because of You. Remind them of Jesus, His sacrifice, and example. f His focus on You and Your Will in spite of the agony He faced. For His strength and humility in times of trial. May it encourage them that they can make it too. May their uncertainty not get in the way of them moving forward and trusting You to direct their path. May their fears not cause them to become stuck in a place where You don't want them to be. When they feel uncertain themselves, help them to feel certain in You. To not just believe in You, but to believe You. I ask this prayer of You, the omniscient, all-knowing God. Amen.

DAY 75

FOR THOSE IN HOSPICE CARE

Oh Father, who art in Heaven, please hear my prayer for those in hospice care. Only You know the exact day of our death. Some of us will meet an unexpected or sudden end to our lives and others find themselves consciously aware of the end approaching. No matter the reason they are in hospice – the natural progression of age, an incurable illness, a decision to not undergo treatment – may the care they receive be comforting, and emotionally uplifting and give them relief from any physical pain. Please tend to their mental and emotional needs and the needs of their family and friends as they process the situation. I pray their time in hospice will not be sad but will be a time where they can celebrate the life they have lived and that they come to know how much they have meant to others throughout their life. May they be told how much they are loved and how much they are appreciated and how much they will be missed. May they be prayed over and blessed by those who know You and love them. Father, I pray for miracles, where unexpected healing and recovery comes. But if it is truly Your Will that their life is coming to an end, I pray that they know You and Your Son Jesus! I pray they will be celebrating with You as soon as they take their last breath on this side of Heaven. Hallelujah! Amen.

DAY 76

FOR THOSE EXPERIENCING DISTRACTIONS

Oh Lord, how the distractions of life can cause so much turmoil. I pray for those who are experiencing distractions of any kind today. Distractions designed by the enemy to steal their joy or cause them to steal someone else's. Distractions of the enemy are designed to disrupt their obedience or completion of an assignment or plan You have given them for their life. Distractions the enemy uses to discourage or destroy their confidence and ones he uses to disrupt their focus. I pray You would give them the ability to recognize these attempts by the enemy and the things of their own flesh that cause distractions. Help them to see where they are allowing their thoughts, temptations, insecurities, and concerns to distract them from Your plans, their goals and even promises they have made to others. Let distractions not interrupt their life today. When they recognize them, may they immediately turn from them and remain focused on what You want them to start, complete, or focus on in each moment of this day. In Jesus name, Amen.

DAY 77

FOR THOSE WHO ARE LOSING THEIR EYESIGHT

What a precious sense eyesight is. Not everyone is born with it. Today I pray for those who have been able to see and are now losing their eyesight. I pray that they will quickly identify any challenges they are having and have access to the medical care they need to properly diagnose what is going on. If there is a possibility of their sight being restored or somehow slowing the progression of loss, I pray that the therapies or medications that can help are available and there is no barrier financially or otherwise to receiving them. If Your Will is for them to lose their eyesight, I pray You would help them accept Your Will and find ways to continue to live a full and functioning life without the ability to see in the way they once did. Heighten their other senses, help them to learn braille, and find ways to see the people and world around them without the use of their eyes. Lift any depression or discouragement that may come from the loss of this sense. Give them a heart of thanksgiving and gratitude for the season of sight they have experienced and help them to show themselves grace as they deal with all the emotions that may come. May their compassion for others who have had a similar experience grow and help them to make connections with new friends who can be a support system as they adjust. In the name of Jesus, Amen.

DAY 78

FOR THOSE WHO ARE HAVING A HARD TIME FORGIVING

Today I pray for those who are having a hard time forgiving. Help them to see that their unforgiveness is disobedience. Your Word tells us over and over again to forgive. It reminds us that we are forgiven and that we should extend that same grace You show us to others. Father, please help those who are still holding on to their anger, their frustration, their hurt, and their pain, to see that it is damaging their spirit and mental well-being. Show them that forgiving, not only will make You proud, but it will also release them from the destructive emotions, bitterness, and turmoil that unforgiveness plants in the heart. May they come before You and share their feelings honestly and without shame and then may they ask for Your strength to let those feelings go. Especially in situations that truly can't be resolved, help them to cast their cares on You and truly forgive the person who has done them wrong without needing an apology in return. If Your Will is that they not only forgive in their heart but also express this forgiveness to the other person, give them discernment of the right timing and the exact words to say. May the other person be receptive and respond with kindness, understanding, humility, and grace. Help them both know if they should continue to be in each other's lives, or forgive and move on. And if this isn't the first time they have forgiven, help them to find the strength to forgive again. In the name of Jesus, Amen.

DAY 79

FOR HUSBANDS

Father Son and Holy Spirit, what a weight You have put on the shoulders of men. There is such beauty in life but it also comes with such responsibility. Today I pray for those men who You have deemed will be called husband. Like Adam who came before them, You have given them the role of lover, protector, and provider for the wives You have blessed them with. They have been called to be a partner in this life to the one woman You created just for them. They have been called to like Christ, align themselves with Your Will and Your ways and lead their wives on a path of righteousness. Their relationship with their wives is to model Your relationship with Christ and Christ's relationship with us. What an honor and what a heavy burden. I know Your Word says that Your yoke is light but in the everyday, I imagine that a husband who tries to do things the right way and in accordance with Your Word has a hard time. This fallen world doesn't seem to give them the same deference that You do. And how hard it must be to lead while also submitting to his wife. Your Word says that husbands should submit themselves to Christ and that husbands and wives should submit themselves to each other. I want to acknowledge that that must be a hard balancing act. So right now, I pray for husbands. All of them no matter how long they have been married I pray You would help them to be at peace in a constant posture of submission to You so that they might lead their wives well and truly love them like Christ loves, unconditionally and with abounding grace. Give every husband the wisdom he needs to discern what is best in his household and to work together with his wife to build a loving home and lasting bond. Help him to be vulnerable with his wife and share his needs, his wants, and his desires. Let his wife's arms be a place of refuge for him away from the pressures he experiences in the world. Help him every day to learn more and more about You and use that knowledge to give him the strength and the commitment to be the husband that You designed him to be. Thank you for those you have blessed to be husbands. I pray they make You so very proud every single day. In Your holy name, in Your mighty name, in the name of Jesus I pray. Amen.

DAY 80

FOR THOSE WHO ARE TRYING TO CONCEIVE

Oh, what a blessing to conceive a precious child. Oh, what a miracle it is every time You allow man and woman to come together to create an embryo that carries a future and Your purpose. The ability to conceive is an expectation until it isn't. Most women and men never consider that they may not be able to create a child through natural means until the reality of infertility becomes a part of their life's journey. You designed women to carry children in their womb, yet even in the Bible there were many women who were unable to...until You intervened. So today I pray for those who are trying to conceive. Whatever the reason is, I pray You would make a way Lord. Touch, heal, and create in them a womb that is perfectly designed for their miracle child. Life is in Your hands Lord, so I ask You to bless their womb with new life. However You do it, through a touch of Your hand or through the hands of doctors that You guide, please bless them with their heart's desire and allow them to conceive like You've done so many times before for women all over the world. For the woman who is feeling discouraged, may Your Holy Spirit draw her to the examples of Sarah, Elizabeth, Hannah, Rebekah, Rachel, and the mother of Samson. From these women may she learn perseverance, submission to Your Will, and grow to trust You and Your timing more. May she feel encouraged and not discouraged by those around her who may not understand how she feels. Protect her self-confidence and remind her that even this experience is a part of Your Will for her life and not a punishment. Help her to believe in her heart that the trouble she is having conceiving is not a reflection of her worth or value as a woman. May she hold her head up high and look to You for direction in navigating this journey. In the name of Jesus, Amen.

DAY 81

PRAYER PROMPT
FOR SOMEONE WHO HURT YOUR FEELINGS

Start by asking God for a clean heart and that He would give you understanding of why they did what they did. Ask Him to help you pray for their needs regardless of how they hurt you. Use this space to make notes or write out your prayer.

DAY 82

FOR THOSE WHO ARE LOSING THEIR HEARING

Father, our sense of hearing gives us the ability to not only communicate and navigate daily life but also to experience the wonder of a newborn baby's cry, the beauty of a bird's song, the peace of a flowing stream, the majesty of thunder and rain and so much more. For those who have experienced these things and now are losing their hearing, I pray You would help them adjust to their new normal. Give them access to medical care, equipment like hearing aids, and other tools so that their quality of life would not be negatively impacted. May health insurance and finances not be a barrier to them getting the resources they need. Help them, their family, and friends to learn sign language if necessary. And may they have peace in knowing that on the other side of Heaven, all their senses will be restored and they will hear the most beautiful sounds of praise for eternity. In the name of Jesus, Amen.

DAY 83

FOR JOURNALISTS AND REPORTERS

Father, for those whom You have tasked with researching, investigating, and communicating information, facts, and news I pray. For journalists and reporters who are able to report in their own words and select what topics, people, or events they cover, I pray they will always write and speak the truth. Not their truth, the truth. Give them insight, wisdom, and integrity. Help them to communicate in ways that are easily understood by their audience. May they share information and stories that inform and uplift, that shine a light on the good and bad things going on in the world. May the information be accurate and worthy of being spread. That what they report convicts us to turn from evil, inspires us to unite for good, and reminds us that we are to love others as You command. And I pray the same for reporters and journalists who don't have the same autonomy and are assigned stories or read teleprompters of reports written for them. What a struggle it must be to sometimes read something in different words than you would want to or even say words you may or may not agree with because it is your job to read what is written. Give courage to those who refuse to report lies and risk their job or careers. For those who knowingly communicate lies or divisive content meant to cause confusion or animosity between people, please convict their spirit and help them choose to not participate in this scheme of the enemy. For journalists and reporters in countries where they can be jailed or worse for reporting the truth, please protect them and continue to give them the determination to risk their own safety so that information can get out to the world. For those who are currently jailed or being held hostage for their work, I ask for their release from captivity and return to their homes. For reporters in war zones who risk their lives to expose the realities that go on around the world, I pray for their courage and safety. My prayer is that those who selflessly risk their lives, jobs, and reputation to seek and report truth would be guided by the Holy Spirit and given discernment of truth and protection as they carry out

Your Will. That those who seek to use their reporting to confuse, divide, destroy, hurt, hate, or manipulate, would be exposed and prevented from being used as a tool of the enemy's schemes. May the history recorded from their work be an accurate reflection of events and not influenced by personal bias. Thank You for the talent You have given them and may they grow in their experience and have opportunities to work for the companies, publications, and networks they dream of. If they aspire to write books or be published in journals, may You give them the perseverance to accomplish those goals. And may whatever they write or report reach the audience that You intend. In the name of Jesus. Amen.

DAY 84

FOR THE CHILDREN OF INCARCERATED PARENTS

Jesus, be a friend to the children of incarcerated parents. Father, be the parent they need in situations where their parent may be absent or not able to participate in their life. Bring other family members and a support system to surround them and care for their needs. May they not feel alone. Comfort them when they miss their mother or father and give them relationships in their life that can fill any void. Give them perspective to help them to process the situation in a way that does not impact their life negatively. Regardless of what their parent is incarcerated for, may the situation not make them feel less than others. May they know that their life is their own and help them be confident in who they are. Help them to see themselves as the person You created them to be, a reflection of You. Help others to see them for who they are and don't allow their opinions to be clouded by the sins of their parents. Protect them from being ostracized for something that their parents have done. Give them discernment about what their relationship with their parent should be. Help them to see them through Your eyes. May they find emotional healing for any hurts or disappointments. Help them to forgive and to love like You love. Whether they stay in contact or keep their distance, may they have a healthy, loving and grace-filled mindset towards their parent and the situation. No matter their age when their parent was incarcerated, I pray that You would not let their parents' situation disrupt the good plans You have for their life. Thank You Jesus. Amen.

DAY 85

FOR THOSE CURRENTLY EXPERIENCING A LOSS OF POWER DUE TO A NATURAL DISASTER

Father, You are God of all. The seasons change because of You. You created this world and the nature and weather we enjoy. Sunshine, rain, snow, heat, cold, no matter the weather, it can bring us peace and joy and laughter but You also allow us to experience storms and flooding and earthquakes; tornadoes and hurricanes and tsunamis, and more. There are some who are currently having their lives upended because of the devastation of a natural disaster. Help me to remember that everyone around the world is experiencing different weather right now and not assume that if all is okay with me, that no one else is suffering. Father, I pray for those who are struggling, and who have lost power from a storm, earthquake, or flood. For those that have no heat. Please keep them warm and safe. And help those with children to find ways to keep everyone occupied as they wait for the power to come back on. We are so dependent on electricity for so many things Father and it's not until we have to go without that we realize how reliant we are on it for so much. For those who have no way to connect to the internet or phone to let their loved ones know they are okay or to call for help. For those who have any kind of damage to their homes or businesses, please help them to stop any further damage and make a way for repairs. For those who are sick and at home or in a hospital Father please help them to get the assistance they need. If it's medication or medical equipment or just a helping hand, please make a way to help them through this time. Father for those who are working to restore power, to make repairs, and all those who are playing some part in helping during this crisis, please give them strength and energy, give them resources, tools, and equipment, and give them patience and wisdom. Please help them to restore power to all those affected. In the name that is above all names, I pray. Amen.

DAY 86

FOR FAITH TO GROW

Father, I come before you praying for us all. Praying for our faith, that it would grow in spite of how we feel. Each day seems to be a wrestling match of trying to take control of our lives versus letting go and obeying You. We desperately want to let go and let God, but You knew when You created us that that would be easier said than done. Our hearts want to trust You and yet sometimes we struggle to match that with our words and actions. Thank You for being ever faithful to us, even when we've been unfaithful to You. Thank you for loving us in spite of ourselves. We love You Father. We love You Jesus. We desire to draw nearer and nearer to You and that our faith would continue to grow. Please help our faith be stronger than our feelings. Let our faith overwhelm us to the point that we seek You first in all things and aren't discouraged from doing Your Will because of how we feel. Our feelings are temporary, they come and go, they change sometimes moment by moment. But You never change. Help us to remember that, Father. In the mighty name of Jesus, may faith among Your people continue to grow and may our faith kindle a flame in others to seek You and grow in faith too. Amen and Amen.

DAY 87

FOR FAMILY UNITY

God, Creator of all, You created woman out of man, and child out of woman. Families are meant to be unified. In our fallen world, there are so many families that have division so deep that it spans generations and seems like it will never be healed. Today I pray that the bonds of families all around this world would be strengthened. That whatever caused the breakdowns in trust, communication and connection would be healed. That family members who are unified would reach out to others who have been shunned or pushed away and extend an olive branch of peace and acceptance. I pray for families who are unified that they would remain so and be protected from the enemy's schemes to disrupt their love and support for each other. That every generation within each family would find hope and inspiration in those who came before. That family members would love and respect each other and extend each other grace. That family secrets or histories that are causing or might cause breaks in bonds, mistrust, hurt or pain would be revealed in ways that allows everyone in the family to heal. Today I pray for unity within families Father. In the name of Jesus, Amen.

DAY 88

FOR THOSE WHO ARE MAD AT GOD

How ironic it is that we can be mad at You Father. But it is a reality that so many people harbor anger towards You. Some recognize and readily admit their feelings, while others are not even aware that the distance they are feeling is because they are mad at You for something You have allowed to happen or even for something that they want that You won't allow to happen. Right now, I pray for those who are mad at You Lord for whatever reason. Like Job, I pray You would humble them and remind them of who You are. May they have the courage to be honest with themselves about what they are feeling and to express that openly to You. Remind them that You are God and there is nothing that they are thinking or feeling that You don't already know about. Remind them that You can handle their anger, even if unjustified, so there is nothing that they need to try to hide from You. Whatever the reason is that they are angry, disappointed or hurt, give them eyes to see that You are always in control and even this is part of Your plan. If they are looking at the situation through a self-centered perspective, expand their vision to see that not everything is about them. Help them see how what they are upset about is for the good of others. Soften their hearts so that through this experience they would become closer to You. If they know You, may this increase their trust and faith. If they do not know You, may this confrontation between their will and Yours be a catalyst to them wanting to get to know this God who controls all better. Thank You Father for not giving up on us, even when we are disrespectful to You. I ask Your forgiveness on behalf of those who are mad at You and pray for them as they go through this Job season in their life. Amen.

DAY 89

FOR THOSE WHO HAVE A LOT OF DEBT

Father, Your Word tells us to pay to all what is owed them; that the borrower is slave to the lender and we should owe no one anything but love. (Proverbs 22:7, Romans 13:7-8) You tell us that those who borrow and do not pay back are wicked. (Psalm 37:21) No matter the type of debt or the reasons it was incurred, I pray this prayer of intercession for those who have a lot of debt. For those with loans for education. For those with loans for their mortgage or car. For those who have medical debt. For those who have credit card debt. For those who have business loans and lines of credit or investors that they owe money to. For those who took a risk and incurred debt. For those who have had to take on the responsibility for someone else's debts. For those who have made bad decisions and are now overwhelmed with how much they owe. For those who are in debt because of a lack of self-control, for those who are in debt because of right decisions, and for those who are in debt for reasons out of their control, please help them all to get a handle on their financial situation. Please, Lord, give them clearness of mind to understand exactly what they owe and what it will take to pay it. Prevent them from adding to their debt as they make a plan to reduce and eliminate it. Give them relief from the mental and emotional strain that debt can cause. Relive their anxiety enough that it does not affect their well-being, but does give them the determination to get out of debt. Every situation is unique and every path out of debt is specific to that person, but God, I pray You would make a way for each one of them. May every person who is struggling with debt reach a point where they are struggling no more. May we all repay what we borrow and give generously. In the name of Jesus, Amen.

DAY 90

FOR THOSE WHO LOST A CHILD THIS WEEK

What pain it is to lose a child. God of all comfort, please comfort those who have lost a child this week. Tend to their heartache and help them to function moment-by-moment as they bear such heavy grief. May they not feel alone and have people in their lives who will be there for them physically to hug them and wipe away their tears. May they have people in their lives who will be there for them emotionally, to listen, and to console them. I wish You didn't allow this pain, but You show us by Your example that sometimes this is a part of Your Will. You sent Your precious son to die for us, so You understand their loss. It can feel unbearable, yet we can bear all things with You. So please stay near to those who have lost a child this week and remain with them now and in the months and years to come. When the acuteness of this pain rises up in an unexpected wave of emotion, please help them to show themselves grace and help others to understand that the loss of a child isn't something that people get over. Help them to maintain and regain their joy even in the midst of this sorrow. Holy Spirit, please help them to reach a place of peace. May they look to You for the strength to still live their lives to the fullest even with this hole in their heart. May their pain not be in vain, use their experience for Your Glory, and to share comfort with others who find themselves grieving the loss of a child in the future. I pray to You, God of all comfort, Amen.

DAY 91

FOR THOSE WITH ADHD

Father, for all those who have been diagnosed with anything that falls under the category of attention deficit hyperactivity disorder, I pray a prayer of intercession. Father what we define as "normal" behavior may not always align with how You would define it. But our human minds prefer to categorize the way we think and behave so that we can understand the people around us. For those with diagnosed or undiagnosed ADHD I pray that You would touch their minds and help them recognize that You designed them that way. That the way they process things isn't wrong, it's just different. Make clear to them that there is a reason that You created them to experience the world around them the way that they do. That their inability to focus or ability to hyper-focus their hyperactivity, or any other traits that come along with ADHD are tools that they can harness to fulfill the purposes You have for their life. May they become superpowers rather than a hindrance. For those who can hyper-focus, use it to help them accomplish great things Lord. For those who have a hard time focusing, may they notice things that others do not and use that for Your good Lord. For those who are hyperactive, may they use their abundant energy to create positive connections with others and be resilient in situations that others find tough to navigate. Also, help them to recognize any ways in which the way they function or process information may be impacting their life or relationships negatively and give them tools to navigate well. Help others show them grace and not judge them or make assumptions about the intent of their behavior. Give those with ADHD confidence in themselves so that they never feel broken or compare themselves to others who do not have ADHD. Help those with ADHD to channel everything that comes along with it and make You proud. In the name of Jesus, Amen.

DAY 92

FOR THOSE WHO WANT TO LOSE WEIGHT

Dear Lord, precious Father, please help those who want to lose weight. Help them to identify a healthy weight goal. Help them to be realistic about their plan to reach it. May they see their body through Your eyes and not the unrealistic expectations that the society that they live in might promote. Give them a "why" that encourages them to persevere when they struggle to stay the course. Protect them from misinformation about weight loss that is so prevalent in our world today. Guide them to resources that will help them make healthy decisions that align with how You designed their body. Give them the determination to take the initiative to be active, exercise, change their diet, or make lifestyle changes that will help them reach their weight goal. Holy Spirit, help them to show themselves grace if they get off track and gently convict them to not give up. May the people in their sphere of influence be a support and encouragement in every way. For those who want to lose weight, Father, I pray they will reach the goal they have set for themselves in Your right timing and gain confidence in themselves along the way. May their perseverance bring Your Son Jesus to mind and draw them to a deepened relationship with Him. For those who already know Him and those who don't, may their weight loss journey not only change their body but may it also renew their mind. In the name of Jesus I pray, Amen.

DAY 93

FOR THOSE WHO FIND THEMSELVES IN A HEAVY SITUATION

Father, Son and Holy Spirit, we all find ourselves in heavy oppressive situations in life. I pray they would be few and far between, but Father, for those who find themselves there now, I pray You would lift their spirits. Lift the weight that is on their shoulders. Remove the weight, that only You can bear. Give them strength to move forward or to be still, whatever is Your Will. Give them what they need to make it through this heavy situation that You have allowed in their life. You have allowed it like You allowed Job's afflictions, so we trust that like You did for Job, You will help them make it through. Father, please give them the relief they need to make it. Renew in them Your hope. Give them Your strength and the perseverance of Christ. Remind them that even this hard situation has a good purpose in Your plan. In the precious name of Jesus Christ, Amen.

DAY 94

FOR WIVES

How special it is to be called a wife. To be designed to be ezer kenegdo to a husband. Of equal value, but with a very special purpose, unique to woman. Father, today I pray for wives, whom You designed because it is not good for man to be alone. You designed wives as suitable helpers, fulfilling needs that men cannot fulfill for themselves. You designed wives to be loved and cared for by their husbands because they are so precious in Your sight. May wives always know their worth and that You call them worthy. May they love their husbands unconditionally as You love them. May they feel loved always and, in every way, have a deep connection with their husbands. Marriage is hard, so Father in those periods or fleeting moments when they feel alone, misunderstood, taken for granted, or unloved, may they feel Your love for them, may they know You understand them, may they know You see them, may they know You are always with them. Help them love and respect their husbands even when they don't feel like it. Remind them that they do that for You and not for him. Help them see that their imperfect husband is perfect for them. Show her the ways You want her to continue to grow to be the wife You designed her to be. May she have a community of support to encourage her through the tough times and celebrate the joys of her union. May she be a reflection of Your love to her husband. May she be his sounding board that he comes to for advice and wisdom. May she be a safe place for her husband to seek refuge from the challenges he faces in the world. You designed wives to be strong. May every wife recognize this and know how important they are in Your plan. Renew their strength each day as they do their best to care for the husband You designed for them. In the name of Jesus, Amen.

DAY 95

FOR GOD-CONFIDENCE

Father, today I am reminded of how Paul talked about being nothing, but in nothing being inferior to anyone else. How he boasted not because of himself, but because of You. Our confidence comes from You Lord. Today I pray that someone who is struggling would have God-confidence. That they would see themselves through Your eyes. That they would see their situation as something that they can go through because You are on their side. That their confidence wouldn't be in their ability apart from You. That they would recognize all their talents, skills, experience and blessings are from You. That with boldness and courage that they would live out each day because they have confidence in You, no matter what their eyes see or what other people say. I pray their God-confidence would help them do things even if they are scared. I pray their God-confidence would lead them out of their comfort zone. I pray their God-confidence would help them always maintain a right estimation of themselves and the situations they find themselves in. I pray that their God-confidence would inspire faith in God in others. For those who feel discouraged I pray God-confidence. For those who are struggling with spiritual warfare, I pray for God-confidence. Help them understand Your Word, Your character, Your Will and Your ways so that in every season and situation they have confidence in You. In the name of Jesus, Amen.

DAY 96

PRAYER PROMPT

FOR A CHILDHOOD FRIEND YOU'VE LOST TOUCH WITH

Start by asking God to bring a specific friend to mind. It doesn't matter if you feel led to reconnect with them or not. Thank God for their friendship. Ask the Holy Spirit to bless them wherever they are and whatever is going on in their life right now. Use this space to journal about what their friendship meant to you as a child or write out your prayer for them.

DAY 97

FOR ARTISTS

How blessed this world is that You created artists. Thank You Creator God for blessing so many of Your children with the ability to paint, draw, sculpt, sketch, mold, design, and use their hands and minds to create things of beauty and wonder for us to appreciate. For all artists of any kind, Father, I thank You for their craft and pray You would guide their creativity to make things that would reflect You. Even for artists who don't know You, may their work illuminate Your existence and majesty for those who see or experience it. I pray artists will be continually inspired and find new and interesting ways to express what they want to communicate through their work. I pray their work would be recognized and if it's Your Will and their desire, that they would be able to make a living for themselves from their craft. Give them access to the tools, materials, and space they need to complete their work. Guide their hands, their hearts, their minds. May others see value in what they do and respect their talent and ability. Thank You for artists Lord, and for how I have been impacted by their work. Give me eyes to see You in what they create. Amen.

DAY 98

FOR FIREFIGHTERS

Father, for those who risk their lives to put out flames, I thank You. What courage You give them to walk into danger to save people, property, and possessions. For the lives they rescue I thank You. For the homes and buildings, they save, I thank You. For the precious possessions they save from destruction, I thank You. Thank You for the selflessness they display. Thank You for their training. Thank You for their willingness to be away from their families and commune with other firefighters who are ready to jump into action when emergencies arise. Please keep them encouraged Father. May Your Holy Spirit abide with them in their firehouse as they wait to be called into action. Give them rest for their bodies and fellowship for their souls. And when they are called to service, please protect them from the flames, from any harm, hurt, or danger. Continue to fill them with the strength and courage they need to do their jobs with the utmost skill. Be with their families and let them not worry about their loved one's safety, but instead be so proud of what they do. And when they are off duty and get to spend time at home, please let them know that their work is not in vain. May they be showered with appreciation. In the name of Jesus. Amen.

DAY 99

FOR PEOPLE WHO HAVE TO FIRE SOMEONE TODAY

Father, how hard it is to have to fire someone from their job. I pray for those who have to do this today. For those who have to fire someone who reported to them and for those who work in human resources and have the job of handling these situations on behalf of a company, give them peace. Remove any anxiety or worry. Prepare them in advance for the conversation and prepare the heart and mind of the person they must let go. No matter the relationship may this difficult conversation be done with respect. I pray You would give them discernment of how to go about it. Help them choose their words wisely. Help them be honest and speak the truth in love. May they not destroy the person's confidence or say things that are hurtful or unnecessary. Regardless of the reason they have to let this person go, may they do it with compassion and grace. Give them patience and ears to hear so that the person feels heard in expressing any disappointment or even anger over the situation. But no matter what the person says or does, may they respond in peace, certainty, and clarity about the decision and why it was made. Please give them the support of the company they work for to provide resources or a severance package or references that will help the person they are letting go to move on to the next opportunity You have planned for them. May they not harbor any ill will towards the person who let them go, but rather accept that this is a part of Your plan for their life. For people who have to fire someone today, give them relief from anxiety, guilt, or fear. May they have peace in knowing that even in this tough situation, they can handle it in a way that honors Your command to love others. In Jesus name, I pray, Amen.

DAY 100

FOR CHILDREN WHO SPEND A LOT OF TIME ON SOCIAL MEDIA

Holy Spirit, I pray for children who spend a lot of time on social media. It is such a normal part of our society today and can have positive and negative effects on children. Please help children and their parents or caregivers maintain healthy boundaries around how much time they spend on social media and which platforms they are allowed to use. Guard them from addiction to using it, viewing it, communicating through it. Give them self-control. Help them maintain clarity in their minds that social media does not reflect real life. Give them perspective on what they consume online, block them from evil and the enemy's schemes to use it to steal, kill, and destroy. May they use social media for good, to shine light into the world, to promote positivity and kindness, to connect with others around the world, and to increase their compassion and expand their understanding of the diversity of the world You have created. Use it to show them they are not alone. Protect them from those who would use it to do them harm. Use it to help them express their creativity. Protect them from those who would use it to convince them that lies are true. Use it to expand their knowledge. Protect them from those who spread misinformation. Use it to expose them to people and cultures that they may never physically get to meet or visit. Protect them from exposure to pornography, violence, crime, hate, and all forms of sin. Father, I live in a time when social media is one of the main ways that the world connects, that entertainment and other content is consumed, that businesses advertise, that friends and families stay connected, and so much more. It is hard for adults to find a balance between the time they spend offline and online, so I especially pray now for children who also have this struggle and don't know a world where social media doesn't exist. Please protect these children and may social media only be something that is used for good in their life. Amen.

DAY 101

PRAYER PROMPT
FOR A CHURCH IN ANOTHER COUNTRY

If one doesn't come to mind, spend some time online looking for the name of church in a country where you do not live. Use this space to take notes about the church you find and then pray for them.

DAY 102

FOR THOSE HAVING SUICIDAL THOUGHTS

Almighty God, I urgently pray for those who are having suicidal thoughts. I rebuke the enemy and his schemes to convince them that their life does not matter. Please prevent them from taking their own life. Immediately fill their mind with Your light, Your truth, and Your love. May their body literally feel Your peace fall upon it and cause them to release the tension and oppression and weight they have been carrying. May they feel Your presence and know that they are not alone, not forgotten, not worthless. Help them see the value You have placed in them from the day of their birth. May they know that even before they were conceived in their mother's womb, You loved them. May they have victory over the spiritual warfare that is affecting their outlook on life. Renew their hope. Give them mustard seed faith that multiplies with each breath they take and reminds them that they can get through anything and that things will get better. If they don't know Your Son Jesus, may this be the moment that they open their hearts and call out to Him. If they do know Jesus, then may this be the moment that they ask Him to be their strength, calling out His name over and over until You are all that they can think about, pushing out any thoughts of hurting themselves. Give them clarity on what they need to move forward, being joyful in hope, finding patience even in the worst of afflictions and situations, and maintaining a faithful prayer life. (Romans 12:12) I thank You in advance for Your grace and mercy upon them and for saving them from making an irreversible choice to end their own life. I also ask You to meet them where they are and bring support from loved ones, mental health resources, and all the tools in Your Power to prevent them from ever feeling this hopeless again. Permanently heal the hurt, pain, stress, depression, and despair that lead them to this place. May they never lose hope again. In the name of Jesus! Jesus! I pray Amen!

DAY 103

FOR SANITATION WORKERS

Father, I thank You for those who work in the sanitation industry. For those who collect and process things that the rest of us throw away. For those who collect garbage, for those who manage industrial or hazardous waste, and for those who work in wastewater treatment or disposal. For all those in this industry whose work I'm not aware of, but whose work impacts my everyday life. I pray that You would watch over them physically and mentally as they do their job. Help them to learn and grow in their area of expertise and give them strength and perseverance to do their job with excellence. Protect them from any contamination they are exposed to. Protect them from all hurt and danger. May they be treated with respect and paid well for their effort. May they have access to health insurance and whatever medical care they need. May those who collect trash feel valued and appreciated by the businesses and people whose homes they collect trash from. For those who process trash that goes to landfills or can be recycled, give them discernment in the best ways to handle what they process to decrease its negative impact on our environment. May those who work with industrial or hazardous waste always have the gear and equipment they need to do their jobs with safely. Thank You, Lord, for protecting them and for how their work protects others. For those who work in any form of water treatment or disposal, help them also to do their job with excellence and increase their understanding of the science behind Your creation. Help them to understand water, how to treat it to make it safe, and how its disposal affects the land. May all who work in the sanitation industry enjoy their work, the camaraderie of their coworkers, and the appreciation of all those who their work impacts. In the name of Jesus, Amen.

DAY 104

FOR BUSINESS OWNERS STRUGGLING TO MAKE PAYROLL

To our Provider, Jehovah Jireh, I ask today for a special blessing of provision upon business owners who are struggling to make payroll. Father, relieve their stress and give them clearness of mind to discern what their options are. Give them insight into what resources are available to them to be able to pay their employees what they are owed. Depending on the situation, Father, I know Your solution may be different, so I can't pray for every situation specifically, but I can ask You to guide each business owner to make good decisions that are best for their team and their business situation. Increase their humility. Give them the courage to be honest with their team and give their team members hearts of compassion and understanding. If there will be a delay in their getting paid, please sustain them financially in the meantime. If they choose to leave the business, may they leave on good terms and still be paid what they are owed. And may the business owner not take their departure personally but be understanding of the situation their team members are in. Help business owners who are struggling to find ways to increase revenue, find investment, or another way to make ends meet and fulfill their obligation to their team members. I pray this situation will be temporary and an experience that they can grow and learn from, helping them to be even better business operators in the future. And that once this struggle is over, the business owner and their employees will have a stronger bond of trust as they work together going forward. In the name of Jesus, Amen.

DAY 105

FOR THOSE RAISING A FAMILY MEMBER'S CHILD

There are so many reasons why one family member may find themselves raising another family member's child. Father, first, I thank You for their willingness to be a caregiver to this child. I pray You would provide them with an open and loving heart towards them. I pray that You would provide them with the financial resources and means to take care of this child's needs and spoil them with some of their wants too. Give them guidance on what this child needs emotionally and spiritually, and help them pour into them. Give them patience in the initial adjustment and bring ideas to their mind of ways that they can make the child's acclimation smooth. Help them navigate any family dynamics that shift or change. May there be no confusion, disruption, animosity, or other negative feelings created in the home because of this situation. May all the family members in the home be united in their love for each other and desire to help this child. If there are other children in the home, may there be no division between them. May they all be treated equitably with love, grace, and compassion in the name of Jesus, Amen.

DAY 106

PRAYER PROMPT

FOR A PLACE THAT EXPERIENCED AN EARTHQUAKE IN THE LAST YEAR

Earthquakes occur all over the world. Some are so devastating that lives are lost and homes, businesses, churches, and whole communities are destroyed. Identify a place that experienced an earthquake within the last 12 months and lift them up in prayer. Use this space to take notes about the specific rebuilding, economic or healing needs the area and its population has or use this space to write out your prayer.

DAY 107

FOR ANIMALS OF THE SEA

Wow, what it must be like to live in the sea! Today I pray for the animals for whom You designed the water to be their home. Every animal that You create has a purpose. I pray that theirs would be fulfilled. May there be peace in the waters both shallow and deep. From the smallest fish to the biggest whale, from the crab to the dolphin, to the otters and octopus...from the turtles to the penguins, to the jellyfish and the seals, there are so many animals of the sea Father. I marvel at Your creativity! For all the animals of the sea that are known and those we have yet to discover, may their habitat be safe. Protect them from man-made contaminants and debris that threatens their health. Protect them from pollution. May they not go hungry. Lead them to find food from the sources You intend in each season. Heal those that are sick and for those that find their way to our shores, guide us in how to care for them so that they can renew their strength and be released back into the waters again. In Jesus name I pray. Amen.

DAY 108

FOR PEOPLE TO HUNGER GOD'S WORD

Like we hunger for food Lord, I pray that we would have an insatiable hunger for Your Holy Word. That people around the world would desire to read it, understand it and live by it. That when we want to feel loved, we hunger to understand how You define it and how You express Your love for us. When we feel alone, I pray we would hunger for Your company and want to get to know Jesus on a deeper level as our personal friend. When we are afraid, I pray we would hunger for Your protection and open the Bible to learn about how to be courageous and not fear. When we are discouraged, I pray we would hunger for Your Holy Spirit and all the encouragement found in Your Word. For guidance, may we seek Your Word. For correction, may we seek Your Word. When we mourn, when we celebrate and for every circumstance, we find ourselves in, may we hunger for how it relates to Your Word. Today I pray that every person on this planet Earth would find themselves hungry for relationship and revelation from You. God Most High, Lord Almighty I pray, Amen.

DAY 109

FOR ORPHANS

Today I come before You on behalf of children who have lost their parents. Please give them comfort and help them to deal with the emotions they are feeling. Whether they are an only child or have siblings, please help them to not feel alone. May they have more than shelter and the food that they need, but Father I pray that You would make them orphans no more. Give them a family to belong to. I pray this would be immediate, but I know that is not always Your Will, so for those orphans that are waiting for a family to call home, please allow them to feel loved and be well taken care of where they currently live. Give them hope that they will not be orphans forever and show them that You have a beautiful plan for their future. While they wait, Father may they celebrate birthdays and holidays and special occasions with joy. May their caregivers show them compassion and be attentive to all their needs. May their resilience in this season of their life be a catalyst for all the amazing things You have planned for them that they can't even dream of right now. Be with all orphans and shower them with an extra special dose of Your care. In the name of Jesus, Amen.

DAY 110

FOR ADULT STUDENTS

Thank You for creating us with minds that can learn at any age. Father, I pray today for adult students. For those who are going back to school to complete a degree unfinished, for those who are continuing their education and going after a new degree or certification, for those who are enrolled in a program as part of a change in their career path and all adult students, I pray You would help them complete what they have set out to accomplish. Give them focus and the ability to set specific time aside for their studies. Give them energy to complete their schoolwork, especially those who are also juggling a job, a family or other responsibilities. Help them to remember the information and concepts they have learned. Give them clearness of mind to understand the material and how to apply it. Help them complete each assignment, help finish every paper, help them take every test. If they struggle with confidence and worry that they might not be able to keep up in class, Lord, I pray You would relieve their anxiety and show them with every class that they attend that that is a lie. If they struggle with taking tests, I pray You would help them understand the reasons and give them tools and support that would help them have the best chance of success. If they struggle with imposter syndrome and think they aren't good enough, I rebuke this lie. Remind them often of why they are in the program they are in and reveal to them what positive effects the completion of this program will have on their life. And may this knowledge keep them motivated on days when they struggle. Please don't allow them to consider giving up. In Jesus' name, Amen.

DAY 111

FOR THOSE SEARCHING FOR PURPOSE

For those who seek direction and are searching for purpose, Father, I pray You would guide their path. Open their eyes to see what is special and unique about them, their life and their experiences. Help them to see the qualities and talents You have specifically designed them with. Help them to connect all of this with the purpose You have for their life. May they know that whatever it is, our ultimate purpose is to bring You Glory, to love You and to love others. Help them see how their earthly purpose fits into the destiny You have designed for their life. Whatever the purpose is that You have for them, whatever the assignments You have for them to complete, whoever the people are that their life is meant to impact, Father help them to know they are important to Your plan. Help them to not measure the value of their purpose against others based on how the world views things. Give them eyes to see their purpose through Your eyes. Give them humility to accept that Your purpose might be different than what they hope or have planned. May those who are aimlessly wandering, uncertain of how they fit in, suddenly, right now see the lighted path that is before them. May they follow it, trusting Your guidance even if it doesn't make sense yet. May they have confidence as the continue to walk it out and not be deterred by what other's think or do. May no one waste their life searching, but rather find themselves and their purpose in You. In Jesus' name I pray, Amen.

DAY 112

FOR THOSE WHOSE HEARTS ARE HARDENED TOWARD JESUS

Father, Son and Holy Spirit, for those whose hearts are hardened towards Jesus, please soften their hearts, open their eyes and ears to see and hear and know You are real and that You love them so very much! No matter the reason their heart has become hard, it does not have to stay that way. They can choose to let You in. Convict them Holy Spirit and show them how much they need Jesus. God show them how You will never give up on them or harden Your heart towards them. Show them that they can always repent and rebuild their relationship with You. While their heart is hardened, may it be chipped away at by others who love Jesus. Through the words, behavior and actions of others, may they see Jesus and start to yearn a closeness with Him again. May whatever has caused this hardening start to fall away until there is nothing left to block them from desiring a personal relationship with Jesus. Father, Jesus and Holy Spirit, thank You for being patient with us when we turn from You. Thank You for always leaving open a way for us to come back to You. I pray that those whose hearts are hardened toward You would recognize that they need You in their life. I pray that their hearts would be hard no more. In the name of Jesus! Amen.

DAY 113

FOR DAYCARE SERVICE PROVIDERS

How precious are those who take care of other people's children. Thank You Lord for their willingness and compassion. May they have the training they need to provide a safe, clean and fun space for children to spend their day. May they have a good relationship with the parents and caregivers of the children in their care, able to communicate clearly and work together to provide what each child needs. May they have a good relationship with the children in their care. May the children listen and respect them and feel safe with them. Give daycare service providers the ability to keep their facility, equipment and toys clean and safe in every way. May any outdoor space where the children play be kept in good condition and secure with fencing or walls to keep the children safe. Please help them to stay up-to-date on any safety, CPR or other training they need. Give them energy to keep up with the kids in their care, to facilitate activities that will help them learn to socialize with others and grow. Please give them patience Lord when they are frustrated or when the kids are just driving them crazy. Help them to deal with every situation with compassion and the utmost of care. Give them rest each night and wake them refreshed each morning with new energy for the day. May they be appreciated by the children and parents and know they are making a difference in their lives. In the name of Jesus! Amen.

DAY 114

FOR REFUGEES

Father, today I pray for refugees. I pray for those who have been forced to leave their country, the place they call home, in order to escape from persecution, war and natural disasters. First, I pray for their spirit, that You would uplift them and give them hope no matter what they are facing. Remove any depression they are experiencing from being forced to leave their home, especially if they have had to leave any family behind. Give them safety from harm Lord as they escape and travel to a place of safety. May they be welcomed and treated with dignity when they arrive. May they experience the best of humanity and be reminded that people do care. Give them shelter and provide for any medical needs they may have. For those who have experienced persecution or war, may they receive the mental health support they need to process what has happened to them. For those who have experienced a natural disaster, especially one where the destruction has devastated their home and they cannot return, please help them to settle in a place where they can rebuild. May they receive the resources they need to re-establish a place for themselves in this world. May all refugees be able to find a new place to call their permanent home or be able to return to their country, whatever Your Will Lord. Today I pray for refugees, that You would show them an extra special dose of Your compassion and love today. In the name of Jesus! Amen.

DAY 115

FOR VICTORY OVER SPIRITUAL WARFARE

Holy Spirit, I call upon You now in the midst of the spiritual warfare going on in the spirit realm. For the warfare we are aware of and the warfare that we have no idea is going on that is impacting people and events all over this world. I thank You that we already have victory in the name of Jesus. I rebuke all spirits that would conflict The Truth of the Word of God. I pray strength and a clearness of mind for all people that we would be aware of the enemy's schemes to steal, kill and destroy. That we would say "not today" and put our trust and hope in You. That when the warfare gets so bad that we don't know what to do, that we would call upon the name of Jesus! Holy Spirit, rise up in those of us who call Jesus our Lord and Savior. May we not be unwise or blind to what is going on in the spirit realm. Help us to be strong and courageous. Strong in the power and might of the Lord! That we are able to withstand every dart that is directed at us and those we love and care for. May we be girded with truth, righteousness and peace always prepared with faith to go into battle. Help us to stand, speak boldly and have unwavering faith no matter the situation. Holy Spirit help us to walk with You no matter what warfare comes our way. In the name of Jesus! Amen.

DAY 116

FOR THOSE WHO ARE UNEMPLOYED

Father, for those who are unemployed I pray that You would provide a new opportunity for them. I pray it would be something that they would enjoy, with a company that treats them well, with coworkers they get along with and with work that is rewarding. I pray it would be something that meets their financial needs and goals. When the opportunity comes, make it so clear to them that it is the one You have planned just for them so that they have no fear of accepting. Give them certainty. Give them confidence to negotiate the terms of their employment, their salary and benefits to ensure that they are being fairly compensated and their needs are met. And when they start their new job, may they do their work with excellence that impresses their employer and makes You proud. In the meantime, Lord, as they wait for You to open this door, give them patience and peace. Be their provider, covering their financial needs. Give them hope as they apply and interview. Help them curate their resume to highlight their skills and experience. Help them to write heartfelt cover letters that get the attention of those who are hiring. Help them express themselves in interviews in ways that make it so obvious what a positive addition they could be to the company's team. May they not be discouraged about the jobs they are not offered. Give them peace in their spirit that the right job will come at the right time. In the name of Jesus! Amen.

DAY 117

FOR WEDDING COORDINATORS

Father, what a fun and rewarding job this is; to help others coordinate the day that they make a covenant before You. Today I pray for wedding coordinators, because the reality is that this job can be highly stressful. To have the responsibility of helping to make someone else's special day perfect. Often carrying the stress and anxiety so that the couple doesn't have to. Father, thank You for wedding coordinators that do so much to help others. Give them listening ears and open hearts to understand what their client's desires are so that they can fulfill them to the best of their ability. Help them to be resourceful to find the vendors who can meet all their client's needs at reasonable prices and with excellent customer service. Help the coordinators with wisdom about how to work with their client's budgets so that no couple goes into debt on their special day. And above all else, Father, I pray that each coordinator knows YOU and regardless of if the couple they are working with knows You, that the coordinators shine Your love into their lives. In the name of Jesus. Amen.

DAY 118

FOR MORE KINDNESS IN THE WORLD

Father God, to the author and finisher of our faith, I come before You to ask for increased kindness in this world. That those who walk by Your Spirit, would do so in a way that displays its fruit of kindness in all they do and say. That even for those who don't know You, that they would act with compassion and love towards others, making an effort to be kind in every situation. That this world would have more kindness than animosity, hostility or hatred. That indifference towards others would not become the norm. That we would not become indifferent to each other's struggles and pain – even if we don't understand or can't relate to what someone else is going through. May kindness not be random, but be purposeful. May it be the standard that people live their lives by. Open the eyes of those who have become bitter towards others and are not able to express kindness. May they be showered with kindness and may it soften their heart. Father, I pray for more kindness in the world and that every person would live by Your command to love one another. In the name of Jesus! Amen.

DAY 119

FOR THOSE WHO ARE EXPERIENCING FOOD INSECURITY

How scary to not know where your next meal will come from. Father, our Provider, I pray to You now for those who are experiencing food insecurity. May they never go without. May they never experience severe hunger. Please provide them with sustenance each day with healthy food and clean water that will be good for their bodies. And please spoil them, Lord, with goodies and treats to enjoy too! If they need financial assistance, please provide it so that they never miss a meal. For families and individuals, Lord, I pray. Relieve their anxiety about where their next meal will come from or if they will have enough. May they find support from family, friends, neighbors, and their community to meet their needs. May there be food banks that are accessible in their neighborhood that are stocked with good food. May this insecurity be short-lived, Lord. May they quickly be in a season of abundance as You make a way and change their situation. In the name of Jesus! Amen.

DAY 120

FOR THE UNITED STATES OF AMERICA

Almighty Father, I come before you today in prayer for the United States of America. This is a prayer for the unity and solidarity of this nation. Father, please forgive us for all our sins. I personally want to first lay mine before You, before asking for anything Father. I seek Your forgiveness and ask You to hear my prayer. Father, I pray specifically for this great nation. No nation is perfect, yet I am grateful and know how blessed I am to call this country my home. I love this country and ask for Your peace to fall upon us. Father, I ask You to do the work that only You can do and that Your Spirit would revive our hearts so that all the people who live in America would treat each other with love and respect. That we would see each other through Your eyes Father, even when we disagree, that it would spark a curiosity to understand rather than division and anger. Father I praise You for the abundance of blessings You have bestowed upon the United States and I ask You to help us be good stewards of them. For those without clean water, food or shelter, for those looking for a job, for those struggling financially, for those feeling lost and alone, Father, I seek You now and ask You to touch their lives, give them hope and provide for their needs. Father, thank You for blessing America and I pray You would continue to do so. In Jesus' name I pray, Amen.

DAY 121

FOR THOSE WHO WILL GET FIRED FROM THEIR JOB THIS WEEK

All knowing Father, I come before you praying for those who will be let go from their job this week. For those who have a sense that it is coming and for those who have no idea and will be blindsided. I don't know the why. Maybe the company has to lay people off in order to survive. Or maybe they are being let go because they have not met the expectations of their role. Or maybe they are being unfairly fired because of some interpersonal work conflict. Whatever the reason, You have still allowed it. You have determined it is time for them to move on from that place. I pray You would help them to accept this situation. Whether fair or unfair, expected or unexpected, help their mind to process the situation and handle it with grace. I pray You have something better planned for them. That a new opportunity would arise quickly that would be suited to their talents, experience, and interests. A job where they can feel welcome and like their contribution is valuable. In the name of Jesus, Amen.

DAY 122

FOR THOSE APPLYING TO A SCHOOL OR EDUCATIONAL PROGRAM

Lord Jesus, thank You for giving someone somewhere the desire to gain more knowledge and education. There is someone right now in the midst of applying to a program. I don't know if it's an associate's degree, a bachelor's degree, a master's degree, a PhD, an MDiv, a special certificate or maybe they are applying to a high school or other academic program. I don't know the specifics, but You do, so I come before You on their behalf, asking You to show up for them in a mighty way! Give them clarity and certainty that what they are applying to is the right path. Give them confidence that with You they will be able to complete it and earn their degree or certificate. Help them cover the cost of any application fees. Give them insight of how to fill out the application and how to collect and organize whatever additional information they must provide. If they have to include some sort of letter about why they want to be accepted, please calm their nerves and help them to write from the heart, expressing their interest, their passion and what the program means to them. May they already have clarity of how You want to use this educational opportunity for Your Glory in their future and how they can use it to have a positive impact on others. If they need references, may they come easily. May they be overwhelmed by the number of people that are willing to vouch for their character, skills, talents and ability. Give them patience once they have submitted their application and give them peace as they wait for the answer. Father, I pray that they would be accepted into the program they desire to attend, yet if Your Will is for them to go elsewhere, may their desire come into alignment with Yours. I thank You in advance for the day they graduate and how they will use their new increased knowledge for good. In the name of Jesus! Amen.

DAY 123

FOR WOMEN EXPERIENCING MENOPAUSE

What a wonder the female body is Lord! How amazing it is to consider how You designed it to work, the phases and stages it goes through in a woman's life. Today I lift up to You women who are experiencing menopause. For those who are in perimenopause and beginning the transition and for those who are in an advanced stage of menopause. For physical symptoms like hot flashes, sleep disturbances, night sweats I ask that You would give them relief. Give them access to treatments to reduce the severity and duration of all the symptoms they experience. For the emotional and hormonal changes that can cause depression and anxiety, I also ask that You would help them to get relief and support so that this would not have a negative impact or disrupt their life in any way. Help them to communicate their needs to doctors, caregivers, friends and loved ones and may they find support, understanding and a listening ear. As they go thru this season, may they not feel alone. And for those who are distraught because menopause for them means an end to their ability to conceive, I pray for Your comfort and peace. Whether they have given birth to children or not, I pray that You would help them find contentment with Your timing and Your Will. In the name of Jesus, I pray, Amen.

DAY 124

FOR NEW PARENTS

Halleluiah Lord! Thank You for blessing first time parents! I pray for them today, that You would help them to be the best parents they can be to the child or children You have created specially to be a part of their family. May their love for their child be instant and unconditional. Prepare their hearts and minds for the days ahead as they figure out what their new normal, their new routine will be. Help them acclimate to the changes, unexpected and expected that they experience. Dispel their fears and anxiety and guide them as they make decisions on how to care for and raise their child. Give them confidence and also humility. When they make mistakes, help them to learn and grow. May everything they do be in the best interest of their child and in preparation for the good future already have planned for them. May they feel loved and appreciated and have a good relationship with their child as they grow. May they have a support system to help them as they adjust. May loved ones come alongside to babysit when they need a break. May You help them provide financially for their new family and keep a safe roof over their heads. When they struggle encourage them. When they rejoice, may they feel Your love smiling upon them. For all new parents Lord, meet the needs of their unique situation and help them to be the parents You want them to be. In the name of Jesus, I pray, Amen.

DAY 125

FOR PEOPLE WHO ARE HAPPY BEING SINGLE

Father, Your Word tells us that there is a blessing in singleness, that those who are single are able to dedicate even more time to You and being a vessel for Your Glory. For those who are happy being single Lord, I pray that You would guide them in how they can do more for Your Kingdom. I pray that You would encourage them so that they are never lonely. That they would have a strong community of friends and loved ones that make their life full. That they would be showered with love. That they would be confident in knowing their desires and that others would accept their preference to remain single without judgment or assumption of their reasons why. For those who choose to be single Lord I pray You would shower them with blessings and opportunities to shine for You. In Jesus name I pray, Amen.

DAY 126

FOR THOSE EXPERIENCING INFERTILITY

Infertility can be so hard to accept Father. So many women in the Bible experienced this and each had a different reaction. Some schemed to find a way to still have a child, some prayed and begged You for a miracle. You blessed so many with the children they desired. Thank You! Thank You for the encouragement and the lessons in their stories. May they increase the faith of those experiencing infertility in this day and age. Help those who have just become aware that it may be hard or medically impossible for them to conceive. Comfort those who are shocked and in despair. Give them hope no matter the journey ahead. For those who You intend to bless to conceive, but are in a waiting season, I pray You would help them endure. If Your Will is for them to keep trying naturally, I pray You will not let them lose hope each month that they wait and do not hear the news they want to hear. May they not feel as though their body or You are betraying them and instead lean into patience and trusting Your timing. If it is Your Will for them to utilize special treatments or seek medical assistance, please help them to become knowledgeable about the options that are available for them. Guide them to a reproductive endocrinologist who knows You and will give them godly advice, show them compassion and care. For those currently trying to conceive and going through an assistive treatment, help them be resilient through the ups and downs of the journey. Stay close to them Lord. I pray they will lean on You. Amen.

DAY 127

FOR FARMERS

Thank You Lord for farmers! Thank You for those who know how to raise animals, grow the food we eat and cultivate crops that are used as raw materials. Today I pray for the farmers, farm workers and all their families. Thank You for the knowledge and skill You have bestowed upon them. For the planning and problem-solving skills, for their patience and determination. For their heavy labor. Touch every inch of their bodies Lord and give them relief from any pain. Lift exhaustion and give them energy every day. Give them sound rest when they slumber and renew their strength. May they be able to take care of their own bodies the same way that they care for the land and the crops and the animals that they raise. Give them relief when they ache and the resources, they need to maintain good physical health. Protect them from the weather, the heat and the rain, snow and wind. Please protect them, their families, their animals, their crops, their homes and their land from damage or destruction from contaminants and natural disasters. Please provide the tools and equipment they need to work their land and to maintain their sheds, barns, fencing and other structures. May their harvests be plentiful and may they earn a fair price for what they sell. May they feel the satisfaction of their hard work providing sustenance for others and know the importance of what they do. Bless the work of their hands Lord. Amen.

DAY 128

Prayer Prompt
FOR SOMEONE WHO HAS PRAYED FOR YOU

Think about someone who has prayed for you recently or in the past and return the favor by using this space to pray for them.

DAY 129

FOR STRAY ANIMALS

Father, we know You created animals to live in the wild. We've built up modern cities and buildings that have limited the areas of nature where they can roam and find food and shelter for themselves. So today I pray for the dogs and cats and other animals that in our modern society we consider strays. Those roaming on the streets, dirty, hungry and not cared for. For those with medical issues, who've been hurt or abused, I pray they would be healed naturally or get the medical attention they need. May someone see them and take pity on them and help them. Giving them food, taking them to a shelter or even taking them into their own home. May anyone who does this be protected from danger, hurt or disease as they try to help. May they have the resources or find the support they need from local agencies, friends or neighbors to address all the needs of the animal. Give them courage to do what they can for stray animals when You convict their spirit to act and help. In Jesus name I pray, Amen.

DAY 130

FOR THOSE CHEATING ON THEIR SPOUSE

Father, today I pray for those around the world who are currently cheating on their spouse. I don't know the reasons why. I don't know their personal pain, trauma, resentments, needs, etc. that got them to a point where they willingly chose to cheat, but I do know that adultery is a sin. So, I pray that You would convict their hearts right now to the point that they immediately stop this behavior. I pray they would repent before You, confess to their spouse and ask for forgiveness. I pray You would give them a deep understanding of themselves and why they allowed this sinful behavior into their life. Help them to be honest and clearly express these things to their spouse with humility if that is what You want them to do in order to rebuild trust and intimacy in their marriage. Give them patience and compassion to listen and respect their spouse's reaction to their confession. Rather than being defensive or expressing excuses for why they cheated, help them to give their spouse the room to express their emotions and any requests for space or time to heal. May the cheating spouse take it upon themselves to reach out for help from a counselor, therapist or pastor to really help them work through this so that they can with confidence promise their spouse this will never happen again. Father, every situation is different, so I pray that You would tailor Your guidance and direction for this person and end their willingness to cheat today. In the name of Jesus, Amen.

DAY 131

FOR THOSE WHO DESIRE A BETTER RELATIONSHIP WITH THEIR CHILDREN

The parent child relationship is such a special one, no matter the age of the children, so Father God, today I pray for those parents who desire a better relationship with their children. Help them find ways to seek to understand their children on a more intimate level. Help them to let go of their expectations of who their child is and instead to see them for who they truly are. Give them ears to listen and Your counsel on how to respond. Help them love unconditionally, while always speaking Your truth. Help them to discipline in ways that are healthy and help their children grow into the women and men You created them to be. Help the children see their parents as loving, even when they disagree with something. May they know that ever instruction or advice given is coming from a place of love, protection, life experience, godly wisdom and care. If there is anger, please lift it. If there is bitterness, please remove it. If there is disappointment, please wipe it away. Please give the parents clarity on how to develop a better relationship with their children and encourage them on the journey to getting there. In the name of Jesus, Amen.

DAY 132

FOR DOCTORS

To The Great Physician, I thank You for earthly doctors, for those You have allowed to be trained in the medical field to care for others. Thank You for their education and training. Thank You for their desire and willingness to heal. Thank You for the specific field of medicine they have chosen. I pray that they understand that their gifts and talents come from You. I pray they know You and that You would guide what they do and say in every patient interaction. Help them deliver good and bad news. Help them to have a good bedside manner, even when they are exhausted or overwhelmed. Thank You for their selflessness to care for others even when they might have personal struggles of their own. For those who are drowning in medical school debt, please make a way for them to pay it and not have to compromise their integrity or limit who they can help for financial reasons. For those with their own practices that are struggling under the weight of all the insurance and licensing requirements that they need to pay for, please make a way for them to be able to cover those costs while also offering their service at prices that patients can afford. Give doctors strength, physically and mentally, to do their jobs with excellence. Give insight and discernment as they diagnosis their patients and plan for treatment. Please guide their minds, hearts and hands in every procedure or surgery they perform. Father thank You for doctors and the skills You have blessed them with. In Jesus' name, Amen.

DAY 133

FOR THOSE WHO ARE INTERVIEWING FOR A JOB

Father, I thank You for the opportunities You will give people around the world to interview for a job this week. May just getting the interview be an encouragement to them. May it remind them that their experience and skills are valuable. You already know if this job is meant for them or not. I trust You and ask that you make Your Will very clear to those who are interviewing and those who are making the hiring decisions. Help those that are interviewing to not be nervous or anxious for anything. Help them communicate their experience, talents, interests and what makes them amazing. Give them courage to ask questions to understand the role, the salary, the benefits and the company culture. Help them discern if this is a place that they want to work and if this job is one that is aligned with the skills that they have and what they enjoy doing. If they are not offered the job, may they learn something thru this process that helps them in future interviews. If they are offered the job, please make a way for them to be offered good compensation, great benefits and join a team where there are opportunities for growth. I pray that those who are interviewing for a job this week would find the perfect role for them. In the name of Jesus, Amen.

DAY 134

FOR COUNTRIES THAT ARE AT WAR

Oh Father, for countries that are currently at war, I pray for peace. I know that You allow wars for reasons that are far beyond my understanding; yet, I wish they didn't have to happen. Today I want to pray for the people of countries that are at war. The innocent civilians that are caught in the cross-fire and who live in harm's way. While the war is raging on, please protect them Lord. Protect them from bodily injury and harm. Protect them from starvation and hunger. Protect their homes and shelters. Be their comfort when they are afraid. Be their peace when chaos reigns. If at any point they have to interact with the opposing side, please be the peace in the situation and don't allow the interaction to result in any violence or pain. If they desire to find refuge in another place until the conflict is resolved, I pray You would make a way of escape. If they desire to stay in their community while the conflict continues, please help them to do that, providing all that they need as they wait for peace. Father for countries that are at war, I pray that the conflict would be resolved as quickly as possible with the least number of lives lost as possible. Father, for countries that are at war, I pray that You would bring about peace.

DAY 135

FOR PRESIDENTS

I can't begin to imagine the real burden each president has carried. Today Lord, I lift up the current president of the United States of America to You. Father, give them wisdom, strength and health. Give them courage and convict their heart and mind to do Your Will. And I pray for every former president and every president yet to come. Father, You know why each one was given that position of authority just like every king and ruler of biblical times. I pray for each of the past presidents that any stress or regret they carry from their time in the While House or the hard decisions they had to make or the threats to their lives or the horrible situations at home and around the world that they were privy to that we will never hear about would be lifted and relieved. That You would speak encouragement to their hearts about the things they did that made You proud and convict their hearts of any sin or disobedience that did not bring You glory. I pray for their health and well-being and that of their families. Thank you for their service to the country. And for future presidents that are yet to come, Father I pray You would prepare their hearts and minds even now for the day when they will take their oath of office. That when they lay their hand on the Bible that it will not just be ceremony, but that they would feel a heartfelt conviction to trust in You to guide their decisions and behavior. Father only You know which presidents of our past actually had a personal relationship with You and Your son Jesus. And only You know which presidents in the future will truly know You. Just like in the Bible, not all those who governed over Your people knew You. But they still fulfilled Your purpose and what You allowed for Your reasons that are far above our understanding. So, I pray that the hearts of future presidents will take Your great command to love others to heart. No matter what they believe, that they would act in ways according to this Holy command. That You would give them discernment and wisdom and that they would fulfill Your Will in the name of Jesus. Amen.

DAY 136

FOR THOSE WHO HAVE HAD TO TAKE ON UNEXPECTED RESPONSIBILITIES

Life is full of the unexpected Father, so today I pray for those who have had to take on unexpected responsibilities. For some it's something new, for some it's something more complex, harder or bigger than they thought they would ever have to handle. Whatever the situation, please reassure them that they can handle it with You. I pray this would draw them closer and closer to You for direction and guidance of how to handle it. May they be encouraged knowing that You trust them to handle it. Give them clarity of thought, light the path that You want them to follow. If it is a short-term responsibility, I pray You would give them strength. If it is a long-term responsibility, I pray You would sustain them through it. May they treat this responsibility with care and not take its importance for granted. Help them to move past the unexpectedness of the situation and take initiative in it. Help them to not ask "why me" and instead ask You what Your Will is and how they can handle this in a way that makes You proud. In the name of Jesus, Amen.

DAY 137

FOR THE STUDENTS OF A SCHOOL IN YOUR AREA

Father, I pray for _____
That this school would be a place where its students look back on their time there with fond memories. That it's teachers and administrators' work make a difference in the lives of its students. That its students appreciate the hard work of the maintenance, grounds keeping and janitorial staff. Where it's cafeteria staff, school counselors, nurses and all other employees do their best to provide a caring and supportive environment to all. Where the security and safety personnel are proud of how they keep the students and the entire school community safe. May the teachers take seriously their charge to educate and go the extra mile to help any students who may be struggling academically. May the students be inspired to do their very best every day. Please keep all the students safe from all harm, hurt or danger. May bullying at school or through social media be quickly stopped and addressed. For students struggling at home for any reason, may this not negatively impact their ability to receive an education. Please give them the courage to speak to a school counselor or administrator and may they be freely given the support or resources they need. May the students that attend this school now and, in the future, have an experience that gives them a hopeful outlook on their future. In the name of Jesus, Amen.

DAY 138

FOR A COUNTRY EXPERIENCING FAMINE

Father, today I come before You, our Provider, to pray for countries experiencing a famine or food shortage of any kind. Please provide sustenance to its people Lord. How hard it must be to live in a place where there is literally no food. Not just no food that you like, but no food at all. Oh, how so many of us in this world take for granted the privilege of being able to pick and choose the food we eat. The privilege of food preferences. How grateful we should be for having access to foods that help us avoid allergies and other intolerances. You designed our bodies to need physical food to survive. Please make a way for the people of these countries to get access to the food they need. I don't know why You are allowing them to experience this famine or how long it will last. My hope is that it won't last long, but in the meantime, while these countries wait, work, trade or negotiate for food, please sustain their people. Help them find ways to survive on what they have and if they have nothing, remind them that they do still have You. Be their food when their kitchen is bear, be their Living Water when their wells have run dry. Sustain the people not only physically but also mentally until food can be available again. I pray You would shower abundance upon them in due time. In the name of Jesus, Amen.

DAY 139

FOR HEALTHCARE WORKERS

Today, I pray for all those who work in the healthcare industry. I pray for those who are often remembered, like doctors and nurses, and also for those who are often taken for granted, like pharmacists, physical therapists, occupational therapists, midwives, medical lab scientists, physician assistants, surgical assistants, orderlies, paramedics, phlebotomists, dieticians, hospital chaplains and so many more. Thank You for the work that they do, the work of their hands that You guide, and their minds that You give wisdom and direction to. I pray that You would help them to do their jobs with the utmost care for their patients. I pray that You would give them adequate rest so that they are able to perform well. For those who are weary from the years they have cared for and served others and for those who are weary from the 2020 pandemic or other high-stress events, renew their bodies and spirits, Father. Help them to process the pain and even death they have seen by recalling more often the miracles, the healing, and the joy they have experienced while tending to the health care of others. Bless them, Lord, in all that they do to help others live a healthy and healed life. In the name of Jesus, Amen.

DAY 140

FOR THOSE WHO WORK FOR THE IRS

Father, today I pray for those who work for the Internal Revenue Service. I think of the tax collectors in the Bible and how the people felt about them, and I imagine that that is similar to how some feel about those who work for the IRS today. But Father, the employees are not our enemy. They, like Your apostle, Matthew, are doing their job and can be used for Your Glory too. Help those who have to file taxes, those who owe money, and those who may feel like the tax laws aren't fair to separate the laws and governmental issues from the people who work at the IRS. Help them to be seen as hard-working people and not enemies. I pray that you give wisdom to those who review, audit, and work in other roles at the IRS. Give them the integrity to do their jobs to the utmost ability that You would give them. May they be fair and exercise good judgment in all things. May their hearts be open to show grace as You would lead them to. May they be proud of their work. Help them in seasons of high stress and increased workload. Help them not to rush through their work or become desensitized, forgetting that behind the numbers, there are people. Your people. In the name of Jesus. Amen.

DAY 141

FOR THOSE WHO HAVE BEEN BETRAYED BY A FRIEND

Betrayal is hard. Trusting someone enough to truly consider them a friend can be a scary thing because we have to open ourselves up and be ourselves, hoping that the other person accepts us as we are. So, when that friend betrays us, we can feel broken. So today, Lord, I pray for those who have been betrayed by a friend. Help them to process what has happened. Please give them clarity and show them the truth, removing any denial that is getting in the way of their ability to fully see the situation for what it is. Help them understand if that was anything that they did that may have contributed to the situation that they can learn from moving forward. May they not repeat these things in other relationships. Were they too trusting or not trusting enough? Did they not see or ignore a sign of warning You sent to try to protect them from the heartbreak they are experiencing now? Help them to have clarity while also showing them where their anger and hurt are righteous and justified. Please help them process their feelings in a way that is healthy and doesn't cause them more pain. Protect them from their betrayer and bring true friends alongside to comfort and support them. Whatever the specifics of the betrayal, please bring peace and resolution into the situation swiftly so that they can forgive and move on. Please don't let this betrayal keep them from allowing new friendships to bloom. I pray they would deepen the true friendships they have and find new ones in new seasons as You ordain. In the name of Jesus, Amen.

DAY 142

FOR PROFESSIONAL ATHLETES

What a fun and challenging career You have assigned to professional athletes! Even before they were born, You designed them to be fierce competitors who are physically and mentally tough. And how creative You are, Father, that You would provide so many different ways for them to make a living. Running, biking, baseball, basketball, volleyball, gymnastics, football, soccer, skateboarding, cheerleading and more. There are those who make a living as bodybuilders, Olympians, boxers, dancers, athletic coaches, arm wrestlers, and synchronized swimmers! Today, I pray for all professional athletes. There are too many to mention them all, but You know each and every one. You know the skills, talents, and strength that they need to be the best at what they do. Give perseverance to the ones who work solo and strong camaraderie to those who are a part of a team. You know, the famous ones and the ones whose names I'll never hear. Encourage them in the ways You know will motivate them the best. Touch them, Lord, physically and mentally, to give them the energy to never give up and continue to train to become better and better in their field. May they be able to earn or win enough money to support themselves and their families. And when their careers are over due to injury, age, or any reason, I pray that You would help them to adjust to their new season of life without feeling like they have lost who they are. Help them now while they are still competing to be good stewards of their earnings and save for the future while they enjoy every experience of today. In the name of Jesus, I pray, Amen.

DAY 143

FOR WOMEN WHO WILL HAVE A MASTECTOMY THIS YEAR

Today, I pray for women who will undergo a mastectomy this year. Father, You already know their names. You already know the reasons for this surgery. Whatever the situation, I pray You would guide them to make the decision that is right for them. I pray their physicians have given them accurate and clear information so that they are well-informed of the benefits and risks of the surgery. I pray they have a high level of understanding of the different options available to determine what amount of breast tissue will be removed. Give them discernment, Oh Lord of if they have selected the right surgeon, and help them to advocate for themselves if they have questions or want to seek additional opinions or advice. Remind them of their beauty and where it comes from while also helping them work through the very real feelings they will have about this surgery and the change to their body. If they choose to undergo breast reconstruction, please guide them in this as well. Throughout this entire journey, give them Your Peace that surpasses all understanding. As they feel all the emotions that come with their diagnosis, the process of making the decision to have a mastectomy and deciding if they want to go through reconstructive surgery, please never leave their side. I pray that they know You are there and can feel Your Comfort and support along the way. I pray that any cancer is completely removed or if this is preventative, that it would be successful in keeping any cancer from forming in their body. I pray they will be at peace going into and coming out of surgery and that their recovery will be swift. In the name of Jesus, Amen.

DAY 144

FOR THOSE WITH PTSD

Today, I come before You, Lord, to pray for those with post-traumatic stress disorder. I pray for their complete healing from the traumatic event that they experienced or witnessed that causes them to be triggered still today. Please ease and completely remove the anxiety they feel. I know You can do this just by speaking a word, and I know that You can also do this through others that You can send into their life to help them heal. So, Father, right now, I ask that You would connect them with mental health professionals that can address their specific situation. Connect them with someone who will ask the right questions, listen and develop a treatment plan, and teach them tools to help them overcome PTSD forever. I know all things are possible with You and that You can take away the power that those memories have in their mind. You can replace those triggers with peace. So that's what I ask You to do today, Lord. Don't allow those triggers to have power over them ever again, give them back the strength they need to process what they experienced and not allow it to control their lives. In the name of Jesus, I pray, Amen.

DAY 145

FOR THOSE WHO ARE TRYING TO STOP SMOKING

Lord, I pray for those who are trying to stop smoking. If they desire to stop smoking or vaping tobacco, nicotine, marijuana, or any other substance, I pray You would remove that desire from them. That they would have the mental and physical strength to resist the temptation because You have completely removed the addictive pleasure that they previously felt. Replace that need with a healthy habit or change in their lifestyle that will benefit their physical and emotional health. If they are smoking to relieve stress, I pray You would open their eyes to other ways to lift the burdens from their minds. If they are smoking as an escape from something, I pray You would give them other ways to find refuge. If they smoke just because it's their way of socializing, help them to resist the temptation even if others around them are indulging.
Help them find enjoyment in socializing with others without the need to smoke. For those who are trying, I just pray that they will not be discouraged and never give up. Even if they stop for a while and find themselves reaching for a smoke again, convict them to remember why they wanted to quit and to try again. May they not feel shamed but instead supported by others who encourage them and remind them that they can do it. Give them strength, Lord, help them persevere. Please help those who want to stop to stop forever. Amen.

DAY 146

FOR THOSE WHO ARE TIRED

Jesus, Your Word says that those who are tired can come to You, and You will give them rest. (Matthew 11:25-30) It also says that those who wait on the LORD will renew their strength; they might stumble, but they will always keep going and never give up. (Isaiah 40:28-31) So, like the birds of the air that You care for so much, that flap their wings and renew their strength as they soar, I pray that You will renew the strength of those who are tired and weary. May they know that this is a normal part of being human and that this feeling does not last forever. May they look to You for their strength and hide away with You alone somewhere where they can be renewed by Your love. Help them to show themselves grace and take time to rejuvenate their soul, body, and mind so that they can again run the race You have assigned just for them. In Your name, Jesus, I pray, Amen.

DAY 147

FOR THOSE WHO ARE STRUGGLING WITH THEIR SELF-WORTH

This world can make people feel worthless. I rebuke the lies that the spiritual forces of evil try to put into people's minds. For those who are struggling with their self-worth, Holy Spirit remind them that You live in them and that You would not reside in a place without value. Remind them that You love them because the Father loves them so much that He literally gave His love, His Son's life for them. May they know that Jesus Christ's death on the cross was because they are worthy of love. Show them in new and unexpected ways that they are valuable, worthy and priceless. That You in Your sovereignty decided they were worthy of creation. The fact that they exist, proves that they are valuable to You and this world You placed them in. You do not waste Your time or energy on meaningless or worthless things. Help them remember this and hold on to this truth when the enemy, other people or even their own mind and flesh tries to convince them otherwise. In the name of Jesus, who sacrificed Himself because they are worthy, Amen.

DAY 148

FOR THOSE WHO STRUGGLE TO FIND HARMONY BETWEEN THEIR WORK AND PERSONAL LIFE

Holy Spirit, I come before You today to pray for those who are struggling to find harmony between their work and personal lives. The struggle is truly real. Thank You for guiding us and leading us throughout each day. Please help those who are struggling right now to hear You and obey as You guide them in how they prioritize their time and how they use their energy and resources. Help them to live by You, The Spirit, making decisions for themselves that produce peace and joy in their lives. Reveal to them how to schedule their time. Show them what things they need to stop doing and what things they should start doing that will bring more peace between their work and personal lives. Give them courage in setting and communicating healthy boundaries to protect their peace. May they carve out time with You daily to check in and ask for Your guidance. And may they protect that time so it never gets stolen away for something else. Help them prioritize people over work, tending to the relationships You have blessed them with. Help them to not take anyone for granted while also being a good steward of the skills and talents You have given them to do good work in this world. May they show themselves grace, knowing that "balance" may not be realistic but "harmony" can be achieved. I pray they find harmony, a comfortable and pleasing rhythm between their work and personal life. Amen.

DAY 149

FOR THOSE WHO ARE DATING

Holy Spirit, today I lift up to You those who are dating. I include all those who are dating Lord, for those who are dating around and those who are dating monogamously. For those who are just having fun and those who are looking for a commitment. For people who are young and old, for all those who are dating Lord, I pray You would guide them and direct their path as they make decisions on who to spend time with, what to do during that time and how long to date. Give them clarity on who is only supposed to be in their lives for an experience or a season and who is supposed to be there forever. Protect each person from danger or harm. Holy Spirit, give them insight into how to stay safe and when to say no to a date or leave a relationship. May no harm, hurt or danger befall them. In each interaction, may each person learn something about themselves, about others and about You. May no interaction be in vain. Use each experience to lead them to the right person You have ordained for their life. Help them to be themselves, confident in who they are and what they want. Let them not be ashamed of their hopes, dreams or desires. May they be open to sharing their heart so they can connect with the person You have designed to be perfectly suited for them. May every man find his ezer kenegdo and may every woman understand the grace, strength and importance that You designed them to have in relationship with man. May they not indulge in any sinful behavior, yet also still have fun on their dating journey as You lead them to the covenant relationship You planned for them. In the name of Jesus, Amen.

DAY 150

FOR PARENTS OF ADULT CHILDREN

Holy Spirit, I pray You would be in the midst of relationships between parents and their adult children. Give the parents understanding of how to love, support, care for and continue to guide their children, while also letting go and letting them find their own way. Give the parents peace of mind Holy Spirit, that they would not worry, but instead rest knowing that You love their children even more than they do and will keep them in Your care. Give them the right words to speak and help them discern the right timing to say the things that they need to say as they continue to give godly advice to their children and share their own experience and knowledge with them. May their children respect them and grown in their understanding of their parents as they experience adulthood themselves. May their relationship become deeper and more intimate as parents and adult children begin to see each other in a new and different light. Especially help those parents who are struggling to let go and let their children be adults. Soften their hearts, Holy Spirit, and help them to have self-control, holding their tongue when what they have to say may not be helpful to their children learning on their own. Give them peace, Holy Spirit, to not be anxious or fearful about their children making their own decisions. And for single parents of adult children, I say a special prayer that You would help them to enjoy their lives, filled with friends and activities that fulfill their passions and interests. Help single parents who have been used to their lives revolving around their children to let go and set healthy boundaries between their lives and their children's lives. In the name of Jesus, I pray, Amen.

DAY 151

FOR ENTREPRENEURS

Today, Lord, I ask You to show special favor to entrepreneurs. I pray for everyone who operates a business regardless of size. For those who are doing it all alone and those who have teams and boards and investors. Today, I pray You would give them clear vision. Help them see where they are, what they have accomplished and what is yet to be done. Give them insight on the path they are forging and discernment on the plans they make and the strategies they employ. Bless their minds with creativity and their hearts with strength, so they can navigate the challenges of entrepreneurship well and make You proud. I pray that whatever their business is, it is something that glorifies You, sharing Your light with this world. When they struggle for ideas, please be their inspiration. When they struggle financially, please be their provider. When they fail, may they learn but not give up. When they succeed, may they give You all the glory. I pray that the lives of those they serve with their business would be made better in some way because of them. May every entrepreneur fulfill their assignment with integrity, always being true to the original mission You put in their heart, no matter how big their business grows. Remind them through the customers or businesses they serve that what they do matters. In the name of Jesus, I pray, Amen.

DAY 152

PRAYER PROMPT
FOR A FRIEND WHO DOESN'T KNOW CHRIST

Use this space to pray for someone you know that does not know Christ as their Lord and Savior.

DAY 153

FOR GRANDPARENTS

First Lord, I thank You for grandparents! That You allow so many to live to see their children's children. What a blessing! Thank You for their lives and I pray today that they would be rich with joy, seeing their children and their children's children thrive. I pray they would have healthy relationships with their entire family. I pray they would be loved and supported emotionally and if necessary, financially by their family. For younger grandparents who are still working, I pray that they would have the ability to spend quality time with their families and enjoy their love and affection. I pray their grandchildren would get to see them at work and be inspired. For older grandparents who are retired, I pray they would also be able to spend quality time with their families and have the physical strength and energy to be actively involved in their grandchildren's lives. For grandparents who don't live in the same state as their grandchildren, I pray they would be able to travel to see them often and have access to other tools like video calls, to stay connected and be a part of each other's lives. May grandparents have the opportunity to pass down their wisdom to their grandchildren, teaching them life lessons that will make a positive impact. May they be respected and not neglected by their grandchildren. May grandchildren never take for granted the blessing of spending time with them. May grandparents pass down family history and stories so that their legacy lives on from generation to generation. Lord, I thank You for grandparents. I thank You on behalf of those who never got a chance to meet their grandparents, their legacy still impacts their lives in ways that they might never know. I thank You on behalf of those who's grandparents are living and have the ability to connect with them right now, today. And I thank You on behalf of those who's grandparents have passed away. I thank You for the time they got to spend with them. I thank You for your grace and mercy throughout their lives. I thank You for all grandparents, Lord. In the name of Jesus, Amen.

DAY 154

FOR HOMEMAKERS

I thank You and pray for homemakers, Lord. For women and men whose priority is to make their homes warm and welcoming places for their families to grow and thrive. For those who stay at home and take care of their homes, run their households, and are the backbone of their family. Some may be stay-at-home parents, some may be stay-at-home spouses, some may have part-time jobs or small businesses, and others may not have employment at all, but they are all important in Your sight. May they all know that they are worthy and important to their family. May they know they are appreciated in all that they do. May they feel loved and cared for, seen and heard. May their effort and work never go unnoticed or be taken for granted. May they feel proud of the work of their heart and hands. May they wake up each day with energy and strength. Help them to be the CEO of their household, organized and showing leadership in everything they do. May their family feel at peace because they know they can rely on them. May each homemaker be a good steward of the home You have blessed them with. No matter the size of their home or their family, help them to be grateful and not take what they have for granted. Help them to have eyes to see what needs to be done to maintain a space that is a welcoming, peaceful retreat from the world for themselves and their family. Give them rest and times of refreshment so that they can continue to pour into their home. May their family return their love with appreciation and care so that they never feel undervalued. May they take pride in their work and see how You use them as a vessel of Your love, grace, and encouragement in the lives of every person who steps foot in their home. Thank You for the homemakers. May they continue to be blessed. In the name of Jesus, Amen.

DAY 155

FOR THOSE WORKING ON THEIR PHD

Oh, how hard it must be to stay the course and complete something like a PhD. For those who are in the midst of working on their PhD right now, I pray that You would give them the determination of spirit to not give up when it is hard. Help them to focus and to gain access to the knowledge they need to complete their research. Open their minds to new ideas and ways of thinking that expand their understanding of their area of study. May this PhD not just be a degree on paper or a goal they accomplish, but let it also be a foundation for the great work You have assigned for them to do in this life. I thank You for their dedication. Please help them persevere. Continue to motivate them and inspire them. If they are also working or juggling family life at the same time, I pray that You would make a way for them to finish all their assignments and requirements while also meeting these other responsibilities. And I pray that for those in financial hardship from the costs associated with their degree, You would make a way for that burden to be lifted. Bless them financially with the resources to pay for tuition, books, tools, housing, childcare, transportation, and whatever they need while they are working on their PhD. Protect them from the enemy's schemes to throw them off course, to distract or discourage them from completion. Remind them when things get tough that this is something You have assigned them to accomplish for Your great purpose and that they can do it, no matter what anyone says. I thank You in advance for this accomplishment, Father. I hope they will celebrate this victory by giving You the glory. In the name of Jesus. Amen.

DAY 156

FOR SOCIAL WORKERS

Today, I pray for social workers, for those who help people and communities in need. They are a group of people with such giving and caring hearts who help so many different people, from young to old, of every race and creed, in such diverse situations. I pray that all the work that they do will honor You, Your Will, and Your Ways. That you would give them discernment in the decisions they have to make on behalf of others and for themselves. Help them to always do what is right for their clients and the communities they work with. Give them perseverance to advocate and fight for what is right. Protect them, Oh Lord, as they sometimes find themselves in unhealthy, hostile, or dangerous situations. Give them courage and strength. Protect their bodies and keep them healthy. Protect their minds and their mental health and help them to persevere even when they deal with trauma. Encourage them, and may they know that their work makes a huge positive difference in other people's lives. I thank You, Lord, for their willingness to use their skills and energy to do what they can to make other people's lives better. Bless them, Oh Lord. In the name of Jesus, Amen.

DAY 157

FOR THOSE WHO ARE UNDER-EMPLOYED OR UNAPPRECIATED

Father, I pray for those who are under-employed and not making enough money. For those who are having a hard time finding enough work to earn enough money. For those whose jobs do not reflect their full skills or abilities. And I pray for those who are employed but underappreciated. The people who have a job that matches their skills and abilities but are not appreciated by their boss or their coworkers. Help them feel valued by You and not be discouraged by men. Those who are not being paid a fair wage that reflects the quality of their work and their level of contribution to the organization's success. For those who should have been promoted but for reasons outside of their control have not been yet. And also for those stuck in the wrong job who want to make a career change but are having a hard time getting potential employers to appreciate what they have to offer. For all people who find themselves in these types of situations, Father, I pray that You would make a way. You are The WayMaker, so I know You can if it is Your Will. Please provide for those who are struggling financially. Bring them opportunities to earn more income to make ends meet. May they be offered promotions or new job opportunities that exceed their personal income goals. Reward them for their hard work and faith in You. May the unappreciated be seen and recognized by those with the power and influence to reward them with salary increases, bonuses, and promotions. I trust in Your timing in every situation, Lord, so I ask that in the meantime, You would be with each person and help them to persevere through their situation. In the name of Jesus, Amen.

DAY 158

FOR CHILDREN WHO ARE BEING BULLIED

Jesus, be a friend to all children who are being bullied. I pray it would stop immediately, yet I know that sometimes these hard experiences are allowed by You for reasons that I can't understand. So, for those who You allow to go through something like this, whether in-person or online, I pray for Your protection over them. Protect their physical bodies and their mental health. I pray the bullying will stop right now. That those who are doing it would feel the conviction of Your Spirit to stop their evil ways and turn to loving others as You command. For those being bullied, may they not believe the lies that are spewed at them. May they know who they are and know their identity is in You. If they don't know You, I pray they come to know You and understand who You say they are. Give them the strength and courage to seek help and let a responsible adult know what is going on. May that person be led by Your Spirit to do whatever needs to be done to put a stop to the bullying. No matter the reasons why it is occurring, help them to have ears to listen to the child that is coming to them and give them discernment in how to handle the situation. May the child's heart and mind be protected from any long-term trauma from the bullying. May they not internalize it but seek out help from an adult or a counselor to talk through what they have experienced and how it has made them feel. Especially for any children who are in situations where the bullying has made them consider suicide, Lord, please intervene and remove all thoughts of depression, worthlessness, or hopelessness from their spirit. Speak to them, Lord, and let them know that they are special and valuable in Your eyes. Let them know that things will get better and help them to make it through each day. Give them peace and courage to go on in the face of adversity. Father, please be with all children who are being bullied, and I pray that You will soon bring it to an end. In the name of Jesus, Amen.

DAY 159

FOR THOSE TRYING TO RESIST TEMPTATION

Father, Son, and Holy Spirit, today I pray for those who are trying to resist temptations and addictions of any kind. My prayer is that they know You and know that with You, they can resist anything. I pray they come to know Your power and strength. Give them will power to run from their temptations, no matter what they are. Being tempted is something that we all experience. Even You, Jesus, experienced temptation. Help us all to be like You and have the clarity of understanding, mental strength, and faith to not give in. No matter how great the temptation, help us to recognize in our moments of weakness that You are greater. Convict our hearts and minds to not indulge, not participate, not initiate, not rationalize, not be deceived. May we also not be ashamed, Father, so that we can talk about our temptations with others who will give us sound, godly advice and encouragement. Please bring people alongside each other to support each other in resisting the temptations we all experience in life. Father, I pray that our behavior will make You proud and that if we slip, we do not fall but instead repent and seek Your forgiveness and strength to help us not to slip again. In the name of Jesus, Amen.

DAY 160

FOR LAWYERS

Thank You for the lawyers who You have appointed to represent and defend others. Father, today I pray that all lawyers around the world would seek justice and godly wisdom. I know that Your law, Your commands, and Your Word are the laws we should follow. I know that some of the laws man has enacted around the world do not align with Your Ways. So, I pray for lawyers who are believers and may struggle to make sense of how to handle situations where human laws are not in accordance with You. I pray for all lawyers that they will have the insight, knowledge, and experience they need to represent their clients well. I pray You would give them discernment of how to handle each case. I pray You would give them the evidence they need to fight for justice. I pray You would give them the resources they need to properly argue their case or represent their clients. Help them to negotiate terms and deals that are fair and in alignment with Your Will. Help them to always do what is right and not be fueled by vengeance or any reasons that are not aligned with Your justice. Give them rest, Lord, when they are weary. Give them peace from stress and anxiety. Give them guidance as they interact inside and outside of courtrooms. Protect them from harm. May they not be traumatized by all the things that they see and experience. Help them to do their jobs with excellence and all the ability You have blessed them with. May they be proud of the work that they do. In the name of Jesus, Amen.

DAY 161

FOR THOSE WHO CAN'T SEE GOD AT WORK IN CREATION

Father, I don't understand how anyone can look around and think that this world is not the work of a thoughtful, creative, and amazing God. For those who think that creation happened randomly and that science is not the human explanation of how You work. For those who can't see You at work in the way that the flowers and trees grow. For those who can't see You at work in the way that the waves of the ocean are designed to only go so far on to shore. For those who can't see You at work in the way that man and woman are designed to fit together. For those who can't see You at work in the way that human beings can reason in ways that animals can't. For those who can't see You at work in the stars in the sky. For those who can't see You at work in the sun and the moon and the planets of the universe. For those who can't see You at work in every breath that they take and every new morning that they experience. For those who can't see You at work in the blessings of their lives and the mercy they have experienced. For those who can't see You at work in how birds soar and fish swim. For those who can't see You at work in the unconditional love of their dog. For those who can't see You at work in the way that their body functions and the abilities that they have. Oh, Father, I pray that their eyes would be opened, their ears would hear, and their minds would be expanded to understand that this world was created by The Creator, who took care to design Creation in ways that we will never fully understand. I pray they would be arrested with amazement and see You at work everywhere. In the name of Jesus, Amen.

DAY 162

FOR POLICE OFFICERS

I praise You, Lord, for police officers. Father, for those who are on patrol, who are detectives, who work behind a desk, and all those positions that I'm not even aware of. Thank You for the heart You have given them to want to protect and serve others. May this mission be deep in their hearts and the focus of everything they do. Thank You for their courage, skills, and talents. I ask that You help them in every situation to use them for Your Glory. Help them help others, bring justice, and promote peace. In this fallen world, those who have dedicated their lives to the service of public welfare face mounting challenges. Father, I especially lift up to you those officers who fight against injustice and corruption amongst their own ranks. Those who are honorable and just but find themselves having to sometimes confront their own to make positive change. Father, I pray that You will give them the courage they need in every situation. Whether in their department or out in the community, I pray You would guide their hearts and minds in righteousness. Father, please protect them as they do the work You have called them to do. May no hurt, harm, or danger come upon them or those they are trying to protect. Give them discernment and clearness of mind when they have to make tough and split-second decisions. Give them wisdom when they investigate. Help them to develop strong and positive relationships in the communities they serve. Father, the career they have chosen is a hard one and one that has many risks. I thank You that there are those among us willing to take these risks to keep others safe. I pray Your hedge of protection would surround them as well. I pray for their protection, that God would give them discernment and wisdom as they make decisions on how to handle the situations and people they encounter, and that God would give them courage. And I pray for peace of mind for their loved ones, who I'm sure worry about their safety. In Jesus' name, Amen.

DAY 163

FOR SOMEONE'S SALVATION

Father today I urgently pray for _____'s salvation. I don't fully know what their relationship with You is Lord. Only You know what they truly believe in their heart. I pray fervently that they come to know Your Son Jesus before they take their last breath. Please forgive them Father for all their sins and may Your Holy Spirit speak to them so loudly, right now, that they cannot ignore You. In the name of Jesus. May they truly accept Your Son Jesus into their heart. I want so badly for them to find the same peace and joy that I have in You. Please draw them to You with Your Holy Spirit, that they might make a bold declaration of their faith and be assured of eternity with You. If there is anything You will for me to do to show they Your love Lord and to be an example to them, please let me know. Show me what to do or tell me what to say the next time I am in their presence. May I always be a positive representative of You in their life Lord. May nothing I do cause them to not want to know You or to doubt my faith in You. Father, I pray for their salvation today. In the mighty name of Jesus, I pray. Amen.

DAY 164

FOR THOSE WHO SEEK DIRECTION

Oh Father, for those who are seeking direction today, those who don't know which way to turn, I pray You would be their compass. I pray You would give them clarity of their next step. I pray You would make their path straight and lit in a way that they have no doubt, no anxiety about which way to go. Bring counsel into their lives from those who know You and can encourage them along their way. May Your Holy Spirit whisper to them when they seek Your Will and Your Way. May their direction be aligned with Your Will for their life. If they are lacking self-confidence, give them God-confidence. Lend them Your strength, so that they can push past any fear they have about moving forward in the direction You have planned for their life. As they follow You, may they feel Your Peace wash over them and give them courage to keep going. In Your Name, Almighty Father, Amen.

DAY 165

FOR STUDENTS ABOUT TO GRADUATE

Father God, thank You for all students right now from high school, to college, in Master's programs and working on their PhDs, who are preparing to graduate. Thank You for how You have carried them through their academic journey and allowed them to reach this moment of culmination. Thank You for helping them be accepted to the program, obtain the classes that they needed, complete coursework, pass tests and write papers. Thank You for the teachers, teaching assistants and classmates who supported and challenged them along the way. For being with them when they celebrated accomplishments and finished assignments. For being with them when they struggled and wondered if they would make it. As they are now in the home stretch and about to graduate, please continue to encourage them that they can make it. May any last assignments that are due be completed with excellence and ease. May they feel Your Spirit with them, showering them with peace in moments that would normally cause anxiety or stress. May their hope be so full with anticipation and excitement for the future You have in store for them. Give them visions of the great things that You have planned for them to do with all the knowledge they have gained. If there are financial concerns, please alleviate them. May nothing get in the way of their graduation. If there is family or personal drama, may it end, so that their focus can be on this goal. If they are working, may their load be light so that they can enjoy this season of celebration. And may they know that it has been You Lord that has made this all possible. Today, I pray for all those preparing to graduate, that they would be proud of what they are about to accomplish and that they have family and friends who celebrate them too. In the name of Jesus. Amen.

DAY 166

FOR THOSE WHO WANT INTIMACY WITH GOD

Oh God, for Your children who want a deeper relationship with You, I pray today that You would honor the desire of their hearts. Especially for those who don't know how to draw nearer, I ask that You would lead them with Your Holy Spirit and guide them into deeper levels of prayer, worship and study of Your Word. That Your Holy Spirit would whisper to them and give them clarity on what they should do to know You more. They love You Lord. Help them to learn how to honor You with all that they are. That they might walk in the Spirit and produce its fruit through their words, actions and behavior. Give them clean hearts and minds so that their thoughts are only of You and Your Ways. May nothing and no one get in the way of their pursuit of more intimacy with You. May they be not discouraged by other people's opinions. May they be not discouraged by the enemy's attempts to put thoughts of comparison in their minds. May they know that Your relationship with them is unique and special and theirs alone. May they not feel rushed or see their relationship with You as a goal that they will accomplish in their time here on earth, but rather a journey that will not be complete until the day that they see You face to face in eternity. May their quest for deepness with You be one that takes them to new unexpected places that strengthen their faith and solidify their hope in all circumstances. Thank You for allowing us to have intimacy with You. The same intimacy I desire with You, I pray You would have with others too. Abba, Father, thank You. Amen.

DAY 167

FOR THOSE WHO HAVE TO MAKE A HARD DECISION ON BEHALF OF THEIR FAMILY

Father God, for those who have to make a hard decision on behalf of their family, I pray that You would quiet their worries, their fears, their concerns and the thoughts running through their minds. Give them ears to hear Your whispers of what the right decision is to make. May they seek Your guidance in making this decision and not be swayed by anyone or anything that is not in alignment with Your Will. Please help them discern what would be in best interest of their family. Help them balance their feelings and Your Will. Give them clarity and relieve them from any anxiety over what the "right" decision is. May they feel Your peace with the decision You lead them to make, even if the decision is or isn't what they prefer. May their family be understanding and trust that their actions are led by Your Holy Spirit and coming from a place of love. May they feel the love and support of the family members that will be impacted by this decision. In the name of Jesus, Amen.

DAY 168

FOR THOSE STRUGGLING TO PAY THEIR RENT OR MORTGAGE

Oh, what worry those who are struggling to pay for their housing feel. To not be certain you can make your rent or mortgage payment causes so much stress and strain. Father, in the name of Jesus, today I pray for those in this situation. Regardless of why, I pray that You would make a way for them to not fall behind and keep a roof over their head. Father, You hold all riches in Your hands and are able to provide in so many ways. Whether it is leading them to find extra work or getting a raise or bonus because of the excellent work they have done, Father, I ask that You help them to make ends meet, not only this month, but in the months and years to come. I pray they seek You for help and in doing so and are open to whatever You want them to do. If they are in a financial situation that they cannot maintain, I pray You would help them to create a plan to reduce their expenses and find a more suitable situation. If they have medical bills or unexpected expenses that are affecting their budget, I pray You would connect them with good financial or legal counsel who can help them find some relief. Father, You know all the details of every person who is struggling to pay their housing costs right now, so I just lift each situation up to You and ask You to make a way. Thank You in advance for how You will care for each one of them. Amen.

DAY 169

FOR THOSE WHO HAVE LOST A LOVED ONE TO POLICE VIOLENCE

What a horrific tragedy for anyone to live through. I can't imagine the pain of knowing that your loved one's death was caused by people whose job is to protect and serve. Father, You know the specific details of each situation, I do not sit in judgment, I only seek to pray for those that grieve and may be fighting for justice for their loved one. I pray for them emotionally and mentally as they deal with seeing or hearing the details of what happened. I pray for them spiritually that their faith would be strengthened and that they would continue to run to You, the God of all comfort. I pray for the families of the police officers involved and what they must be going through. I pray for the officers whose actions caused the death and pray they would confess their part in this to You God and that they would accept whatever Your justice is in this situation. Oh Lord, I pray for all police officers that this would not make their jobs harder but that it would give the good officers courage and boldness to call out and stand up to the bad. For the family and friends who have lost their loved one, please help them to deal with the unimaginable complicated emotions they must be feeling. Help them to continue to handle all things with grace and be role models to us all of how to not respond to evil with more evil, but instead to look to You and speak peace in spite of our anger and pain. In the name of Jesus. Amen.

DAY 170

FOR THOSE WITH LEARNING DISABILITIES

Father, I come before You today, praying for those with learning disabilities. People of all ages, babies yet to be diagnosed, children and adults. I pray for them all. For those babies whose learning disability will not be discovered until later, I pray now for their family, for their parents, their teachers, their doctors, for everyone who is involved in their care. Please give them eyes to see and understanding to discern that there is something special about this child. Help them to identify and put in place early any help or resources this child will need to develop and live a full and fulfilled life, not limited by the disability You have allowed as part of Your design. I pray for all people with learning disabilities, that they would have the access to whatever they need to live without limits on their ability to accomplish whatever Your Purpose is for their life. Thank You for the abilities You have given them and may Your Holy Spirit speak to their hearts and minds, so that they know that You love them and created them the way You have for a special reason. May they never feel that their learning disability is a curse of mistake. May their loved ones, friends and neighbors treat them with love and respect and never as less than. May they be encouraged by teachers to reach for the stars and never be limited by what other people may think. Father, I don't know why You allow some to be born with or to develop learning disabilities, while others don't, but I do know that nothing You allow is wasted. Everything is a part of Your perfect plan, so I trust in You and lift those with learning disabilities up to You today. In the name of Jesus, Amen.

DAY 171

FOR PEOPLE TO USE THEIR TALENTS FOR HIS GLORY

Oh, Father, today I pray for those who are not using the talents and skills You have given them for Your Glory. For those who have a desire to but don't know where to start, I pray You would give them direction. Guide them in the steps they should take and the plans they should make. For those who don't have the confidence to start or don't think they are worthy of being used for Your Glory, please bring someone into their life who will speak faith and God-confidence to their spirit and kindle a flame that will push them to act. For those who have gifts and talents that they don't realize are from You, please humble them to see You at work in their life and open their eyes to ways they can be good stewards of the talent they have, not using it only for worldly pursuits, but also in ways that will build Your Kingdom and uplift other believers here on earth. Please convict those who are currently using their God-given talents for evil or purposes that are against Your Will. Open their eyes to see and repent and turn to You. Today, I pray that every person all over the world would have a moment of awakening to see how You designed their talents and skills to be used for Your Glory and make the choice to do everything they can to make that happen. In the name of Jesus. Amen.

DAY 172

FOR THOSE CRUSHED IN SPIRIT

For the broken-hearted and crushed in spirit, I come before You today, Father, Son, and Holy Spirit. Father, may they see the situation that has caused this feeling clearly. Help them to understand what has happened with a right perspective. Not overblow or without Your truth. Jesus, please be their friend, drawing them to Your Word and scriptures that will help them to know that they are not alone and that although their spirit may feel crushed right now, it is not broken. Remind them that You have been through much worse than what they are going through now and that You gave Your life so that they might have eternal life. May they know that You are walking with them through the wilderness or pain that they are experiencing, and You will never forsake them. Remind them that if whatever is crushing their spirit is something that has happened to them or a loved one or if it is something that was caused by them, that You love them just the same. Holy Spirit, please speak to their spirit and comfort them. Uplift them Holy Spirit so that they would start to feel relief from whatever is crushing them. In that relief, please help them to hear Your Whispers that can guide them to a place of contentment and joy that can fix the broken and damaged places in their heart. I pray for those who are crushed in spirit and hope You will lead them to a place of peace. In the name of Jesus. Amen.

DAY 173

FOR THOSE WHO ARE NOT TREATED WELL BY THEIR FAMILIES

Oh, Father God, Your design is for family members to love one another and support one another through good times and bad. Your design is for families to be led by God-fearing elders who love You and Your Word and can teach the younger members in Your Way. A family is meant to be a safe place of refuge from the world's wickedness and a support system to navigate life. So today, Father, I pray for those who are not treated well by their family. Those who are not shown the love they should have. Those who are shunned for whatever reason and not loved unconditionally. For those who are abused or abandoned by the family that was meant to care for them. For those who have been hurt by their family members or feel unseen or unheard. Father, I don't know any of the circumstances or reasons, but none of these matters. What matters is that You call us to love. You call us to love our neighbors as ourselves, and how much more do You implore us to love our flesh and blood. There can be disagreements or conflicts within a family, yet we are still called to love one another. There may be truth spoken that is hard for a family member to hear, but there must still be love. For those who are not treated well by their family, whatever the situation, I pray that You are in the midst of those relationships. That You would convict, mend, and heal. I pray that You would guide each member in how to treat each other well, no matter the situation. That no matter the situation, they would each feel and show love to one another. In the name of Jesus. Amen.

DAY 174

FOR HUMAN RESOURCES PROFESSIONALS

For the people You have gifted to manage the most precious resource You created, Father, today I pray. I pray for those who work in Human Resources. The people managers, whose job it is to ensure that others are in the right positions that align with the skills and talents You've given them. The people managers whose job it is to make sure that employees are supported and given an honest assessment of their work in order to excel in their role. For the people managers, whose job it is to help other people managers be great leaders and inspire their team to do great things. For the people managers, whose job it is to ensure fair working conditions, health and wellness benefits, and fair wages. For the people managers that navigate interpersonal conflict on behalf of others and remove obstacles that get in the way of employees getting their job done. For the human resource professionals that recruit, hire, and fire. For the ones that often put the needs of others before their own and are sometimes overlooked for their emotional strength. Today, I pray for human resource professionals in all industries and roles. I pray You would continue to give them the knowledge of laws, guidelines, and human nature that help them to do their jobs with integrity and compassion. I pray You would give them strength and patience when they are resolving conflicts that others do not have the ability to resolve on their own. I pray You would give them the support of their company in all they do and provide them with the courage they need to address each challenge. I especially pray that they would be fulfilled by seeing the positive impact that they have on so many lives, knowing that their role is vital to the success of the company they work for and to the success of so many people. May they feel valued always. In the name of Jesus. Amen.

DAY 175

FOR THOSE WHO ARE LONELY

We are never alone because You are with us, Lord, yet there are times when we all feel lonely. I pray today for those who are lonely and especially for those who are lonely and do not know You, Jesus, as a friend. May those who feel lonely feel an unexplainable peace right now, Lord, that leads them to draw closer to You. May they wonder what it is that lifts their spirit and makes them feel a peaceful presence. May this intrigue drive them to search for You and connect with Your Holy Spirit that dwells in us. May they come to know that feeling of loneliness as an indicator of their distance from You and desire to draw near, read Your Word, pray, and reach out to connect with others who know You so that they don't feel alone. If there is anything that is causing them to unconsciously pull away from others who are trying to reach out, please help them to break down those walls. If they are feeling lonely even amid their family, friends, co-workers, or community, please help them to express how they are feeling with someone who will take the time to listen and know them on a deeper level so that they don't feel lonely anymore. Give them the courage to reach out to others and protect them from rejection when they try to make new friends. Please bring people alongside them who have common interests, especially in You, and may these friendships be a sweet balm to their souls. May they truly come to know in their spirit that You, Jesus, are their best friend because there is no greater love than the love of someone who would lay down their life for a friend. Remind them that this is how much You love them and that You sent Your Holy Spirit so they would never be alone. In Your Name, I pray, Amen.

DAY 176

FOR THOSE WITH SCHIZOPHRENIA

Father God, our Creator, You designed our brains to be so amazing and intricate and complicated. We have been able to explain so much with our scientific studies, but there is so much we still don't understand. And we don't know why You allow some people to experience the challenge of schizophrenia and others don't. I come before You today, praying for those who you have allowed to experience delusions, hallucinations, disorganized speech, and thoughts. Please be with them, Father, speak to them, and calm their minds. Whether through Your miraculous touch, through the medicines You have allowed us to develop, or through psychotherapy, I pray that those with schizophrenia would find relief, peace, and a right mind so that they would be able to function well and have a good quality of life. That they would be able to develop relationships, express their thoughts and needs, care for themselves independently, and fulfill the work on this earth that You designed them to do for Your Glory. In those times when they are struggling, please protect them and those they interact with from harm. May they not hurt themselves or others. I rebuke the voices that would cause them to do anything that would put them or anyone else in danger. May those who interact with them treat them with kindness and understanding. May they always have access to the medical resources they need to stay in their right mind and have the support they need to battle this thorn You have allowed in their side. Help them to stay connected with reality and hear Your voice over all others, guiding them each day. May they not feel ashamed because this is not something that they caused. May they instead have the mental strength they need to take one day at a time, knowing they are loved and worthy of Your love and the love of others. In the name of Your precious Son, Jesus, Amen.

DAY 177

FOR SPOUSES WHO ARE LONELY

Oh, Father, marriage is such a beautiful part of Your design. For a husband and wife to be joined together by Your love and the gift of Your grace. How special each should feel that You created them to be one before they even knew each other existed. Yet there are times, even in the best of relationships when a spouse can feel lonely. The distractions of life can cause one spouse's focus to be outside of the home, and they can become neglectful of the other's needs and desires. The financial struggles of life can cause spouses to become so stressed that they each pull away from one another, thinking that if they don't talk about it, it would be easier. Emotional, intellectual, and sexual intimacy can begin to wane as the years pass by, and the passionate fire that was there on the day they said "I do" can be almost extinguished. But God, what You have joined together, let no man put asunder. Today, I pray for spouses who are lonely. I pray for husbands and wives who don't know how to express their feelings and needs to each other. Please give them the words and the courage to ask for what they desire. And give the spouse they are asking a kind and open heart to hear and a desire to meet their spouse's needs, even if they don't understand it fully. I ask You to protect these unions from the enemy's attempts to use these feelings of loneliness to drive such a deep wedge between them that they begin to feel it's unrepairable. Holy Spirit speak to the lonely spouse's heart and mind, reminding them that God is able to fix whatever is causing the loneliness in their relationship. Help them to trust the time and the work it might take to reconnect with their spouse and to know that it is worth it. May their feelings of loneliness be temporary, and may they always remember that You are what binds them with their spouse, so they are never alone. In the name of the Father, the Son, and the Holy Spirit. Amen.

DAY 178

FOR THOSE WHO RIGHT NOW ARE HAVING VIOLENT THOUGHTS

Father, I come before you today against the principalities, rulers of darkness and wickedness Your Word tells us that we wrestle against. I know our minds were created by You for good and justice, righteousness and love. And yet, there are those who are plagued with thoughts of wickedness that lead to violence against themselves and others. Others in their families, their communities, their homes, their schools, their workplaces, the world - Father, please send Your Holy Spirit right now into their minds and destroy the ability of the enemy to plague their thoughts with evil. Replace the violence they obsess over with peace. Convict their souls to seek help. May those that they reach out to hear them and take them seriously and give them or help them connect to the support they need to remove those violent thoughts completely from their mind. I pray that You would immediately remove those thoughts from their mind, yet I know Your Ways and not my ways. So, for some, it may take time, therapy, or even medication to help rid them of these thoughts permanently, so as this process is being worked through, Father protect those that they come in contact with that no hurt, harm, or danger would befall them. In the name of Jesus, God be their protector, Amen.

DAY 179

FOR ADOPTIVE PARENTS

What a blessing adoption is! To show Your Love goes beyond blood and that we are meant to love everyone and care for others and give them a family and a home. Today, I pray for adoptive parents. First, I thank You for their hearts. You have placed in them a desire to welcome a child into their family and love them as their own. Oh, how they model how You have adopted us as Your sons and daughters! The adoption process can be so hard, and there is so much I could pray for in that, but today, I want to pray for their patience and their strength as they raise the child or children they have adopted. Whether a child is biologically yours or not, parenting is challenging at times. And especially for the adoptive parent who has to make so many decisions as they raise this child with an added layer of concerns. Their adopted children may be their only children, or they may have other biological children in their family. Please help them to treat all their children equally and raise them to love one another like blood. Help the adoptive parents to understand the uniqueness of their children and to recognize and appreciate the traits and qualities that may be different from theirs. If their adopted children are of a different culture, race, or country, help them to navigate raising their children to know who they are in all aspects. Help them to celebrate the beauty of their differences and help their children to connect all of who they are in a way that they don't feel disconnected from a part of themselves. Father, please send a special blessing to adoptive parents, and upon their homes, may they always feel the presence of Your Holy Spirit. In Jesus' name, Amen.

DAY 180

PRAYER PROMPT
FOR A MIRACLE IN SOMEONE'S LIFE

Take a moment to think about someone you know who has been hoping for a miracle for a long time. Pray for them that God's answer will be "yes."

DAY 181

FOR ADULTS STUDYING FOR THEIR GED

Today I pray for adults studying for their general education development test. Thank You Lord for giving them the desire to continue their education and please help them to accomplish this goal. May they feel supported and encouraged by their family, friends and community as they take classes and study. When things are hard, remind them that they can do it. Please give them determination to preserve. May they know that accomplishing this will help them in their future endeavors. If they are also working or caring for a household while going to school, please help them to find time to balance all their responsibilities. May they have time and quiet to study. If there is any subject, they struggle in, I pray that someone would come alongside them to help them learn and understand the material. I pray that as they are preparing to take the test, that they allow themselves to daydream about the possibilities that having their GED might open up for them. When they take the test, I pray they feel no anxiety or worry, but that instead, the answers would flow from their mind because they are so prepared. I pray that pass the test and feel a huge sense of accomplishment. I pray they are celebrated by their friends and family and know how proud of them You are. In Jesus' name, Amen.

DAY 182

FOR THOSE WHO DON'T HAVE ACCESS TO HEATING OR AIR CONDITIONING

Father, how we can take for granted the creature comforts we have. Today, I pray for those who don't have access to heating or air conditioning in their homes. Some have one and not the other. Some have neither. There are those who don't have it in their homes, but have the ability to visit nearby public places, like a shopping mall or a coffee shop or even a friend's home, to cool off or to warm up. But there are those who live in places where even that is not an option. So today I pray for those who have no option but to endure through cold, even freezing temperatures. Today I pray for those who have no option but to endure through heat that can cause dangerous levels of heat exhaustion and dehydration. For those who can't take public transportation, or walk, or drive to a place to find relief. Father, please touch their bodies and help them to make it through what they are experiencing physically. Help them mentally to handle what they are experiencing as well. Being physically uncomfortable can really mess with your mind, so I pray You would bring them peace, patience and relief. I pray that the resources and funding needed to provide their community with protection and relief from the weather of their climate would come, so that they don't have to live in these conditions forever. In the name of Jesus, Amen.

DAY 183

FOR THOSE CONSIDERING COMMITTING A CRIME TODAY

Father, I do not know the reasons why, but for those that are considering committing a crime today, I pray. I pray that You would arrest their mind and thoughts and convict them that what they are considering is not what they should do. May they feel Your Presence and a strong sense in their spirit that they should find another way. No matter the reasons they are considering this illegal path, please help them to find another way, a way of righteousness. If they are in desperation, please send relief that meets their needs. If they have accepted the enemy's lies that this is the only way to survive, please break those lies down in their minds and help them see that You have a better path for them to walk. Give them a glimpse of the hope You have planned for their future that will cause them to immediately desire to know You more and walk in Your Ways. If there are bad influences in their life and they feel stuck, like they have no other option but to commit a crime that they have been pressured into, please release this pressure and help them to think clearly and see that they have the strength and intelligence to choose another path. Give them courage to walk away, especially in situations where they are committing crimes with others. Help them to be Your Light in those situations and even turn others away from the sins they are considering committing. Father, in this prayer, I do not judge them, because I know nothing about what has brought them to this moment, but for those considering committing a crime today, I ask that You turn them in another direction and don't allow their plans to succeed. In the name of Jesus, may they hear from Your Holy Spirit right now and follow You. Amen.

DAY 184

FOR HOW WE USE TECHNOLOGY

First, I come before You Lord, giving thanks for the amazing technological advances that You have allowed humanity to achieve. Wow Lord, I am in awe of the fact that we have been able to imagine and create so many things like hardware, software, computers, the internet, artificial intelligence, augmented reality, virtual reality, cell phones, and so much more. These things have made our lives easier in some ways and harder in others. These things have helped us connect and caused us to feel further apart. These things have led to innovations that have improved education, healthcare, transportation, manufacturing and so much more. These things have also affected employment and job opportunities. Technology can be used as a blessing to spread Your Word and it can be used to spread evil. So today, I pray for how we use technology currently and in the future. Please touch the hearts and minds of those who develop it and give them foresight to see the future impact of their work and make good choices about what they create. Help them to find applications of technology that benefit the world and give them the integrity and courage to not allow what they have created to be used for evil. Help those of us who use technology to not allow it to become an idol. It is so easy to rely on these things in place of relying on You. It is so easy for us to think we can't possibly make it in life without the technology we have become so accustomed to. Please help us to discern where our reliance on it is getting in the way of relationship with You. Father, especially for Believers, I pray that you would help us hold fast to Your Word and our study of it would not be influenced by changes that may be made to its electronic format. Please protect it from being manipulated and help those who seek to understand it be led to right and accurate translations. For those websites, apps and other technological resources that proport to share it, may they be held to account for keeping it true to Your original language and may we all never find ourselves without a printed copy of the Holy Bible in our homes. In the name of the

Father, the Son and the Holy Spirit. Amen.

DAY 185

FOR THE WORLD TO COME TO UNDERSTAND THE TRUE MEANING OF LOVE

Your Word tell us that there are two commandments that are more important that all others. This is because they are the foundation of all others. You tell us to love You, Our Lord and God with all our heart, soul and mind and put no other gods before You. You tell us to love others as we love ourselves. Without loving You and loving others, we cannot live by Your other commands. Love is the key to everything. In this world, it can sometimes feel like we've forgotten what love really means. We seem to have watered it down to something that doesn't include sacrifice, humility and selflessness. We have somehow separated it from forgiveness, kindness and grace. We have made it something that we think we can decide if others deserve or not. We have fooled ourselves into thinking that love is conditional. We have believed the lie that if we love someone we also have to accept or agree with everything they say or do. But that is not how You love. You love us even when we don't show You love. You love us even when we are disobedient and sin. You love us even when we disappoint You. You love us without condition. You love us despite our flaws and bad choices and selfishness. Your love doesn't mean that You accept all these things, You still speak truth to us, You still convict us, You still allow consequences of our choices and decisions to occur, but You love us through it all. Father, today I ask that You would help me and the whole world come to a deeper understanding of what Your Love really looks like in practice. Help us know the true meaning of love. Help us see it in the life and sacrifice of Jesus. Help us understand and live by it in the way we love You and others. Help us to love ourselves the way You love us and extend that to others. Jesus, today I pray that this world would come to understand the true meaning of love. Amen.

DAY 186

FOR PEOPLE IN THE PROCESS OF MOVING

For all those that are in the process of moving I pray that everything would go smoothly. I pray that they would have the help and resources that they need to pack and prepare. Whether they are moving by choice or because of a situation they did not choose, I pray You would give them peace about the move and that the space they are moving into will be filled with peace before they arrive. I pray that the stressors that come with moving would be removed and they would feel at ease throughout the process. If they are moving a short distance, across a country or across the globe, I pray for their safety and traveling mercies. I pray that the possessions and furniture that they are moving would all be transported with care and arrive without damage. I pray that nothing would be lost. I pray that the process of turning off or turning on utilities would be easy and they would not run into any complications. I pray that they are moving into a place that is within their current means to afford, so that there would not be any financial stress. I pray that they would feel at home in their new place and quickly find a new routine and connection in the surrounding community. If there are children involved who might have to change schools or make new friends, I pray that their transition would be smooth. I pray that would have more excitement than apprehension about the changes and that they would quickly feel comfortable and make new friends easily. For those that are in the process of moving, Father, You know all their concerns and needs. I pray that You would meet them today. In the name of Jesus, Amen.

DAY 187

FOR JUDGES

Father, Your Word highlights for us the importance of those who You have allowed to fulfill the role of judge in the lives of Your people. Judges in Your Bible are people who have been given the authority to make godly decisions and provide guidance, often as prophetic messengers of Your Will and teachers of how Your Word is meant to be applied in life. In our current era, we have judges who preside over legal proceedings and make determinations of what aligns with the law and what does not. These decisions are based on our human judgment and the shifts and changes in our culture. They are not always aligned with Your Will or Your Word. So today, I pray for judges, not only in my own country but around the world, who have been given the authority to make decisions that impact so many. Their decisions impact Believers and non-believers alike. I pray that every judge would have a relationship with You. That they are open to hearing from Your Spirit as they consider each case. That they are led by their conscience and Your commandment of love and not just the law of the land, which can be flawed. Give them discernment in the decisions they make. Help them to see the short and long-term impact and consequences of each decision. Help them to act with fairness and no personal bias. Help them to be open to hearing all of the information presented and making decisions that are right and just in Your eyes. When they make a mistake, help them to act with humility to correct it. May their hearts never become hardened to the people that come before them. May they always speak truth and not be influenced by evil or fall prey to lies of the enemy or our worldly culture. Please protect them mentally and physically in their work from anyone or anything that seeks to prevent them from doing their job to the best of the ability You have given them. Give them wisdom, courage, and integrity. May every decision they make be laced with love. If they don't know You as their Savior, may they come to know You and honor the trust You have put in them. In the name of Jesus, Amen.

DAY 188

FOR THOSE TRAPPED IN HUMAN TRAFFICKING

Father, today I come before You, asking You to step in and end the evil of human trafficking in this fallen world. I pray for those trapped in this. Please rescue them now, Lord, end this bondage, this form of slavery that they are stuck in. I pray fervently for their physical and mental freedom from those who hold them captive. Until they have freedom, please be with them and protect them from physical and mental harm. Foil the plans that others have on their lives. Disrupt the evil plans to use these human beings, and may they be set free or rescued. For those trapped in this situation who do not have family or friends, I pray that they don't feel hopeless or alone. I pray that somehow, in Your sovereign power, You would uplift their spirit despite the reality of what they are going through. For the families who are desperately trying to rescue someone, please give them the information, the resources, the support, and the strength to persevere in the fight to break their loved one free. For the authorities who are fighting this evil, please make all their plans succeed. Help them to remain resilient and focused, give them wisdom and insight and courage to do everything they can to end this terrible practice of human trafficking. Oh, for those who are trapped in this, Father, please be their strength. Give them victory, may they break free and be blessed with a bright and joy-filled future. In the name of Jesus, Amen.

DAY 189

PRAYER PROMPT
FOR A PLACE THAT EXPERIENCED FLOODING IN THE LAST YEAR

Think about or research to learn about a place that recently experienced flooding and use this space to make notes about their ongoing needs and pray for them.

DAY 190

FOR PASTORS TO PREACH THE GOSPEL

Father, today I fervently pray for pastors. That they would be dedicated to the continual study of Your Word, no matter how long they have been preaching. That they would never feel that they know it all, but that they would always be curious to learn more and go deeper. That they would have a right estimation of themselves, knowing that they have been called by You, but they are not You. Knowing that they have wisdom, but that it is nothing without Your wisdom. Knowing that they have knowledge, but not all knowledge so that they are humble and always seeking Your direction on what they should say to the people You have called them to shepherd. That they would preach the Word of God and not things that are made up by influence of the culture or the enemy. That they would humble themselves and never become puffed up. That they would always point people to You and not to themselves. I pray for their courage to preach the Gospel even when it goes against the trends of the culture. May they preach it with love and kindness, even when they're communicating hard truths. Give them the words to communicate to the specific people that You allow to hear the sounds of their voice so that it would penetrate their hearts and encourage them to seek a deeper personal relationship with You. May they have a community of support from other Believers who pour into them and challenge them to go deeper into Your Word and deepen their own relationship with You. Iron sharpening iron, as Your Word says. Today Lord, I lift every pastor up to You, around the world, and give them wisdom, strength, courage, and encouragement to fulfill the great commission You have assigned them. In the name of Jesus, Amen.

DAY 191

FOR MISSIONARIES

Lord, I pray today for those that You have given a heart to go out into all the world and spread The Gospel of Jesus Christ. For these special people who choose to spend their time and in some cases their lives, reaching out to new communities and telling them about Your Word and Your love. I pray for their protection as they travel. I pray for guidance and clarity of where they should go and who they should evangelize. I pray for financial provision, that their needs would be met. I pray You would give them wisdom in what to say, the timing to say it and the words that they use. I pray that You would keep them humbled at heart, to follow You and listen to Your Holy Spirit to guide them in everything they do and say. I pray in advance for the communities You will send them into, that they would be welcomed and open to the message. And I pray that each missionary would not pour so much of themselves out to others that they neglect their personal relationship with You. Keep them focused on the Great Commission and not distracted by any man-made rules of the organization they're affiliated with. Help them to be good representatives of Christ in everything they do and say. Give them the physical strength and energy they need to do any work that You desire them to do as a service to the communities they engage with. Help them to be respectful of the cultural heritage of the people they meet, remembering that they are there to spread The Gospel, not to westernize the people. May every missionary be encouraged and persevere through every situation they find themselves in. May they make You proud. In the name of Jesus, Amen.

DAY 192

FOR PETS

Thank You Lord for pets and the joy they bring to people's lives. For cats, dogs, birds, hamsters, rabbits, guinea pigs, fish, reptiles and all household pets, I hope they are content. We don't speak their language or fully understand what they think or feel, but I hope that they are happy and live lives they enjoy. May they be well cared for and properly fed. May they have shelter from storms and a cozy spot in their home to call their own. May they not be neglected or mistreated in any way. May they be given healthy food and treats that nourish their bodies. You designed them in the garden and we have taken them out of their natural habitat for our pleasure. I pray that they would feel loved and not feel lonely in any way. If possible, pray they have opportunities to spend time in play with their kind. That dogs and cats would be able to go to parks or kennels or visit the homes of others where they can interact with their kind. That pets like birds, or fish or reptiles or rabbits would not be alone and have another like them in the home. Help us as humans to empathize with our pets to make sure their needs are met physically and emotionally, remembering that they are living creatures that do not just exist for our pleasure. Lord, thank You for pets and their seemingly unending love for people. I appreciate how that reflects Your unconditional love for us. I pray for pets all over the world today. In the name of Jesus, Amen.

DAY 193

FOR MECHANICS

What an important job mechanics have! Father, today I pray for all mechanics. I pray for those who work on aircrafts, cars, motorcycles, buses, trains, boats, and all forms of transportation. Father, I ask forgiveness for any time that I've taken for granted their work and how important it is to our lives and physical safety. Thank You for the talent and skill You have given them that allows them to do their jobs with excellence and care. Thank You for their wisdom and intelligence that helps them to identify issues and troubleshoot problems. Their work helps other people's lives run smoothly, because packages get delivered and people can get from one place to another. Their work can often be overlooked and they are sometimes not treated with the same respect that we give other professions, so help us to remember how reliant we are on what they do and to show our appreciation. They work with their hands and often have to position their bodies in uncomfortable ways to complete their work. Please touch them and give them relief from any aches or pains. Give them the physical strength they need. May they have good medical coverage and have employers who support them in proactively caring for their health and wellbeing. May they be paid a fair wage that aligns with how hard they work. And may they feel valued by their customers or their company. May their experience and knowledge be respected and listened to. Please care for all mechanics Father. In the name of Jesus, I pray. Amen.

DAY 194

FOR MARRIAGE COUNSELORS

Today, Father, I come before You to pray for marriage counselors. What a blessing they can be to those who are struggling in their relationship and need guidance. I pray that You would give them the wisdom to help each couple according to their specific needs. I pray You would give them ears to hear not only what each spouse is saying, but what they are feeling. I pray You would speak to and through them so that their insights and advice would be aligned with the truth of Your Word. Give them the courage to say the hard things with kindness, in ways that each spouse would be open to hearing. Help them understand their clients not only as couples who are one, but also as individual people with their own baggage, desires and needs. I pray that all marriage counselors would focus on the goal or repairing relationships and helping them to be healthy. May they continue to grow in their own education around counseling best practices and tools that will provide the best results for their clients. May they maintain an unbiased perspective and treat each spouse equally, giving them a safe, comfortable and supportive space for them to be honest about how they are feeling. May every marriage counselor have success in their practice, resulting in couples completing sessions and not needing counseling anymore. And may the counselors always have enough clients to maintain their business, doing work that honors Your Will for husbands and wives. In the name of Jesus, Amen.

DAY 195

FOR THOSE WHO HAVE GREAT WEALTH

Jesus, I call upon Your name today and pray for those who have great wealth. Thank You for blessing them with the financial means to do great things here on earth. We know that Your Word says the love of money is sinful. I acknowledge that not all those who have great wealth are lovers of money and that there are many ways that people attain great wealth. There is no judgment in my heart today, only a desire to ask that that wealth would be used for Your good purposes. That those who have great wealth would share it with those in need. That those who have great wealth would use it to solve problems that can improve life here on earth. That those who have great wealth would use it to support organizations that doing work that You deem as good. For those who have great wealth to humbly seek You to understand how they can be good stewards of what You have provided. I pray that they understand that it ultimately has come from you and that it should be used for Your Glory, not their own. Father, I pray that those who have great wealth all around the world would come to know You and use that wealth in accordance with Your Will. In the name of Jesus, Amen.

DAY 196

FOR THOSE WHO ARE DEPRESSED

Father God, today I pray for those who are experiencing depression. It can feel like a heavy weight pressing consistently down on the head, mind, body, heart, thoughts, and breath. It's a pressure that seems like it just won't lift. It can be so hard to get relief. And yet, although they may be feeling pressure from every side, help them to realize that they are not crushed. They may feel alone, but help them to see that they are not abandoned. They may feel down, but show them that they are not destroyed. Depression can be physically exhausting, but You say You will renew their strength, so help them to lift their eyes to You and put their hope in You. Arrest the negative thoughts that run through their mind. Give them the ability to take every thought captive and make it obedient to Christ Jesus. May they meditate on what is lovely and true. For those feeling like they are drowning in hopelessness, remind them that You have a special future planned just for them and that no matter how they feel, the Truth is that Your Grace is sufficient. May their weakness in this season make room for Your Power. Help them to keep moving forward. Walk with them as they take one day, one moment at a time, with their eyes focused on You. I pray that they feel Your love, right now, in this moment and feel the depression lift from their spirit. I pray that they know You and love You and that You will work all things out for their good. Thank You in advance Father for helping them through this affliction. In the name of the Father, the Son and the Holy Spirit, Amen.

DAY 197

FOR THOSE CURRENTLY IN THE HOSPITAL

Father God, today I ask You to be with those who are currently in the hospital. You know each situation and the care and healing that each person needs. I pray You would attend to their needs and use the minds, hearts, hands, and feet of the medical professionals and staff of the facility to restore their health. Give those in the hospital the courage to advocate for themselves and the wisdom to make decisions about their treatment or procedures. May they have a support system of family and friends that is an emotional support and helps them to navigate their situation. May their accommodations be comfortable and conducive to physical and mental well-being. May their minds be clear of worry or fear. Please perform healing miracles in situations that seem dire. Please fill the operating rooms, hallways, patient rooms, emergency rooms, and waiting rooms with peace. May any financial burdens of medical bills or insurance be sorted out and resolved quickly so that it does not cause any anxiety and they don't have to make health care decisions based on what they can or can't afford. I pray that those who are currently in the hospital do not feel lonely. I pray that there are believers they cross paths with that encourage them and show them the love of Your Son, Jesus Christ. I hope that they know You, but if they don't, I pray that their experience would bring them closer to You, the Great Physician. I pray that everything will go smoothly and that their time in the hospital won't be any longer than it needs to be. I pray when they are discharged, they are full of joy and praise You for what You've done. In the name of Jesus, Amen.

DAY 198

PRAYER PROMPT
FOR A MARRIED COUPLE YOU KNOW

Ask the Holy Spirit to bring to mind a specific husband and wife for you to pray for. Use this space to make note of some scriptures about marriage and use them in your prayer.

DAY 199

FOR WOMEN WHO HAVE HAD AN ABORTION

Father, I come before You to pray for every woman who has had an abortion. I ask You to search my heart and mind for any judgment or assumption I have regarding this and give me a pure heart. This prayer is one of love and care for them. I don't know each situation, but You do Father. I do know that there can be spiritual, mental, and physical effects for women who have gone through this. So, Lord, I pray that they know You. I pray they know that You care for them. I pray that they know how much You love them and that no matter what has happened in their life, that they know You want relationship with them. I pray that there is no fear or shame that keeps them from bowing before You and talking to You about whatever they are going through. I pray that they have someone who knows You in their life who they feel safe going to, to talk and process what has happened. If they need professional support, I pray You would connect them with a therapist who can help them work through what has happened and move forward. If there have been medical complications, I pray for healing. Father, each situation is unique and complicated and You know every detail. Let others not stand in judgment and make these women feel shunned or alone. May they find compassion and experience grace, knowing that Your Mercy is new every morning. Father I lift these women up to You. In the name of Jesus. Amen.

DAY 200

FOR THOSE WHO WORK MULTIPLE JOBS

Juggling multiple jobs can be stressful Lord. I come before You today to pray for those who are working for more than one employer or who have side jobs on top of working full-time. Father for those who are working multiple jobs just to make ends meet, I pray You would give them strength and energy to be able to do their best at each of their jobs. I pray if it's Your Will, that they would be able to get a raise or more hours at one job so that maybe they can just work one job. For those who are working multiple jobs to make extra money for a specific purpose, I pray that You would reward their determination and help them quickly achieve their financial goal. For all these people, please help them to still find time to rest and renew their strength. May they still have time to spend with family and friends. Give them relief from any guilt they feel about spending so much time working and may those they work so hard for show their appreciation and understanding. May their bosses at work recognize their efforts and treat them well. May each job they work be enjoyable and in alignment with the good plans You have for their life. In the name of Jesus, Amen.

DAY 201

FOR MENTAL HEALTH PROFESSIONALS

Holy Spirit, today I lift all mental health professionals up to You. I pray for psychiatrists, psychologists, therapists, counselors and anyone else who works in this field. I pray that they would know You and be guided by You in how they care for the people that You bring into their work. I pray that they continue to study new methods and techniques to help others restore and increase their mental well-being. I pray that You would give them discernment to know what to say, when to encourage, when to challenge, when to seek advice from their peers and colleagues on how to handle situations with their clients or patients. I pray You would give them ears to listen to not only what people say, but the meaning behind their words. I pray You would give them a heart of compassion and patience when dealing with others who they may personally dislike, but they are assigned by You to professionally help. I pray for their protection physically and mentally. May they have outlets and support to process their own feelings and not let those get in the way of their work or impact their personal life. In situations where they are not the right fit to meet their client's needs, please give them courage to refer them to someone else who is better suited to help. For all mental health professionals, I pray that they would be able to also have time and space to care for their own well-being. They pour out so much for others, Holy Spirit, I pray that You would be their peace and pour into them when they are weary. Renew their spirit and determination to help others each morning. In the name of Jesus, Amen.

DAY 202

FOR KIDS WHO WANT TO MAKE MORE FRIENDS AT SCHOOL

Jesus, school can be a lonely place without friends to hang out with, laugh with, have lunch with and study with. For children who don't have any or don't have many friends at their school, I ask You to give them divine appointments with other kids that would allow them to connect in new and meaningful ways. That any nervousness that keeps them from talking to each other would be relieved. That you would bring them together around common interests like music, art, reading, sports, and other activities they enjoy. Make these friendships genuine and ones built on care and trust. And if you will, may these friendships last a lifetime and be of benefit in ways they can't even imagine right now. For every child around the world who longs to make more friends at school, I ask You to intervene and make this a possibility for them. Thank you, Jesus, for being a friend to the friendless in all circumstances. May they also feel your love and develop a friendship with You. Amen.

DAY 203

FOR THOSE WHO WORK AT YOUR LOCAL GROCERY STORE

Father, thank You for the employees of my local grocery store. I specifically pray for them today. There are some I recognize each time I go in and there are others I probably never notice. Those that work in the back of the store, receiving deliveries on the loading dock that I will never see. You know them all by name Father, so I ask You to bless them. I hope that they enjoy what they do and feel valued by their company. I pray that they are paid a fair wage and have good benefits that meet their medical and personal needs. I pray for they are treated well by their co-workers and management as well as the customers in the store. Their work allows myself and others to purchase food and the necessities of daily life. May I never take their work for granted. May I show appreciation, by saying "hello" and making eye contact with those who work at my local grocery store, so that they feel seen. Give those who work in every role patience when dealing with customers that may be rude or disrespectful in their interactions. Help them to resolve customer service issues with kindness. May there be camaraderie amongst everyone who works at this store. Please remove any tension or division between them. May the management of the store foster a workplace that is built on excellence and enjoying the work that they do. May they celebrate each other for a job well done. Please also protect those that work at this store from hurt, harm or danger. May this store be a safe place for all that enter it. In the name of Jesus, Amen.

DAY 204

FOR GARDENERS AND LANDSCAPERS

Father of All Creation, I come before You today in prayer for gardeners and landscapers. For all those who plant, care for and maintain plants of every kind. For those who design and build beautiful outdoor spaces with grass, trees, plants, flowers, waterfalls, pathways, and ponds. May they be inspired by the beauty of Your Creation and find peace as they work with their hands. Give them great creativity in their work, no matter how simple or complex the areas are that they maintain. Protect their bodies from aches and pains and give them the physical strength they need to do their work. Supply them with the tools and the resources they need to care for the spaces and places that You have given them responsibility over. As they plant, remind them of Your love planted in their hearts. As the plants grow, may their understanding of You grow also. For those that don't have a relationship with You, may the wonder of the gardens and lawns they maintain, kindle in them a desire to know the God who spoke the world into existence. Give them glimpses of what the garden of Eden must have been like. Give them deep understanding of the sacrifice Your Son Jesus accepted on their behalf, in the garden of Gethsemane. May they know how much they are loved and may their mustard seed of faith be strong enough to move mountains. In the name of Jesus, I pray, Amen.

DAY 205

FOR THOSE WHO ARE SCARED TO GO AFTER THEIR DREAMS

Father God, You are the dream creator. You designed our minds in such a magnificent way that we can dream about the future and the possibilities that we hope it holds. Our not knowing can sometimes be frustrating, yet it also gives us the opportunity to wonder and hope and make plans. Today I want to pray for those who are scared to go after their dreams. They think them in their mind, they hope in their heart, but something is holding them back from acting to make that dream a reality. I know that only with You can their dreams come true, so I hope they know You and feel comfortable being open and honest with You, praying often about their dream and asking for your guidance in the next steps they should take. Give them courage to take that next step, even if they are scared. May they feel courage from Your Holy Spirit and from the people You have placed in their life to be their dream defenders. If they are scared because others don't support their dreams, help them to put others concerns or doubts in perspective. For valid concerns, help them to seek ways to address them. For invalid concerns, help them to ignore them and move forward with faith in You. Whatever their dream, please bring resources and support and opportunity into their life that helps them in their pursuit. May their dreams align with Your Purpose for their life. Where there may be misalignment, help them to see the path that You have for them and fill them with excitement about walking it with You. In the name of Jesus, Amen.

DAY 206

FOR GUARDS WHO PROTECT GOVERNMENT BUILDINGS

Father, before the incidents of 2021, I admit I never thought about or prayed for those who protect our capital or any of our government buildings. So today I want to say a special prayer for those in law enforcement and who work in security that don't get the recognition and appreciation that others in more visible roles do. I want to pray for those who do this work not only in the United States of America, but also around the world. For those whose job it is to protect their government's buildings, institutions and the people who work within them. I thank You for their willingness to serve and protect. I pray You give them strength and help them to perform their duties with excellence, strength, wisdom and compassion. Give them alertness and the ability to sense danger and the courage to address it. Help them to maintain their training, always learning the most up-to-date security and law enforcement practices so that they feel confident in their ability to step up to any conflict or address any threat. May they take their responsibility seriously while also having joy in their spirit. Encourage them when they need it. May those that work and visit the place that they protect acknowledge them and say "hello" so that they don't feel taken for granted. Protect them from harm hurt and danger as they protect the people, the buildings, and other things that we value, but let them know that they are valued too. In the name of Jesus. Amen.

DAY 207

PRAYER PROMPT
PRAY A SCRIPTURE OVER SOMEONE ELSE'S LIFE

Pick a scripture that is meaningful to you and pray it over someone else's life. Use this space to make note of the scripture you chose and who you prayed for.

DAY 208

FOR THOSE WHO ARE BLIND TO THE TRUTH

Oh Father, there are so many in this world who are blind not only to Your Truth, but to the truth in general. Our fallen world doesn't collectively acknowledge You. First, I pray for those who do not accept Your Word and the truths that are found in it. For those who don't know You and those who do. For those who read Your Word and come away with a wrong understanding of what it says. Open their eyes Lord, to the meaning of Your Word. Help them to discern between Your Truth and the enemy's lies. Help them recognize when Your Truth has been perverted or is being used for selfish gain. And for those who are just unable to see the truth of reality Lord. I pray for them also. In this life, it is so easy to be distracted by what is going on in the culture around us. It is so easy to be drawn to information and people who agree with us and never consider that what we believe may not be reality. Help us all to see with clarity what is going on in the world and within our spheres of influence. Open our eyes to biases we have come to believe are true. Convict our spirits to seek out truth and reality and diverse perspectives on topics and situations, so that we always can see the truth. Protect our hearts and minds from the enemy's attempts to use lies to pit people against each other. May we see with Your eyes and understand with Your Truth the realities of the world in which we live. In the name of Jesus, Amen.

DAY 209

FOR HEALING IN RELATIONSHIPS BETWEEN SIBLINGS WHO ARE ESTRANGED

Father, it is a blessing to have siblings and yet it is not always easy. Today I pray for those siblings who are estranged. Those who are not getting along, not speaking to each other or who have cut of their relationship completely. Father, You know their situation. You know what has caused this fracture in their unity. There may be real hurts and deep wounds that have created their estrangement. So, I ask You Father, the One who knows all, to heal all. I pray for willingness to reconcile. I pray for openness and trust. I pray for grace and forgiveness. I pray for understanding, honesty and transparency. I pray for humility and repentance. I pray for patience and if needed that a neutral party would step in and be a facilitator between these siblings to help them in this journey towards reconnecting with each other. You don't make mistakes Lord. You made them siblings for a reason. I pray that they are open to fighting through the heartache, hurts and disappointments to create whatever relationship they are meant to have according to Your Will and Your Plan. I pray You would give them mental and emotional strength and make it clear to each one what their role is in the healing. Every sibling relationship is different, some are close, some are just cordial, but whatever their relationship is meant to be, I do not believe You mean for them to be estranged from one another, so Father, I ask that today would be the day that the re-connection would begin. Please do what only You have the power to do. In the name of Jesus, Amen.

DAY 210

FOR THOSE WHO ARE BEHIND ON THEIR TAXES

What a stress it can be when we are not able to pay our taxes. Father, Your Word tells us to pay what we owe. It may not always seem fair to us, but Your Word is clear. Today I pray for those who are struggling and behind on paying their taxes. I pray that You would make a way for them to catch up. I pray they would not be overwhelmed. I ask that they would receive sound financial advice about how to address the situation. I pray they would be diligent in following the advice and that this would alleviate any stress that they feel. I pray that once they are back on track, that they continue to make good financial decisions and set aside what they need to so that they do not find themselves in a similar situation again. May they be blessed by their determination to take care of this situation. Reward their obedience to Your Word and let them share their testimony of how they made it through with others so that they would point them towards You. Taxes are such an earthly thing and yet they are a reality of the world we live in. I also pray for those who make decisions in the tax code that impact people's lives and financial well-being. Give them wisdom and compassion and help them make the tax codes more equitable to the people of their city, state and country. And may the money that is collected from taxes be put to good use, not squandered or used for evil. In the name of Jesus, Amen.

DAY 211

FOR THOSE WHO ARE NOT ACTING ON AN ASSIGNMENT GOD HAS GIVEN THEM

Lord, I come before You today, praying for those who are aware of something, some action, some goal, something that You want as the priority on their to-do list, yet, they have not prioritized it. It may be difficult; it may be easy. It could be a quick thing or a long-term project. But whatever it is, it's important to You and one of the things You created them to accomplish for Your Glory. So, I pray for those who are not acting on an assignment You have given them. Today, may Your Holy Spirit convict their heart to action. May they take a step towards the goal. May they be reminded that they have everything they need to fulfill the assignment. Open their eyes to see that what they think they don't have, they do have a path to get. Nothing is impossible to those who believe in You and Your promises. As Your Word says in John 16:21-24, may they know that the struggle or pain they might experience on the journey will immediately turn to joy when the assignment is complete. In the name of Jesus, Amen!

DAY 212

FOR THOSE WHO ARE STRUGGLING WITH THEIR FAITH

We all struggle sometimes. Even Your twelve did! Struggling with faith means we have faith. Even if it's just a mustard seed, You say that's enough. So today, I pray for those who are struggling with their faith. First, I thank You for the faith that they have and their awareness of You in their life. I pray that their wrestling draws them into deeper relationship with You. May they humbly submit to Your Will and come to a personal awareness of Your faithfulness throughout their life. Help them process whatever has caused this crisis of faith and see their circumstances accurately. Protect them from the lies and attacks of the enemy and from confusion from their own flesh. Increase their trust in You by reminding them of how faithful You have been and continue to be. As their trust increases, may their faith increase and their hope abound. In the name of Jesus, Amen.

DAY 213

PRAYER PROMPT

FOR THE FAMILY OF SOMEONE WHO PASSED AWAY LAST YEAR

Grieving takes time. There is a family who lost someone last year and is still struggling with grief. Think of someone who passed away last year and pray for their family and loved ones. Use this space to make a note of the family you prayed for or to write out your prayer.

DAY 214

FOR THOSE WHO HAVE RECEIVED A RECENT DIAGNOSIS

Today, I come before the Great Physician, to lift up those who have recently received a medical diagnosis. Some may have been experiencing symptoms and this diagnosis is the clarity and answers that they have needed. For others the diagnosis might be a complete surprise that they feel blindsided by. For others, they have been wanting an answer, but this isn't the answer they wanted to receive. Whatever the situation, please bring them peace. Touch their minds Lord, and slow down their thoughts, so that they are not jumping to conclusions about their health, their treatment or the prognosis. Give them the confidence and ability to get a second opinion so that they have complete clarity and confirmation of the diagnosis. Help them to think rationally and not make decisions about their care from a place of emotion. Give them hope for healing and a peace that surpasses all understanding given the situation they face. And may that peace serve as a testimony to all they meet of Your goodness in their lives and their trust in You in spite of their diagnosis. I pray for their family and friends who will support them, encourage them, comfort them and give advice. Give them strength and knowledge and wisdom. And for the doctors who have to communicate diagnoses, give them courage, compassion and kindness. Help them to treat each patient with care and take the time to answer all their questions and address their concerns. For those who have received a recent diagnosis Lord, I pray that they would feel You by their side and seek You as they navigate their feelings, decision making and medical treatment. In the name of Jesus, Amen.

DAY 215

FOR THOSE WHO CANNOT AFFORD TO RETIRE

Dear Lord, so many people work so hard all their lives and find themselves in a situation where they cannot afford to retire. Each situation is different. You know how they found themselves in this position. It is not my place to judge or assume. What I can do is pray. Everyone wants the ability to enjoy the fruit of their labor. Many dream of retiring so that they can spend more time with the people they care about, enjoy their hobbies, and start new ones. Some want to travel and see the world. Some want to continue to work, using their talent to help others and doing good work that may not pay the bills. Whatever their plans, I pray for those whose financial situation will not allow them to retire. Father, please make a way out of no way and allow them to retire. Help them see a way that they can stop working and still afford to live. Connect them with resources and people who can help them create an achievable plan to meet their retirement goals. And for those for whom that is not Your Will, I pray that You would help them to be able to work in a job that they enjoy, that covers their expenses, and allows them enough discretionary income to still enjoy their lives. May they be able to spend time with their friends and family, travel if that is their dream, take up a hobby, or volunteer their time. May they experience seasons of rest even if they are never able to fully retire. In the name of Jesus, Amen.

DAY 216

FOR THOSE WITH A CHRONIC ILLNESS OR WHO EXPERIENCE CHRONIC PAIN

Holy Spirit, please touch the minds and bodies of those who experience chronic pain or live with a long-lasting, reoccurring illness. Oh, Father, to be told that nothing will change. How discouraging that must feel. To live each day knowing that the pain or illness you experience will never go away. Father, for Your children going through this, please lift their spirits when things get hard. On the days when they feel well, give them so much joy they feel like they could burst! And on the days when they don't feel well, give them the mental and physical strength to push through. I pray that they have something that gives them relief. I pray that they have emotional support from loved ones. I pray that they have access to the best medical care possible. I pray that they know You and know that what they are experiencing isn't a punishment or a curse. Help them to see Your love for them and give them the answers and comfort they need if they are asking You, "Why me"? May they see their own value, strength, and beauty. May they inspire others who don't live with chronic pain to be more understanding and compassionate to the challenges that others face. May they never lose hope. May they never give up. May they always be encouraged. In the name of Jesus, Amen.

DAY 217

FOR THOSE WHO WORK IN FREIGHT LOGISTICS

Father God, thank You for those who work in logistics and those who work on, in, or around cargo ships, planes, trains, ports, and docks. Thank You for the talented people who figure out how to get all types of goods, medicine, food, etc., from point A to point Z while going through points B to Y. For the captains and pilots and conductors. I am grateful for those who communicate across time zones, various languages, currencies, shipping laws, and import/export rules to make sure that things get where they need to go. I pray that these people are not taken for granted and are paid a fair wage and well respected for their hard and often complicated work. I thank You for the skills and experience You have given them to do their jobs with excellence here in my country and abroad. Thank You for the customs agents at our ports of entry who inspect cargo containers and keep us safe. For the men and women who unload goods and move them from one carrier to another to help them reach their final destination. I pray for all those who work in freight logistics, Lord, that they would know how important they are to keeping commerce and the world economy moving. Thank You for these men and women and all that they do. In the name of Jesus, Amen.

DAY 218

FOR THOSE WHO ARE DIVORCED

God, our Father, today I lift up to You those who are divorced. I pray that they have clarity about the reasons for the dissolution of their marriage. That You have spoken to their hearts and minds, and they have worked out with You and unresolved feelings, resentments, anger, or disappointment. I am praying for those who are already divorced so the decision has been made. I pray You would not allow this divorce to define who they are or how they see themselves. Help them to deal with whatever led to the divorce and not let it get in the way of who You have called them to be. I pray that they do not have an adversarial relationship with their ex. No matter what happened. Help them to let go and move forward for their own mental health and well-being. Help those who feel unlovable to see that You love them. Help those who feel defeated to know they have victory. For those who have children, guide them in how to co-parent in a healthy way that prioritizes the needs of their children. May their children not feel like they have to choose but instead feel loved and supported by both of their parents. Divorce can complicate lives. Father, I pray You would uncomplicate every situation. May Your Holy Spirit guide those who are divorced in their particular circumstances. In the name of Jesus, Amen.

DAY 219

FOR CREATIVES

Creativity comes from You, Oh Lord! How creative You are! The Creator of Heaven and all the earth. The Creator of the universe and all that exists in it. Today, I pray for those who consider themselves creatives in whatever medium. May those with creative ability in art, in writing, in strategy, in product development, in design of any form, in technology, in poetry, in cooking, in gardening, in teaching, in anything Lord, help them to create beyond what they think is possible. Help them to continue to be inspired and bring new things to life. Help them to dream and not limit themselves to what has been created before. Encourage them to challenge themselves to come up with even better ideas and improve on things that already exist. May their creativity be valued and acknowledged, through Your blessings and earthly rewards. May they not be discouraged by others who don't believe in them or don't have faith. May creatives use their talent for good and Your Glory. May they know that their creativity comes from You and is inspired by Your creation. And today, Lord, especially for those who have creativity but are afraid to use it or express it. Give them a dose of courage so that they will let the talent You have placed in them shine. In the name of Jesus, Amen.

DAY 220

FOR THOSE WHO ARE FALSELY IMPRISONED

Father, for those who are currently falsely imprisoned, I pray You would give them the strength to endure. Please don't let them lose hope or give up on gaining their freedom. I pray that they have people in their lives who believe them and are fighting alongside them for justice. Until that day that they are free, Lord, I pray You would protect them from physical harm and mental anguish. May the truth come to light, Father, and may it come soon. Whether in jail or being held hostage, I pray for their release. I pray that they are not forgotten by the system, their government, or their friends and family. Help them remain confident in their innocence even when others lie about them or believe things that are not true. While imprisoned, I hope they draw closer and closer to You, Father. I pray You are their hope and their strength. I pray that they come to know Your Word so intimately that they believe Your promises without wavering. I pray that the life of Paul and others in the Bible will give them strength and courage to keep up the fight for freedom. I pray that at Your right appointed time, Lord, they would be freed. I pray that they are blessed with many days, months, and years to live the life that has been stolen from them behind bars. I pray for freedom of their minds right now, God, that though their body might be restrained or restricted, their mind is able to wander and ponder thoughts of You. And I pray that those thoughts bring them peace while they wait. In the name of Jesus, Amen.

DAY 221

FOR THOSE WITHOUT ACCESS TO CLEAN WATER

Jesus, You are Living Water. The physical water we drink, clean with, bathe with, garden with, and more reminds us never to take for granted our access to You, the spring of living water that gives us everything we need. In John 7:37-39, You tell us that anyone who believes in You will receive the Holy Spirit and not be thirsty. I believe in You and come before You today to pray for those without access to clean physical water. It is a basic necessity for life, essential, like my relationship with You. I pray that those around the world who right now are living in drought, whose water source is contaminated, who don't have access to plumbing or have the tools or resources to purify the water that they clean, bathe, and cook with, would be protected physically from any physical harm or disease. I pray they will soon have a clean water source. That individuals, organizations, churches, and companies around the world would invest in helping every person have access to clean water. I pray that no one will die of thirst. I pray that anyone who is having skin irritations because of unclean water will be relieved of discomfort. I pray that anyone who is experiencing health problems because of unclean water that they have to drink or cook with will be healed. I pray You would bring rain to those in drought and help them to collect and filter the water for their sustenance. Holy Spirit, I pray that those who have access to clean water will not take it for granted and conserve where they can so that there is enough for everyone. Father, Son, and Holy Spirit, You are Living Water, please provide physical water for all those in need. Amen.

DAY 222

FOR THOSE WHO ARE BITTER

Our Father, bitterness can be a disease that takes over every cell of our bodies and causes us to physically, mentally, and emotionally break down behind walls we've erected that block our hearts and minds from allowing forgiveness, peace, and healing in. It rots away the fullness of joy that You designed us to receive. Today, I pray for those who are bitter. Whether the reasons for their feelings are justified or not does not matter. I just pray that they would be convicted and comforted by Your Holy Spirit to release what they are holding onto so tightly. That You would help them work through their feelings in prayer, with understanding of Your Word, and if necessary, with the help of a mental health professional who can help them see that the bitterness is eating away at the possibility of joy in their future. Whether they know You or not, I pray they would be drawn to read the book of Ruth. That they would draw insights into their anger or sadness that has allowed bitterness to take root. That they would see Naomi's Mara season and realize they are like her, choosing an affliction that You don't want them to carry. In this journey of letting go, may they have a companion like Ruth who sees past the bitterness, encourages them, and sticks by them as they work out their emotions. I pray they will soon break free from the bitterness that strangles their joy and find peace again. In the name of Jesus. Amen.

DAY 223

FOR THOSE WHO ARE STARTING A BUSINESS

Father God, thank You for the seed You've planted in those who are starting a business. I pray that they have a clear vision of what You want them to do. That they are inspired by good, and their endeavor will bring them joy, fulfillment, and financial blessings. Whatever the business does, produces, or provides, that it would be with excellence. Give each entrepreneur the courage to persevere when challenges arise. I pray they have or are willing and able to gain the knowledge and expertise they need to operate their business and meet its goals. I pray they have a clear idea of what success looks like for their business that is not clouded by what others are doing. May they have high ethical standards and do everything with integrity. May they be a great leader to any employees they hire and a pleasure to any vendors they work with. Guide their decision-making, Father, and may their businesses bring You glory. In the name of Jesus, Amen.

DAY 224

FOR TEACHERS

Today I pray for teachers Lord. Thank You for gifting them with the ability to teach. May their desire to impart knowledge and truth grow each time they stand in front of their students. Help them to be experts in the subjects that they teach and be lifelong learners themselves, never thinking they know it all. May they never become bored with the material they teach. Inspire them to challenge their own understanding and to challenge their students to do the same. Keep them open-minded to new and innovative methods to engage with their students, while not abandoning the tried-and-true methods that work. I pray they have good relationship with their students and the student's parents or guardians. Give them compassion for tough situations they may face and provide them with the support they need to support their students. I pray that they have supplies, tools, equipment and resources they need. I pray that their classrooms are clean and comfortable, with proper ventilation and seating for every student. I pray their classrooms are a safe place where the only concern is learning. I pray they feel Your Spirit of peace as soon as they step into their classroom and that You would protect them and their students always. I pray that none of their students go without the books they need or food in their bellies. That nothing would distract each student from being able to focus on the knowledge that their teacher is sharing. Father, please give each teacher the right words to say to encourage and uplift their students. Father, may each teacher get to see and experience the fruit of their labor and the positive impact their teaching and interaction with their students has had. May each teacher feel seen and respected by their students and the administration. May they be paid a fair wage that reflects the extremely important role they play in the education of their students. Please bless teachers here where I live and around the world. In the name of Jesus, Amen.

DAY 225

FOR THOSE WHO ARE HAVING CAR TROUBLE TODAY

How frustrating car trouble can be! Lord, I pray today for those who are having unexpected or ongoing car trouble today. First Lord, thank You for blessing them with a car. I acknowledge this is a luxury that not everyone has. May they give thanks to You, even in the face of the inconvenience that this issue is causing. Please help them remain calm and rationale and come up with a solution. I pray that the car would be fixed quickly, but that may not be Your Will. If there is somewhere they need to get to right now, Father, I pray that You would give them access to another form of transportation to get where they need to go. Remove any prideful thoughts of not wanting to take public transit, or ask to borrow a friend's car, or use a ride share. May they be able to get where they need to go, even if it means walking or riding a bike. Whatever the trouble is with their car, I pray that it would be able to be fixed in a timely manner and that they would be able to afford any costs involved. Father, I don't know why You are allowing them to experience this car trouble, but I know even situations like this are used as a part of Your grand plan for Your Glory. Help the people who are experiencing car trouble today to not let the situation steal their joy. Remind them that You are in control and will make a way for them to get to the places where You want them to go. Remind them that keeping them from being behind the wheel of their car today might just be a blessing in disguise. May they trust You and give You thanks, even in the midst of this inconvenience. In the name of Jesus, Amen.

DAY 226

FOR THOSE WHO WORK AT THE POST OFFICE

Father God, thank You for those who work at the post office. I pray today for those who work at my local post office, for those who work at post offices around the country and around the world. Each person plays an important part in allowing people to connect, communicate and live our daily lives. Although so many things in this world have gone digital, we still need the postal service, so I pray for those who work there. For those who sort and handle packages. I pray that You would give them eyes to see and make sure that packages are on the right path to their destinations. I pray that You would touch their bodies and protect them from any physical pain or danger. For those who work in the front office interacting with customers, I pray You would give them patience and kindness of heart. May they do their jobs with a joyful heart and receive kindness and appreciation from customers in return. For those who drive letters and packages and all sorts of mail between distribution centers, please keep the safe on the roads and may they not feel lonely. For pilots who transport mail on planes, may they take off and land safely along their entire route. For the carriers who deliver the mail to its final destination, I ask You would help them to do their jobs with excellence, making sure each item gets to the right address in good condition. Protect them as they get in and out of their vehicles and walk through neighborhoods and cities. Father, for all those who work at the post offices around the world that are behind the scenes and make sure the logistics and computer systems and everything else runs smoothly, please shower them with blessings and let them know that they are appreciated. In the name of Jesus, Amen.

DAY 227

FOR PEOPLE WHO ARE BUYING A NEW HOME

Father, thank You for the opportunity You have given those who are buying a new home! May they not take for granted what a special blessing this is. I pray that they are financially prepared and have received good counsel regarding what they can comfortably afford, the size of and location of the homes they are considering. The home buying experience can be emotional Lord, so please help them to balance their feelings and intellect so that the decisions they make are well thought out and in their best interest long term. May they be able to afford the home they need and that You would shower them with some of their wants too. Please keep from buying any home that is not in Your Will and please bless the right home in such a mighty way that they can feel Your Holy Spirit as soon as they walk across the threshold. Give them clarity and peace when they walk into the home that is meant for them. Please thwart the enemies attempts to dissuade them from buying the home You want them to have. Make a way for them if the negotiations get tough. May this home be safe and in good condition. May this home be a place of refuge away from the outside world for the people who will live there. May this new home be a place where they will create memories that last a lifetime. Father, please watch over and guide those who are buying a new home. In the name of Jesus, Amen.

DAY 228

FOR EVERYONE WHO USES SOCIAL MEDIA

Father, social media has become a normal part of everyday life in much of the world. It is a place we go to be social, to connect, to express ourselves, to learn, to be entertained, to shop, to sell, and so much more. Like all things, You can use them for Your good. I thank You for those who use social media to do positive things. I thank You for those who use it to encourage and build others up. I thank You for those who use it to connect people who are lonely and in search of community. I thank You for those who use it to share The Gospel and stand for truth. I thank You for all those who use it to glorify You and reach people outside of their community. I thank You for the ways it brings people together, yet I also acknowledge how it is also used for evil and to keep people apart. So today, I want to pray for everyone who uses social media in any form. For those who use it personally or for business. For those who use it responsibly and those who are addicted. I pray for everyone today. Father, please convict each person and help them to identify what their relationship to social media is. If it's an idol, please destroy it. If it's a distraction from what You have called them to do, please remove it. If it's damaging their mental health, please crush the lies and negative thoughts and help them see Your Truth. Where it has caused hurt, please send healing. If it is being used for Your Glory, amplify it. Help everyone, including me, to understand that social media is not life. Help us understand that it is something we can opt out of and have no fear of missing out. In the name of Jesus, Amen.

DAY 229

PRAYER PROMPT
FOR THE LAST PERSON YOU SAW

Take a moment and think about the last person you saw on the street, on a bus, in a store, or even on TV. You may not know their name, and you definitely don't know their needs, but God does. Jot down a description of who the person is and where you saw them. Then, write a prayer for them. Everyone has needs and desires. Everyone has joys and struggles. So, even when you don't know the specifics of someone's life, you can lift anyone up in prayer.

DAY 230

FOR THOSE WHO DON'T HAVE A SUPPORT SYSTEM

Father, thank You for being my support system. Even when I don't have anyone else, I have You. Today, I pray for those who don't have a support system. For anyone who feels that they don't have friends or family in their corner cheering them on. For those who can't rely on anyone but themselves when times get tough. First, Father, I pray that they do know Your Son Jesus. That they know Him as Savior and as friend. That they feel Your love and support from Heaven even if they don't feel it here on Earth. I do ask that You change that for them. Father, please bring someone into their life who supports them unconditionally and someone who they can support unconditionally in return. I pray that if there is hurt that has caused them to not be willing to be supported, that You would soften their heart and help them to be open to trust again. I know You don't want us to live this life alone, so please, Father, bring them a true friend whose support is an example of Your love in their life. For those who have a support system but don't recognize it, Lord, please crack the ice around their heart or the wall of protection they have put up and help them to let others in. Open their eyes to see the people in their lives who will selflessly support them with encouragement, time, and personal sacrifice in whatever way they need. May they not take these people for granted. May they find peace and joy realizing that they do have someone they can rely on. And may these people be good stewards of the trust that has been put in them. May they be gentle with this person's heart and be guided by You in the ways they show their support. Father, for those who don't have a support system or don't recognize the one they have, I pray that soon they will feel supported so that nothing can get in the way of the plans that You have for their life. In the name of Jesus, Amen.

DAY 231

FOR TRUCK DRIVERS

Father, today I pray for all truck drivers. I pray for their protection as they drive and when they stop along the way. Keep them alert on the road and provide safe places for them to stop and get rest. May their sleep be deep so that they awake feeling refreshed and ready to go. Protect the drivers and their trucks physically. May they not be in any accidents. Help them to avoid any collision. If it is Your Will to allow something to happen, protect the drivers from all harm. As they drive their routes, may their trucks not be damaged in any way. Please help them to make sure their trucks are mechanically maintained, operating properly, and in good condition. May any service or repairs that are needed happen in a timely manner and not cause them any financial strain. May their trucks be comfortable for them to sit in for long periods of time so that their bodies are ergonomically supported. I pray they have medical coverage or access to affordable medical care to make sure that they are healthy and able to find relief from any aches and pains. I pray for their physical safety when they stop for breaks or meals. I pray that You would cover and be with them when they are in unfamiliar surroundings. I pray that You would be with them mentally, especially if they spend long periods of time on the road alone. If they listen to the radio or other forms of entertainment while they drive, I pray You would lead them to positive content that uplifts their spirit and helps them enjoy each journey. For those who are away from their loved ones, their families, or their friends for long periods of time, I pray they will have access to ways to stay connected via phone or video. I pray that in times when they have to go out on the road but want to be at home, You would encourage them. They would not worry about their loved ones, knowing that You are with them. Father, I don't know all the challenges that truck drivers face, but You do, please cover them, hear their prayers, and meet their needs. In the name of Jesus, I pray, Amen.

DAY 232

FOR THOSE IN A STRESSFUL COURT BATTLE

Holy Spirit, I pray peace for those in the midst of a stressful court battle. No matter what the issue is or who is involved, I pray that You will bring just resolution quickly. Let the experience not be adversarial between the parties. Help them to disagree and express their legal arguments without hatred. Encourage them to give the battle to the Lord and let You fight on their behalf. For those who have righteousness on their side, relieve their stress by challenging them to put their trust in You. For those who do not have righteousness on their side, relieve their stress by helping them see the error of their ways and being open to finding a resolution that is just. I pray not only for the parties involved but also for the lawyers, judges, jury members, and others who are involved in each case. I pray that You would alleviate their stress as well. Help them to do their jobs with a clear mind and understanding of the law and the facts of the case before them. Give them Your wisdom on how to conduct themselves and handle their role in the court battle. May they not feel stressed but instead at peace because they are following your guidance on how to handle this case. For all those who are involved in a stressful court battle, I pray for relief from anxiety, hope over fear, and that justice will prevail. In the name of Jesus, Amen.

DAY 233

FOR THOSE WHO PLAN TO DO EVIL

Today, I pray for those who plan to do evil. I pray, Father, that their plans will be thwarted. That their minds would be turned towards Your Truth, and all desire to destroy, hurt, disrupt, cause harm or pain would dissolve away immediately. That whatever is causing them to have these desires would be healed. That anyone who is in their sphere of influence and has an inkling of what they are feeling or going through would be a voice of reason and, if necessary, seek help from counselors, psychologists, psychiatrists, family members, friends, support groups, law enforcement or others to ensure that no evil is done and the person gets the help they need to see the error in their thoughts. Give them the strength to be bold. Father, You tell us to pray for everyone, even our enemies. So, I pray today for anyone around this world who wishes to do anyone else harm. I pray today for anyone around this world who wishes to destroy a structure, a building, or a place. I pray for those who want to do evil in order to terrorize others. I pray for those who want to do evil because of hate. I pray for those who want to do evil because of misplaced love or idolatry. For all those who want to do evil for any reason, please take over their minds and convict them of these thoughts. Protect them and those around them from any harm, hurt, or danger. Put them on a path of righteousness, for Your name's sake! Amen.

DAY 234

FOR THOSE WHO WORK IN NURSING HOMES

Thank You, Lord God, for those who work in nursing homes and care for others who are unable to fully care for themselves. Please bless those who are selfless in doing this work and use their energy to help others have a better quality of life than they could have on their own. This work can be mentally, emotionally, and physically draining, so Lord, I pray that nursing home employees would have access to good health care for themselves so that they can get the care they need to stay healthy and do their best work. I pray that they know the joy of You, Lord so that they can be a light to those they care for who are experiencing a dark season. Please help them to do their job with excellence, Father, providing the best care. Give them the right words to speak in every situation. Give them the physical strength to help those who need their strength to move, to sit up, and to enjoy activities at the nursing home. Give them patience when dealing with difficult people. May they not take the disrespectful or bad behavior of others personally. Help them seek everyone through Your eyes, knowing that even when they do their best, sometimes it won't be appreciated. I pray they enjoy the team of people that they work with and have a culture of teamwork and respect. I pray that they can work a schedule that is conducive to being able to take time off to relax and rejuvenate so that they are never trying to pour into others' lives from an empty cup. Help them to identify any issues at the nursing home and give them the courage and determination to propose solutions and work with others to make things better. May they be blessed for all the ways they are a blessing to others. In the name of Jesus, Amen.

DAY 235

FOR THE PROTECTION OF POLITICIANS

Father, I thank You for those who serve in political roles here in my country and around the world. I pray that all politicians will know You and that their hearts are focused on doing good in this world on behalf of the people they serve. For those who don't know You as their Savior, I pray that Your Spirit will still guide them in all they say and do. For all politicians, Lord, I pray that they would maintain an attitude of service that comes from a place of love and compassion. Please remove any pridefulness or selfish ambition that would get in the way of acting justly, loving mercy, and walking humbly. (Micah 6:8) I pray for the protection of their minds against the attempts of the enemy to do anything that would not make You proud. I pray for their physical protection at this time when it seems like violence is increasingly becoming a way that people are choosing to address political disputes. History has shown that this is not new, BUT GOD, it seems like it's becoming more common all around the world. So, I lift up every politician to You today. Ones I agree with and ones that I don't. The ones whose words uplift and the ones whose words tear down. For the ones who stoke the flames of discontent and the ones who speak peace. You tell me to pray for everyone, so I will not sit in judgment; instead, I will lift every politician up to You in prayer. Today, I ask for their protection. I don't wish harm or any danger to come upon anyone. Please protect all politicians and those who work in politics today. In the name of Jesus. Amen.

DAY 236

FOR THOSE WHO RESEARCH CURES FOR DISEASES

Father God, in this fallen world, You have allowed so many diseases that affect our bodies and our minds. You are the Great Physician and can cure everything in the blink of an eye. I pray for those who are suffering with any disease right now. I pray for their healing and relief from all pain. But I know that it is not Your Will that every person who has been diagnosed with a disease will be cured. In my humanity, this is really hard to accept, but I do understand and trust that Your Ways are above ours and Your reasons are for our collective ultimate good. Today I pray for all those who are researching cures for diseases. I thank You for their desire to do this work. I thank You for the intelligence and education and discernment You have given them. I pray that You would provide the tools, resources, team, willing participants and funding that is needed to do their work. I pray that their work would not be in vain and that You would reward their determination and perseverance with answers to the problems they are trying to solve. I pray that You would help them to see patterns in their research and make connections to various studies that would deepen our understanding of how our bodies work and are affected by disease. I pray You would give them understanding that is beyond the way that our human minds think, so that they can see solutions to the health problems that we face today. I pray that amazing discoveries will be made by those who are trying to find cures for diseases that we have been plagued with for years. And I pray that these cures would be made available for all those who need them, not getting caught up in unnecessary red tape, politics or greed by pharmaceutical companies or health insurance providers. I thank You in advance for the breakthroughs these researchers will make. In the name of Jesus, Amen!

DAY 237

FOR VETERANS

Lord, I am so grateful for those who have served my country. Those in every branch of the armed forces who have dedicated time to serving and protecting their country and those who live in it. No matter how long they served or in what capacity, I thank You for the work that they did and the physical and mental energy it took. I thank You that they completed their service and pray for them now that they are no longer on active duty. I pray that they have family and friends who love and support them. I pray that any physical injury they experienced has been healed or has been treated so that they have the ability to live a full and active life. I pray that any mental trauma that they endured is being treated and healed by whatever means You say is best. I pray that they have access to the physical and mental health services that they need and that these are covered by their veterans' benefits or the job they are currently doing. If they are retired, I pray that You would provide them the financial means to pay for any medical care they need that the government does not currently cover. I pray for those who run the departments responsible for veteran's affairs. I pray they would fight to make sure that veterans have excellent care and support. That they would be given the funding they need and distribute it wisely into programs that directly help veterans. I pray that every veteran would have a roof over their head and not go without a meal. I pray that they would be safe from harm here in the country that they protected. I pray that they would feel the sincerity of others who thank them for their service and truly feel loved and appreciated. In the name of Jesus, Amen.

DAY 238

FOR PEACEMAKERS

This world can feel like it is full of chaos. The enemy seeks to disrupt our ability to seek peace and act with compassion towards one another. It can seem like the angriest and most divisive voices are the loudest, BUT GOD, I know that with Your still small voice, You speak peace. So today I pray for the peacemakers. For those who refuse to be pulled into the chaos. I pray for those who choose love over hate. I pray for those who turn the other cheek even when their anger is righteous. I pray for those who are courageous enough to step into the chaos and speak peace. I pray for their spirit, that You would encourage them to keep going and never give up. I pray for their minds, that You would protect them from the lies of the enemy and of the flesh that tell them that peace is foolish and impossible in this fallen world. I pray against the spirits of discouragement and fear that try to make them question why they even try when it would be easier to "go low" like everyone else. Guide the peacemakers Oh Lord, all over the world, who keep their eyes on You and their thoughts filled with Your love. Help them to keep going, continuing to be peaceful warriors fighting on Your behalf. Give them rest when they are weary and renew their spirit when it wants to give up. Help them bring peace in the lives of individuals, peace in the relationships within communities, peace in the public discourse and peace in this world all over Earth. I thank You for the peacemakers, Father and ask You to bless them in Jesus' name. Amen.

DAY 239

FOR PEOPLE TO BE GENEROUS

Father, You have blessed us each with so much. Please help us to be generous with all You have given us. Let us be generous with our time, talents and treasure. May we give from a cheerful place and not from guilt or obligation. May we put others before ourselves knowing that You are our provider. Help us to act with generosity and selflessness. Help us to not hold on so tightly to material things that others need. Help us to see the difference between our needs and our desires so that we prioritize making sure others needs are met before our wants. Help all of us be more generous Lord. Help us to spend less time on things like entertainment and more time volunteering. Help us to use our skills and talent to do pro bono work to help others. Help us to use some of our discretionary income to feed, clothe and provide shelter for those in need. Help us to not have blinders on to the suffering of others in our family, our community, our country or around the world. Guide us in the areas where we can have the most impact. Help us to see and meet needs that are spoken and unspoken. Father, help us all to be a generous people, caring for our neighbors as we hope to be cared for ourselves. Amen.

DAY 240

FOR THOSE WHO WORK AT SHELTERS

Today I pray for those who work at any type of shelter that helps those in need. For those who work at shelters for those experiencing homelessness, shelters for women, children and men who have been abused or trafficked, refugee shelters and emergency shelters that have been set up to help those affected by natural disasters, war or famine. Father, thank You for the work that they do. Thank You for those who are paid and who volunteer. Please give them the mental strength and emotional energy to do what they do. Help them to process all the pain and suffering that they see and hear about without letting it take the joy from their spirit. Keep them filled with Your joy so that they can help others without becoming mentally overwhelmed and burning out. May those who work at shelters be given the training they need to be of service to those interact with. May those who work at shelters receive the resources and support they need to do their work with excellence. Give them discernment in how to handle difficult conversations and situations. Protect them from physical harm. May they never feel that their work is thankless or take it personally when someone they try to help doesn't appreciate what they offer. For those who work at shelters Father, today I pray that they would know how proud of them You are for being the hands and feet of Jesus. Amen.

DAY 241

FOR THOSE WHO MANAGE OTHERS

Lord God, today I pray for people who You have entrusted to manage others. Help them to understand their role as leaders and to appreciate the trust that has been put in them. May they be filled with compassion. Give them wisdom to understand the individual people that report to them and how they can motivate them to do their job with excellence. Give them insight into each person's skills and experience and the value of their contribution. People management is hard Father. Give them patience and empathy. Open their ears to listen and their mouths to clearly communicate. May they lead with honesty and integrity. May they have someone who encourages them so that they are motivated to show up with energy and optimism for the short and long-term goals they need to accomplish. When they have to deliver feedback that may be hard to hear, give them the right words. Help them find a way to hold each person accountable while also showing them appreciation for the areas where they are doing a good job. Help them not get tangled in office politics or unfruitful drama between employees. Protect managers from burnout Lord. May they be able to take vacations and get a break from their work. Touch their minds and bodies now and remove any stress. May they cast their anxieties on You and trust You to make a way, even in the most complicated or challenging situations. For those who manage others, I pray they will set a positive example for those who You have placed in their care. In the name of Jesus, Amen.

DAY 242

FOR THOSE CURRENTLY IN A TREATMENT PROGRAM

Thank You God for treatment programs. Thank You for those who have put them together and have a heart for helping others overcome substance abuse and addiction. Thank You for the research that has gone into the development of programs that work. Today, I pray for those currently in a treatment program. First, I thank You for getting them there. Especially for those who were resistant to it. I thank You for making a way for them to get the help that they need. I pray that they would not be angry or resentful but instead see this as an opportunity to improve their quality of life and their overall wellbeing. I pray that they would be open to and engaged in each part of their treatment. Jesus, I pray that they know You as friend and Savior and never feel alone. I pray they are not scared, but feel comfortable in the program whether inpatient or outpatient. May they immediately start to feel relief from their struggle and have the inner desire to persevere. I pray that their bodies would detox quickly and safely. I pray that they would experience improved physical and mental health during the program. I pray that they would feel supported by the staff and medical professionals that they interact with. I pray that they would have the support of family and friends during and once they complete their treatment. On days when they want to give up and leave, stop them Lord. Help them to stay in treatment and fight for themselves. May they know they are worthy Lord. May they feel how much they are loved. With Your help, may they break the cycle of substance abuse or addiction that brought them to this place. May it be broken forever, so that they never have to go into treatment again. In the name of Jesus, Amen!

DAY 243

FOR ADOPTED CHILDREN

What a blessing for a child to be adopted! Thank You Lord for their adoption and the family who has made them their own. I pray that their acclimation into this family is smooth. I pray that they are safe and well taken care of. I pray that they have everything they need and loved on with things that they want too. I pray that they know how special they are to their family and to You. If they are in a home where there are biological children, I pray that they don't feel any different or less than. May all the children in the home live as siblings, with no hierarchy between them. I pray the love of their forever family heals any hurt or feelings of abandonment that they have. Help them to deal with any feelings of grief or loss they might feel. May the love of this family fill any empty spaces in their heart left by their life experiences. Whatever Your Will is for their relationship to their birth parents, siblings or extended family, I hope they are at peace with it. If there is interaction between their birth family and their adoptive family, I pray that there is peace, mutual respect and an overwhelming desire to put the needs of the child first. And Father, I pray a special prayer for adopted children who struggle with their identity. For those who have been adopted into families that don't look like them, speak a different language, have different cultural or ethnic traditions. The diversity of Your people is amazing, yet You created us to love You and love one another. Help adopted children to understand who they are and not be disconnected from their full heritage. Help their families to learn about, celebrate and when appropriate teach their adopted child about their culture. May the children feel comfortable and confident to explore all of who they are and never feel they have to codeswitch to be loved and accepted. Please bless all adopted children Father. Amen.

DAY 244

FOR THOSE WHO TEACH THE BIBLE

May those who teach the Bible always be aligned with Your Truth. Father God, thank You for those who You have given the gift of teaching. Especially for those who have chosen to teach Your Word, helping others to understand Your character, Your commands, Your teachings. May they never stop learning. May they never thing that they know everything. Give them an ongoing thirst for more knowledge and may they continue to seek Your wisdom. May they not just be teachers of the Word, but also doers of it. Modeling the behavior that they teach about. May we know teachers of the Bible by their fruit. Give them insights that go deeper and help them to explain them in ways that are easily understood. May Your Holy Spirit be their study partner, leading them to what You want them to study for their own spiritual growth and helping them discern what from their studies is meant for others. Please prevent them from becoming prideful Lord, or from not being able to sit under the teaching of others. May they see themselves as Your vessels, pouring out knowledge that only can come from You. May they stay true to Your Word and keep their minds from being clouded by the culture. Help them teach the Truth in love. May they never be ashamed of The Gospel. May they never use The Gospel as a weapon. May they never use The Gospel for power or manipulation. May their hearts and minds always be in a posture where they are ready to receive a Word from You that they can pass along to others. For all teachers of the Bible, help them to know what to say and how to say it. May their study time with You be rich. May their teaching be captivating and point people to You. May they speak life into people who are in darkness. May they speak life into people who desire to understand You more. May their teaching help all who hear them live a life that glorifies You. In the name of Jesus, Amen.

DAY 245

FOR THE BIRDS OF THE AIR

How beautiful is Your Creation! The birds of the air vary in size and variety, yet they all soar to heights I cannot reach on my own. You designed us to have our feet on solid ground. Every creature has a unique purpose in Your design. Today, I pray for the birds of the air that remind me of the refuge I can find under Your wings, of the renewing of my strength that allows me to soar to new heights in my life. I pray for the little sparrows that remind me of how much You love and care for me. For all the birds of the air, I pray that You would protect them and help them to survive as our climate changes around the world. Protect them from extreme heat and cold. Please make a way of escape when natural disasters occur. Protect their habitats from destruction caused by human industrialization. Provide for them a new, safe home if they are displaced that protects them from extinction. Keep them from being harmed by the pollution we've created and the chemicals and pesticides that we use around our homes and in industrial settings. Father, each type of bird has a special purpose in this ecosystem You designed. Help us as humans to not take them for granted. Help us to care for the birds of the air the same way You do. In the name of Jesus, Amen.

DAY 246

PRAYER PROMPT
FOR A PLACE THAT EXPERIENCED A TORNADO IN THE LAST YEAR

Think about or research to learn about a place that recently experienced a tornado and use this space to make notes about their ongoing needs and pray for them.

DAY 247

FOR THE WIVES OF PASTORS

Today I pray for pastor's wives. I thank You for the support and love that they give their husbands. I thank You for the encouragement they give them and how they uplift them when they are struggling. I thank You for all the times that they prioritize their husband's care over their own self-care. So today, I pray that they will have sincere and trustworthy confidants. Friends that they can rely on and go to for encouragement of their own. I pray these friends would give them godly wisdom and not judge their feelings but instead pray with them and for them. I pray that the wives of pastors around the world would feel appreciated by their husbands, their families, their church families, their communities, and their friends. I pray they would know their identity in You and know how worthy they are of love and respect. I pray they would have time and space to rest and renew their own spirit regularly so that they are never pouring out to others from an empty cup. I pray that they would never have to wear a mask and suffer through anything in silence. I pray they never feel alone and are able to find the support they need in every situation. I pray You would speak to them directly and guide them as they make decisions for their family. I pray that their husbands would love them like Christ loves His Church. Father, I pray that whatever their spiritual gifts are, that they will be amplified for Your Glory. In the name of Jesus, Amen.

DAY 248

FOR THOSE STRUGGLING IN SCHOOL

For those who are struggling in school, Lord, please help them to identify what the obstacles are. Give them clarity on what needs to change and how to go about addressing it. Some may struggle with focus, some may struggle with study habits, and some may struggle with the teaching style they are experiencing. Some may struggle with the physical school environment or with the school culture. Some may struggle because of how they are being treated by classmates or teachers. Some may struggle in school because of things outside of school in their family or personal life. Some may struggle with a particular subject they are studying. Some may struggle with the level of coursework or the amount of homework. Some may struggle because they are trying to balance school and work or school and extracurricular activities. Whatever is causing the struggle, Lord, I pray that You would give them a clear path to make it through. Connect them with those who can give them good advice and tools to remove the stumbling blocks in their way. For all students at any level of education, early education, primary, secondary, post-secondary, vocational, and beyond, please resolve whatever they are struggling with. Please don't let anything get in the way of their learning and continuing to progress as far as they want to go. You know each person's struggle in detail, Lord, so please make a way that addresses their specific needs. In the name of Jesus, Amen.

DAY 249

FOR THOSE WHO DON'T KNOW JESUS

Oh, what a joy it is to know Jesus! Lord God, today I pray that every person comes to know Your Son and His indescribable love for them. Thank Yo,u Jesus, for loving me so much that You gave Your own life so that I could have a relationship with Your Father and experience the indwelling of The Holy Spirit. My prayer is that everyone will accept You so that they can experience this for themselves. For those who don't know Jesus, I pray that they are convicted by Your Holy Spirit with a desire to learn more. Give them a curiosity to understand Jesus' ministry here on earth and lead them to read the New Testament for themselves. In that reading, I pray their interest is piqued to want to learn even more and that as they are drawn into the study of Your Word, they also become connected with other Believers who will come alongside them and encourage them. May they be protected from discouragement from anyone who professes to be a Christian yet judges them or scolds them for asking questions as they seek to learn. May they not see those who do not represent Your teachings well and allow that to turn them away from You. May they come to know You, God, Your Son Jesus, and the Holy Spirit for themselves. May their eyes and ears be opened; may their heart be softened. May they experience the joy and peace that comes from knowing the Truth. I pray that those who do not know Jesus will come to know Him soon and very soon. In the name of Jesus, I pray, Amen.

DAY 250

FOR THOSE WHO NEED A BREAKTHROUGH

I pray for all those who are desperate for a breakthrough. Father, I pray for those who have been praying and seeking You and are trying to patiently wait for Your Will to unfold. I pray You will provide a breakthrough very soon, yet I also pray that You will give continued strength, patience, and guidance to those whose breakthrough is in the future. I pray that they will not give up. I pray that they will not lose faith. I pray that they will never think that You have forgotten about them or forsaken them. I pray that they see You at work in their situation, even in the midst of this trial. I pray that they can see the mountaintop from the valley they are in and keep moving towards it as Your Spirit guides their pace. For those who You want to be still, help them to accept Your instruction. For those who You want to take a specific action or follow a path, kindle in them a flame of initiative and perseverance. May those who need a breakthrough never feel powerless, remind them that their power comes from You and never runs out. Protect them from the enemy's attempts to use their situation to tempt them to doubt or, like Sarah and Abraham or Jacob and Rebekah, take matters into their own hands. May they each day put on the full armor of God and be ready for the spiritual battle, knowing that they do not fight alone. When they feel discouraged and want to give up, please remind them that You are with them and that in Jesus, they already have the victory, it's just a matter of time. In the name of Jesus, Amen!

DAY 251

FOR ARTISTS WHO ARE STRUGGLING FINANCIALLY

Thank You, Lord, for the artists who You've blessed with such a beautiful gift. Their talent comes from You, and they have a heart to express themselves in such creative ways. Our world needs the beauty of art and the inspiration and hope it can give. The art that artists produce can bring us joy. It can challenge us to think. It can inspire us to use our creative gifts to express our thoughts and emotions. Yet, the way our world values art and those that create it is so subjective. Being an artist of any kind, using any medium, can be a hard way to make a living. Today, I pray for those artists around the world who are struggling financially. I pray they will never have to stop producing their art in order to survive. I pray that You would allow them to make enough money to live comfortably. If they have a family, I pray that they can make enough money to contribute to their household income. Father, if it's Your Will that they have other employment, I pray that You would make a way for them to balance their job with their desire to produce their art. Give each artist guidance and clarity about whether they should pursue their art full-time or take on employment to help make ends meet. I pray that they will not be discouraged by those who do not believe in them or support their work. I hope that they know You and express Your love in the art that they produce. I pray that their art will bring them joy and peace and that others will feel it when they see what they have created. Please help artists who are struggling financially, Lord. In the name of Jesus, Amen.

DAY 252

FOR THOSE WHO HAVE A LOVED ONE WHO HAS DIED IN WAR

Today, I pray a special prayer for the loved ones of civilians who died in a war. So many innocent people are killed when the place that they live in, work in, or travel to becomes a warzone. Today, I specifically pray for their loved ones who mourn their death. How helpless they must feel that they couldn't do anything to help. How senseless it must seem that their loved one was taken by a situation out of their control. I pray that You will help them to grieve. Help them to process any anger they feel. Please help them to process any survivor's guilt. May they not feel alone. Give them others they can talk to that empathize with their pain and can comfort them. If they are currently living in that same warzone, please protect them from all harm and danger. Help them to not live in constant anxiety or fear. Father, I pray that the war will end, but if that is not Your Will, then I pray that they will be able to escape to a safe place. I pray that You would provide for their needs. For those whose loved ones have died in a warzone where they were working or traveling temporarily, I pray for the same comfort in their grief. I pray that they are able to bring their loved ones remains home and that You would guide them through all the arrangements without adding to their grief. Father, for all those who have lost a loved one in a warzone, I pray You would help them to mourn their loss and celebrate their loved one's life. In the name of Jesus, I pray, Amen.

DAY 253

FOR WOMEN WHO EXPERIENCE ENDOMETRIOSIS PAIN

Father God, please give relief to women who experience the pain of endometriosis. Don't allow them to be dismissed when they seek help. Give them confidence to advocate for themselves with their doctors, so that they can find the right treatment to manage their symptoms. I pray that their lives are not negatively impacted from this condition. I pray that they are able to find enough relief that they do not have to miss out on activities with family and friends. I pray that their symptoms do not get in the way of them being able to work. I pray that when the pain is hard to handle, they would be met with understanding and compassion from others. I pray they would not feel alone in being able to express how it impacts their life so that they can find solutions and work-arounds. If their pain is so unbearable that they decide with their doctor to try surgery, I pray for their safety. I pray that the surgery would be a success! Father, I thank You that most women who experience endometriosis are still able to conceive. Please uplift the spirits and encourage those who are trying to conceive right now. I pray that You will bless them with the children that they desire. For those whose endometriosis prevents them from conceiving, I pray that You would still help them to conceive in whatever way is according to Your Plan. When that pain comes each month, give them comfort from the physical and mental suffering it brings. In the name of Jesus, Amen.

DAY 254

FOR THOSE WHO HAVE BEEN SEXUALLY ASSAULTED

Father God, today I pray for those who have been sexually assaulted. I pray for all women, men and children who have experienced any form of unwanted sexual contact or behavior. I pray that they do not suffer in silence, but are able to report what has happened to them and seek help. Please bring people alongside them to protect and guide them through the process of making sure they are safe from whoever has assaulted them and have access to the mental health resources they need to heal emotionally. Give them strength and courage, reminding them that they did not deserve what happened to them. Remind them that the person who did this to them is the one who should be ashamed. Let them not feel powerless to get justice and may they receive good counsel about the steps they should take. Help them to not blame themselves for anything that happened and to know they are worthy of real love and respect. If they were assaulted by someone they know, I pray that they are believed by the people they know in common. I pray they are immediately protected from any further harm. Please walk with them as they heal, do not allow this experience to be a stumbling block in their sexual relationships in the future. Help them to be well in their body, mind, heart and spirit and live a joy-filled life in spite of this. In the name of Jesus, Amen.

DAY 255

FOR DENTISTS

Today I pray for those who help us with our oral health. I thank You for dentists and dental hygienists who diagnose and treat pain, decay and hygiene issues with our teeth and gums. I pray that You would give them the ability to correctly identify issues and provide guidance to their patients on what to do. Give them good eyesight and help them to read x-rays. When they are cleaning teeth, may they be diligent in the process of removing anything that could lead to gum disease or tooth decay. When performing procedures like fillings, crowns, root canals, extractions or dental implants, help them to do it with excellence and compassion towards their patient's tolerance for pain. Keep them healthy and protect them from sickness or disease that could be spread from their patients to them. May they always have access to masks and the protective gear they need as well as properly functioning equipment to do their work. May the work that they do be appreciated by their patients so much that they recommend them to friends and family. May each dentist have enough patients to make a good living and support their staff as well. May they continue to learn and grow in their craft, educating themselves on new research, technological advancements and techniques. Please give them the physical strength they need to do their work and help them get plenty of rest. For dentists that have their own practices, I pray You would help them also as business owners and meet each one's specific needs. In the name of Jesus, I pray, Amen.

DAY 256

FOR FATHERS OF YOUNG CHILDREN

What a blessing to be a father. God, You are The Father of all. Thank You for allowing men to experience being a father here on earth. May they walk in Your Ways and parent their children with the same unconditional love and grace with which You love them. May they teach and correct, share their wisdom and guide. May they always impart the truth to their children with love. I lift up fathers of young children to you today and ask that You guide them in the decisions they make for each child. I pray You would give them insight into their children's unique personality, intellectual and emotional needs. I pray You would give them the ability to communicate with their children in a way that builds the bonds of trust and honesty. I pray that their children would see them as a safe place to take refuge from the challenges they face. I pray they would run to them for advice and guidance, knowing that their earthly father, like their Heavenly Father, always has their best interest at heart. I pray that fathers of young children would have the support they need to parent well. May they be encouraged by their family and friends when they are feeling overwhelmed. Please give them an outlet of self-care that allows them to renew their spirit so that they can be emotionally available to meet their children's needs. May they feel appreciated by their children and know how much they are loved, even when it may seem that their children are being disobedient or rebellious. Please help fathers of young children be a reflection of You in their children's lives. In the name of Jesus, I pray, Amen.

DAY 257

FOR THOSE WHO RUN NON-PROFITS

Lord, today I pray for those who start or operate nonprofit organizations. First, I thank You for their heart to do something to benefit others. I pray You would bring others to work alongside them that share the same mission and can help their vision become a reality. If they have a board of directors, I pray that they would be respectful to each other, appreciating what each person brings to the table and always focused on how they can work together to achieve the mission. Please place genuine team members and board members in their organization that do not act out of ego or personal ambition, but have a heart for service. I pray that the work of their hands, minds and hearts would result in the betterment of individual lives, the uplifting of communities and the world to thrive. Although they are a not-for-profit organization, they still need money to fulfill their mission. I pray that You would bless their fundraising efforts and provide the financial resources they need to live, run the organization, and pay for its initiatives. I ask You to call their attention to any grants that they are qualified for and help them to fill out the applications. If they host events or sell goods in order to raise money, I pray that You would give them guidance in how to do this ethically and in the most economical way possible, so that the maximum amount of profit can go into doing their work. When they feel discouraged, please encourage them. When they feel tired and worn down, please give them rest and renew their determination to keep going. Inspire them with the testimonies of the positive impact their work has so that they stay on the path You have asked them to walk. In the name of Jesus, Amen.

DAY 258

FOR THOSE WHO ARE CONSIDERING DIVORCE

Father, the marriage relationship between husband and wife is meant to reflect the relationship You have with Your Church. Throughout the Bible, You show us that that relationship is not easy. Yet You love us, even when we hurt You. You love us, even when we disappoint You. You forgive us, even when we have committed the most horrible sins. You may not love what we've done, but You never give up on us. I pray today for those who are considering divorce right now. For those who are tired of crying, tired of fighting, tired of being taken for granted, tired of being lied to, tired of not being respected, tired of not being loved and treated with value. Today I pray for any spouse who is considering ending their marriage. Father, I don't know the history of what has led them to this place, but You do. You know why they were joined with their spouse. You know the vow and commitment they made. You know if they or their spouse has kept it or broken it. You know how hard relationships are and what You intend for their relationship to be. Father, I pray that those who are considering divorce are talking to You. I pray that they know You and are praying to You and seeking Your guidance and direction. I pray that they are not being swayed by the opinions of others who do not have their best interest at heart. I pray that the people who are speaking into their lives are being honest with them and speaking the truth with love so that they have honest and unbiased advice about their circumstances. Whatever their situation, I pray that if it's Your Will, You will fix the broken places in their relationship, that You would convict both spouses about the things they need to repent of that would allow them to move forward. I pray that they are able to get back to the love they had in the beginning of their relationship and that they would both be willing to put in the time and effort to get back there. Yet, whatever decision they make, may it be Your Will Father. I pray that all hurts are healed and that You are in the midst of it all, whether they stay married or get divorced. Please Jesus, Amen.

DAY 259

PRAYER PROMPT
FOR SOMEONE YOU FIND IT HARD TO LOVE

Who comes to mind? Is there anyone you struggle to love completely and unconditionally? Use this space to first ask God to give you a clean heart the desire to love as He loves. Then pray for them.

DAY 260

FOR THOSE WHO ARE JEALOUS OF OTHER PEOPLE'S MARRIAGES

Father, there are times when we all fall into the trap of envy. I ask You to examine my heart to identify if I have felt envious of other people's marriages. Marriages of people I know personally, strangers I see, or even celebrity couples that I don't know in real life. Today I pray for all those who experience jealously of other people's marriages. In those moments when we have envious thoughts, I pray You would convict us right away. Give us clear eyes so that we can see that what we see on the outside is not always what's going on behind the scenes. For those who are single and want to be married, may they be inspired instead of jealous. May these couples give them hope and a sense of excitement for the special spouse You have planned for them. For those who are married, may they celebrate the other couple instead of covet what they have. Let envy not cause husbands and wives to take for granted what they have in their own relationship. When they see something good that they want in their own marriage, please guide them in how to cultivate it with their spouse. Help everyone find contentment in knowing that what You have for them is for them and that although it might look different than someone else's marriage, what they have is beautiful and brings You Glory in a unique way. Instead of envy, may we all say a prayer of thanksgiving and praise You when we see relationships we admire. In the name of Jesus, Amen.

DAY 261

FOR VALET DRIVERS AND PARKING LOT ATTENDANTS

Father, today I pray for those who work as valet drivers and parking lot attendants. I don't often think to pray for them, so I lift them up today. For those who work these jobs around the world, I pray for their safety as they usually work outside or inside of structures. Protect them from accidents as they drive, move or park vehicles. Protect them from any danger in the streets or parking lots where they work. Protect them from the elements if they work outside or sit in a booth all day. Protect their minds from boredom, by allowing them to entertain themselves or have good conversation with their co-workers or customers. Give them joy in their work. As they care for the vehicles or property they are entrusted with, I pray that they would be treated with kindness by customers. I pray You would give them patience with those that are rude or dismissive to them. I pray that any technology they use in their work would work properly and if there are any issues, that You would give them the knowledge and skill to fix them quickly. May customers not take them for granted, but express their gratitude by saying thank you or offering a tip when appropriate. I pray that the drivers and attendants are paid a living wage and that all their needs would be met. Thank You for these people who make it easier for us to go about our day-to-day activities by providing a place for us to store our vehicles. In the name of Jesus, Amen.

DAY 262

FOR THOSE EXPERIENCING HOMELESSNESS

For those who do not have a place to call home today, Lord I pray. For those living on the street, in a car, in a shelter. For those moving from hotel to hotel. For those couch surfing because they cannot afford a place to stay. I pray for all those that are experiencing homelessness. Around the world there are so many children, women and men who need a home. If they are living outside or in a car, I pray that You would give them an opportunity to stay in a safer and more stable place. Please make a way for them to live in a shelter or a hotel or be taken in by the kindness of a stranger so that they are able to have access to the basic necessities of life. May they be able to bathe regularly, eat three meals a day and have shelter from the outdoors. While they are in this place, please give them the support and determination in their spirit to find a way to sustain themselves financially so that in Your right timing they are able to move into a place they can permanently call home. For those who are working but not making enough money to afford rent, I pray that You would make a way for them to be given more hours or increased pay or a new job that would provide enough income for them to move into an apartment. For those who are living in hotels or on couches of family and friends, I pray that You would provide a way for them to also make enough income to afford a more stable living situation. I thank You for the roof they do have over their heads and pray blessings on the place they are staying and the people they are staying with. For those who are without a home and also struggling with mental illness, Father, I pray that they would be brought into their right mind so that they have a desire to seek the help they need. I pray that reputable organizations would come to them and offer housing opportunities that include mental health care. I pray that they would take them up on these offers. I pray that they would have access to the psychiatrists and medications or treatments they need to keep them in their right mind and allow them to enjoy a fresh start in life. For those who are without a home and also struggling with an addiction, I pray that You would perform a miracle and they would wake up tomorrow with no desire for that substance. I pray that their mind would clear and they would be convicted in their spirit to seek help to make their fresh start in life as well. Father, I pray Your physical protection over all those that are experiencing homelessness. Protect them from abuse, violence and all forms of danger. For those who have already experienced or witnessed abuse or violence, I pray You would be their comfort. Help them to not fear. May any trauma they have experienced living on the street be lifted from their spirit and healed. Father, for those who are so discouraged that they feel You have forsaken them, I pray that they would have a rekindling of their faith. May they call out to You again and experience Your faithfulness in their time of need and affliction. Father, I pray that there will one day be a day when no one in the world is without a home. That everyone has a roof over their head and food in their belly. Until that day, I pray You would be with every person who is experiencing homelessness and meet their needs. Please sustain them until You make a way for them to have a home. In the name of Jesus, Amen.

DAY 263

FOR PEACE INSIDE HOMES

For homes where there is warfare, I pray for peace. I rebuke the spirits of division and anger that have made their way into anyone's home. I ask You to banish them now in the name of Jesus! I pray for forgiveness and understanding inside of every home. I pray Your Spirit of peace would fall on all homes, especially those where arguments are a regular occurrence. Please touch the heart of each person who dwells inside each house and connect it with the others they share that home with. May they enjoy each other's company and desire to spend time together. May they be curious to know what is going on in each other's lives so that they can support each other. May they treat each other with respect and all be aligned in how they care for their home and the possessions in it. Protect each home from any outside influences that try to disrupt the peace. Keep those people or evil spirits from crossing their threshold. I pray for peace inside each home today, Lord. Please show each person in the home how they can cultivate peace and guide them in acting on that today. Amen.

DAY 264

FOR VETERINARIANS

Thank You for the doctors who care for animals. Thank You, Lord, for the expertise You have given them. I thank You for their education and skill. I thank You for their patience with their patients and the people who bring them to be examined or treated. Please give veterinarians the knowledge they need to diagnose and treat the animals in their care. May their jobs bring them joy and lots of laughter. Lift their spirits when they have to deal with a sick or dying animal. Encourage them and help them to be an encouragement to the people who love those animals. Guide their hands as they do their work so that it may be done with excellence. Help veterinarians stay aware of new advancements in science, medicine, and all aspects of animal care. Give them physical energy when they are tired and the strength to handle the animals in their care. I pray that they will have enough clients to make a good living and that they will feel fulfilled in their work. I pray You would protect them from any sickness or disease that could be passed on from an animal to a human. May they feel at peace with the tough recommendations they have to give and the decisions that they have to make. May everything they do benefit their patient's well-being. Thank You for placing them in this line of work. I pray that they feel appreciated and know that their care of animals is important and valued. In Jesus' name, Amen.

DAY 265

FOR ANIMALS IN YOUR LOCAL SHELTER

For the animals in shelters that are local to me, I pray that they would be well cared for and find a forever home. If they were dropped off at the shelter by their owner, I pray that they do not feel a sense of abandonment or separation anxiety. I pray that they were dropped off with the intention of them finding a better living situation. If they have any behavioral problems that caused them to be left, I pray that the shelter would have the resources to address them so that they can be adopted by another household. For those that were strays or removed from bad living situations, I pray that they are happier in the shelter. I pray that any abuse, sickness or disease they experienced is healed and that the shelter becomes their safe space. I pray that all the animals at the shelter feel loved and are provided healthy food that nourishes their bodies. Lord, I pray that You would give each animal in the shelter a forever home in Your right timing. In the name of Jesus, Amen.

DAY 266

FOR THOSE WHO WANT OR NEED TO GAIN WEIGHT

Father, You create each of us uniquely beautiful. Male and female, You know every hair on our head and every inch of our skin. You know our frame and the right amount of weight that is healthy for our bodies to be well. Today, I pray for those who want to or need to gain weight for whatever reason. Please help each person to have an understanding of what their ideal weight is and how to attain it. We often think about those who want or need to lose weight, but there are some who have trouble gaining weight, those who want to gain weight so they can compete in sports, and those who wrestle with their body image or struggle with eating disorders. For all of them, I pray that You would help them to rightly see themselves physically. I pray that You would give them knowledge of what weight is healthy for them. I pray that You would give them a support system of people who will encourage them on their weight gain journey. I pray You would remove any mental blocks, lies of the enemy, or distorted beliefs they have about their weight. If they struggle with shame or comparison, I pray this will be lifted from them. I pray that they will see their bodies as Your beautiful and unique creations and want to do whatever they can to maintain their physical well-being. I pray that You would protect them from negative content on social media, in entertainment, and in society in general that would give them a distorted sense of what is a healthy weight for them. Please give them access to resources that can guide them in how to gain the weight that they need. Give them self-control and discipline to stay the course when moments of discouragement arise. Please help them to stay motivated and encouraged on their healthy weight journey. In the name of Jesus, Amen.

DAY 267

FOR FOSTER CHILDREN

Jesus, today I pray for foster children in my country and around the world. You know the specific reason they have become a part of the foster care system. I pray for that they would receive the emotional and mental support that they need from their foster parents and the agency who placed them. Specifically, for those who were removed from an unsafe home environment or who experienced abuse or neglect, I pray that they would find stability, attentiveness and unconditional love in their foster home. I pray that their foster parents would be patient and compassionate. If they are in a home where there are other children, I pray those children welcome them with loving arms and make every effort to help them acclimate into the family. For the foster children who are having a hard time adjusting, I pray that You would draw them close and remind them that they are loved and worthy. Help them to work through their feelings about their situation and the reasons they are in the foster care system. I pray that they won't have to move around a lot and You would give them a sense of stability. For those who do experience multiple placements, I pray that they are able to become acclimated quickly and that it does not disrupt their ability to go to school or maintain friendships. If they are returned to their family, I pray that the situation that caused them to go into foster care is resolved and fixed once and for all. I pray that they would return to a healthy and loving home environment that is financially stable and safe. Today I pray for foster children Lord. You know each one's unique situation and need. Please meet it today and bless them greatly. In Your name I pray, Amen.

DAY 268

PRAYER PROMPT
FOR A SPECIFIC PASTOR

Who is a pastor you have heard of, but never heard them preach? Who is a pastor you have watched online a few times, but don't consistently follow? Who is a pastor you've heard a scandal about? Pick someone who is not the pastor of the church you currently attend and pray for them. Pray for them, their family, and the congregation of their church. Pray for their relationship with God and how they represent Him to others. Use this space to note who you prayed for or to write out your prayer.

DAY 269

FOR THE ENVIRONMENT

What a world You created! Father God, I can only imagine what Earth looked like on the seventh day. How clean the air must have been, how fertile the soil, how clear the waters and how lush the plants must have grown. When I look around now, I can see and feel the changes in the environment. There is pollution in the air, contamination in the soil and water has to be filtered so much to be made clean. The climate of this planet continually changes effecting temperatures and seasons. So today I pray for the environment. No one person or one country can control it. That is the way You designed this world. Our air and oceans connect us. Help us to work together to reduce the negative impacts we have on the environment. Help every nation to all share the same vision for a world that has clean air and water. Break the chains of politics and isolationism that makes any nation believe that what it does doesn't affect the environment of other nations. Let not money, selfishness, power or control get in the way of what needs to be done. Open eyes, hearts and minds to consider and agree on ways that we as humanity can do a better job of caring for this planet You created for us. Please perform a miracle in the health of our planet Father and the space around it. Help us be a good stewards of the Earth. In the name of Jesus, Amen.

DAY 270

FOR SOMEONE'S HEART TO BE OPENED TO GOD'S LOVE TODAY

Father, I want to pray today for those whose hearts are closed to You. I pray for those who had a relationship with You, but because of hurt, pain or disappointment, their heart has hardened. I pray for those who have never had a relationship with You, but because of what they have seen people do to hurt, shame or control others, in the name of Christianity, they have turned away from wanting to learn Your Truth. I pray for those who for whatever personal reasons are scared to accept that they are not in control and that there is not just a god, but One God, that is omnipotent. I pray for those who have been through something traumatic and still want to believe, but have closed their minds off to Your Love because they can't accept that the God that loves them so much would allow what has happened in their life. I pray for everyone who's heart is closed to You, that it would be opened today. That they would experience Your love in an undeniable way today. I pray that they would allow themselves to think about You. I pray they would feel a desire to connect with You. I pray they would feel a pull to read the Bible and be led to a passage that would speak right to their need. Father, when their start to open, I pray they would seek fellowship with other Believers and that those people would welcome their curiosity and questions with open arms. I pray that those they seek guidance from would not do anything to make them consider closing their hearts again, but would instead hear Your Holy Spirit guiding them in what to say, how to lead and how to support them on their journey into deeper relationship with You. I pray that someone's heart would be opened to Your love today. In the name of the one who died to show Your love for us, Amen.

DAY 271

FOR KIDS WHO ARE TRYING OUT FOR A SPORTS TEAM

Thank You Lord for the desire You have placed into the hearts of children who are interested in joining a team sport. For the kids who have to try out to make a team, I want to pray today that their experience would be positive. I know that no every child is going to make it onto the team, yet I do hope that they know that they have done their best and that they receive constructive feedback if they do not make the team that will fuel their passion to improve their skills rather than discourage them from trying again. May the adults in their life use the experience of trying out for a team as a life lesson that will help them far into adulthood. Whether they make the team or not, may they understand that hard work and dedication are important, yet, life is not always "fair" but God still has a good plan for them. Of course, I wish every kid who wants to be on a team could be chosen, but I know this isn't how things work. So, I thank You for every child who makes the team they try out for and I pray that every child who doesn't make the team will be uplifted and encouraged even in their disappointment. I ask that all kids who are trying out would feel worthy and valued. I pray that there would be no intimidation or bullying during the process. I pray that those who are making the decisions about who makes the team or not are doing it in a way that is equitable and unbiased. And I pray that they would speak truth in love to the kids and parents who do not make the team. Father, You know what team sport experiences You want each child to have and at what age. Please lead them to teams that will benefit their physical and mental wellbeing. In the name of Jesus, Amen.

DAY 272

FOR THOSE WHO HAVE CANCER

God, I come before You on behalf of all those who have been diagnosed with cancer of any kind. First, I pray for complete and total healing. I pray that all cancer would be removed from their body and their health would be fully restored. I know this is not Your Will in all circumstances, even though I wish it was. I accept this, even though I don't understand it. For those who are not miraculously healed by Your hand, I pray that they would still be healed by medical intervention and treatment. I pray that they would be diagnosed at an early enough stage that surgeries or treatments like radiation therapy and chemotherapy are able to be successful at completely eradicating all disease. I pray You would be with those that have to go through a surgery on any area of their body, like their prostate, throat, skin or breasts. I pray You would give them and their loved ones peace and help them cast their anxieties on You. Guide their doctor's hands to perform the procedures with the excellence only You can give. Help them through their recovery whatever it entails. If there is reconstruction needed or if their quality of life is impacted, I pray that You would walk with them through this. Bring the support and resources they need to help them process how this disease has impacted them emotionally. Father, help them financially as well. Please don't let them experience any medical debt in order to get the treatment that they need. Every person's experience is different Lord, so I ask that You meet their specific needs as they go through this experience. And Father, for those who Your Will is not for them to be healed, I wish this wasn't so, but I pray that they and their loved ones know You and trust Your Divine reasons for allowing this. I pray that You would bless them and help them to enjoy whatever time they have left. I pray that they already know You or come to know during this time so that they have peace that even after they take their last breath, they will live in a joy filled eternity with You. It is hard to accept that this is a reality for some, that You will not heal them, but I will still trust Your Will Lord and pray that they trust it too. In the name of Jesus, Amen.

DAY 273

FOR SEXUAL INTIMACY BETWEEN HUSBANDS AND WIVES

Father, You designed such a pure and beautiful way for man and woman to connect through sexual intimacy. Today I pray for husbands and wives, that this would be an area that would be vibrant and fruitful throughout their relationship. May the flames of their sexual desire for each other never be extinguished. May their intimacy be fruitful in producing love, joy, peace, patience, kindness, gentleness, goodness, self-control and faithfulness in their relationship with one another. May they trust each other fully and love each other with their whole hearts, no matter what their physically bodies look like now or change over time. Help them to always see beauty and be attracted to each other's physical form. May their sexual intimacy be just important to them as their intellectual and emotional intimacy. Please Lord, use all these things to bring them closer and closer as one. Inspire each spouse to find new ways to bring each other pleasure, putting the other before themselves. May they feel safe with one another so that they can ask for what they need. Let no outside influences cause division between them. Guide them in honest conversations about their desires and help them to determine what is right for their relationship. Remind them that the intimacy between them is designed by You. I pray that their sex life is satisfying and they have no desire for anyone other than each other. Father, You know each couple You have joined together, please protect them from allowing any issue they are having in this area pull them apart. If they are struggling to work through things together, please guide them to godly counsel that can help them reconnect again and rekindle their physical desire for one another. In the name of Jesus, Amen.

DAY 274

FOR BROKEN FRIENDSHIPS

What a sweet balm to the soul a good friendship can be! What a blessing and important role friends play in our lives. Father, some friends are only in our lives for a season and others are meant to stay connected with us forever. When the bonds of friendship are broken, for whatever reason, it can be so hard to forgive and move on or to repair and move forward. Your Will is different in each situation. Some friendships are broken because You are protecting us or need us to create boundaries from negative or unhealthy influences in our lives. I pray that You would help those who have broken friendships to identify what caused the break and have clarity of if they should attempt to repair it. If You want the friendship to be restored, I pray You would convict their spirit of what the steps are they should take. If they need to apologize, give them self-awareness, humility and courage. If they need to ask for an apology, give them courage, the ability to show grace, divine timing and the right words to say. Give both friends open hearts and ears to hear each other. Help them to let down their guards and let go of any bitterness or hurt that has created a wall between them. Help them both to see why You want them to stay in fellowship and give them the patience and perseverance to work through whatever the issues to get back to the genuine friendship You desire for them to have. Father, I pray for restoration of friendships today that will glorify You. Especially for those who are meant to be in each other's lives to help each other fulfill Your Purpose for their lives. In the name of Jesus, Amen.

DAY 275

PRAYER PROMPT

FOR THE DELIVERY PERSON WHO MOST RECENTLY BROUGHT A PACKAGE OR MEAL TO YOUR HOME

What would we do without those who deliver packages and meals to our homes!? Father, I thank You for the last person who delivered something to my house. I am thankful for the privilege of being able to utilize this service. I'm thankful that their work allows me the convenience of not having to go out and get what I need. I'm thankful that this service helps those who are sick and shut in or not physically able to go get things themselves. I'm thankful for these delivery people who fight traffic and carry heavy packages so that others don't have to. I pray for all those who do this type of work, but specifically today, I pray for the last person who delivered something to my home because....

DAY 276

FOR PEOPLE WHO WORK AT YOUR PUBLIC UTILITIES

Thank You Lord, for the people who whose work allows the place where I live to have water, electricity, gas, communication lines, sanitation, waste disposal and other public utilities. Their hard work in the office and out in the field benefits me personally and my community. Please keep them safe as they work. I pray that they are provided with the safety gear and well-maintained equipment they need to do their jobs. Let no physical harm come upon them, especially when they respond to emergency or natural disaster situations and are trying to restore service. For those who work long hours and do a lot of manual labor, I pray that You would give them times of rest and rejuvenation for their bodies. I pray that their long work hours would not get in the way of their relationships. I pray they are able to take paid vacations. I pray that they are paid a good and fair wage for the work that they do. I pray they have medical insurance coverage and other benefits like a pension or 401k. I pray that You will give them opportunities to continue their education and training so that they have job security as new technologies and innovations are introduced. I pray these new innovations would help bring down costs for consumers but not eliminate the jobs of these workers. May new technologies help public utility workers do their jobs with increased efficiency, less stress and less physical strain to their bodies. May technologies be a tool they use versus something that replaces their role. For those who work in the office, I pray that they have a healthy work environment and comradery amongst their co-workers. I hope that all those who work for my public utilities enjoy what they do and feel fulfilled by the work of their hands. I pray they feel appreciated and not taken for granted. Please give me an opportunity to personally thank one in the coming days. In the name of Jesus, Amen.

DAY 277

PRAYER PROMPT
FOR A CITY YOU DON'T LIVE IN

Think about a city you don't live in, better yet, a city you have never lived in. Lift the city and those that live in it up in prayer. Use this space to make note of different things you want to pray about or to write out your prayer.

DAY 278

FOR PEOPLE WHO WORK IN TECHNOLOGY

Thank You for technology and the people who work in various fields of it. Thank You Lord, for allowing our brains to have such understanding of scientific information and conceptual knowledge and to use it to create such amazing things! Even with our limited knowledge as human beings, You help us to apply it in ways that positively affect our life here on Earth. Today I pray for all those who work in technology of any kind. I pray that You would guide them in their understanding and help them use it for Your good. That You would open their minds to how it can be used to make life better for their fellow man. I pray that the technologies they create would be accessible to those who need them most. Please make them accessible financially and also physically. If a beneficial technology is created in one place and desperately needed by people in another place, I pray You would create a bridge that helps to meet the need. I pray You would prevent anyone from creating technologies that will negatively impact humanity in the short or long-term. For those who have already introduced a dangerous technology, I pray that You would convict their minds and help them see the importance of preventing their creation from being used in bad ways. Please do not let fear or profit or selfish ambition get in the way of their focused determination to find solutions and fixes to stop the negative impacts. For those who You plan to use to introduce new technologies that will benefit the world, I pray that they know the sound of Your voice and seek Your guidance as they work. I pray they would have access to the funding, people, resources and tools they need to bring their ideas to fruition and that they would use what they have created for good. Help them to protect it from anyone who would want to use it for evil. Father, for people who work with technologies that I understand and those I don't, please be their guide. In the name of Jesus, Amen.

DAY 279

FOR THOSE CURRENTLY TRAVELING

Father, I pray Your protection over those who are currently traveling all over the world. No matter how near or far their itinerary will take them, I pray that You would go before them and make each place safe. I pray that You would go with them and guide them along their way. I pray that their route would be smooth and there would be no disruptions or detours, but if You allow those, then please give them patience and keep them on the path that you want them to travel. For those who are traveling for work, I pray that their trip would be a success. For those who are traveling for vacation, I pray that they would truly be able to take a break from their worries and responsibilities and enjoy the time away. For those who are travelling to visit family or friends, I pray that they would have a great time of fellowship and get to spend lots of quality time with those they care about. For those who are traveling to attend a funeral or because a loved one has passed away, I pray that You would bring them comfort in their grief and allow them to celebrate the life of the ones they have lost. For those who are traveling for school or an educational experience, I pray that You would use this trip to open their eyes to all You have created and that their knowledge would grow. For those who are traveling to help someone in need, I pray that they would be a blessing and able to serve with a cheerful and giving heart. For all those who are traveling for any reason Lord, I pray You would bestow travelling mercies upon them. In the name of Jesus, Amen.

DAY 280

FOR THOSE WHO DON'T HAVE ELECTRICITY RIGHT NOW

Father God, this prayer is for those whose power is out or don't have electricity right now. Wherever they are in the world, I pray first for their safety. I pray that not having electricity does not put them in any danger. I pray that they are able to function and live until their electricity is restored. I pray they are able to keep food from spoiling so that they can eat. I pray they have things that they can eat that do not need electricity to be cooked or prepared. I pray that if they are in a cold environment, You would provide a way for them to stay warm. If they are in a hot environment, I pray You would provide a way for them to stay cool. If the loss of electricity has caused them not to be able to leave their home, I pray that everything they need is already there. If the loss of electricity impacts their ability to work, I pray that they would not be financially impacted. If the loss of electricity has cut off their ability to communicate with others, I pray You would make a way for them to still connect and let their loved ones know they are okay and also get access to information about when the electricity will be restored or shelters that have been set up in the meantime. For those whose lives depend on access to electricity, for those who use medical devices as a part of their daily lives, I pray that they have access to batteries, backup generators, stored solar power or other forms of electricity to help them survive. Father, I pray that electricity would be restored very soon for everyone who does not have it. Please make a way, in the name of Jesus, Amen.

DAY 281

PRAYER PROMPT
FOR A POLITICAL PARTY YOU ARE NOT A MEMBER OF

This prayer is your chance to lift others you may or may not agree with up to God and ask Him to give them wisdom and knowledge. Ask Him to give you understanding and help you show them grace and kindness. Ask Him to help them achieve the things that they are doing that are aligned with God's Will and make Him proud. Pray for their peace and protection between them and others that disagree with them. Write your prayer in this space.

DAY 282

FOR THOSE WHO WORK FOR THE SPACE PROGRAM

What a universe You have created Father! How expansive and magnificent it is. The small parts of it You have allowed us to reach are just a taste of all that it is. The truth of what else is out there is beyond our imagination. Today, I pray for those who have made it their mission to explore this universe. I pray for astronomers, scientists, physicists, engineers, technicians, meteorologists, mathematicians, technical writers and astronauts. I pray for those who work at the National Aeronautics and Space Administration (NASA), Jet Propulsion Laboratory (JPL), Cape Canaveral, Kennedy Space Center, Vandenberg Space Force Base, Wallops Flight Facility, Keweenaw Rocket Range, Mojave Air and Space Port, SpaceX and all of the other places in the United States and around the world that study the universe and launch people, rockets, telescopes, satellites, and other equipment into outer space. I pray for the safety of those who travel beyond our atmosphere and those who live and work in the International Space Station. I pray for traveling mercies and that they would have the things they need to stay safe and healthy physically and mentally while they are away from Earth. I pray that those around the world who work in this industry in any way would work together for the common good of all the world's people. I pray You would help us understand that all that has been created was created by You and none of us "own" space. I thank You for all that You have allowed us to learn about space and the celestial objects in it. I pray You would guide those who work in the space program to the places and things in this Solar System that You want us to learn. Help us to understand how all the objects are related and learn things that would benefit humankind here on Earth. Protect us from what You don't want us to understand, from the knowledge that is meant for You alone. I thank You for those who You have given the ability and great responsibility to explore what's out there and I pray through it, they come into a deep understanding of the Creator of it all. In the name of Jesus, Amen.

DAY 283

PRAYER PROMPT
FOR SOMEONE WHO HAS ENCOURAGED YOU

What a blessing to be encouraged. By a friend, a family member, someone you work with, or even a stranger you pass on the street; when people share words that encourage you it can change your perspective, your mood and your whole outlook on life. Who is someone who has encouraged you? Take a moment now to pray for them. Thank God for them and that they would be encouraged too! Use this space to note who encouraged you and what that encouragement meant to you.

DAY 284

FOR MUSICIANS

Music is a beautiful form of worship and a way we can communicate with You Lord. Parts of the Bible are written in song! Today, I pray for musicians. I thank You for their talent and creativity. I pray that it is used for good and that it ultimately brings You glory. I pray that You would encourage those who are just starting out or learning to play a new instrument. I pray they would have access to the instrument they want to learn and helpful instruction. I pray they would have time and a place to practice. I pray that professional musicians would continue to get better and better in their craft. I pray that they would be able to keep their instruments in good condition and have the financial ability to pay for any needed tuning or repairs that they are not able to do themselves. I pray that they would have opportunities to perform and that those who hear them would enjoy it. I pray that those who do this for a living would be able to make enough money to live comfortably and take care of or contribute substantially to their household. I pray that they would be able to enjoy their work and play the type of music that they love. For musicians who are a part of a group or a band, I pray there would be peace and mutual respect between members. I pray that You would remove any spirit of jealousy or unhealthy competition between them that could cause division. I pray that all musicians would find an audience for their work and not be discouraged. Please flood their minds with creativity and give their bodies the strength to play their instruments with passion. I pray that their music would be a balm to someone's soul that helps them celebrate life, love others, get through a hard time or remember a special moment. In the name of Jesus, I pray, Amen.

DAY 285

FOR THOSE WHO HAVE BEEN UNJUSTLY ACCUSED OF A CRIME

Father God, I pray fervently for those who have been unjustly accused of a crime. How it must feel to know that You are innocent, yet others are speaking lies about you. I pray that You would touch their minds and help them stand strong in their innocence. I pray You would provide the legal support they need to defend themselves. I pray this legal support would be good godly counsel giving them advice and helping them make decisions that are in their best interest. I pray that they would have the support of friends and family so that they do not feel alone in this situation. I pray that You would protect them from persecution and make a way for their innocence to be proven beyond a shadow of a doubt. I pray that they would not be found guilty in the court of public opinion, online, or in social media. I pray that no lies about them are spread. I pray that they are treated as innocent and proven innocent without even having to go to court. For those who You do allow to have to go to court, I pray that You would give them peace and strength and patience to withstand the proceedings. I pray that You would give their attorney the ability to defend them well, clearly communicating the true facts of the case and proving their innocence. I pray that the judge and jury would have open eyes and minds and the ability to discern the truth. I pray that all those who are currently being unjustly accused of a crime would have their situations resolved in their favor soon. I pray that all those who have been unjustly accused of a crime in the past are living fruitful and joyful lives, not burdened or traumatized by what happened to them. Please give victory and justice to all those who are innocent of the things they have been accused of. In the name of Jesus, I pray, Amen.

DAY 286

FOR OPHTHALMOLOGISTS

Father, I come before You to pray for eye doctors. I thank You for the talent and training of all eye care professionals. Thank You for the discernment You have given them to provide care, diagnose and treat the health of our eyes. Today I would like to say a special prayer for those who have completed the additional years of medical school to become ophthalmologists, licensed to perform surgeries and medical treatments on patients of all ages. I pray for those in my country and around the world who do this work. I pray for those who work at hospitals, in their own private practices, those who work for non-profits and for aid organizations. Thank You for helping them complete this additional training and guiding their eyes to see what their patients need. Please guide their hands as they perform such delicate surgeries. May they feel a sense of peace and calm as they work. Help them to focus and complete each procedure with excellence. I pray that they would have the ability to provide care to patients who are in need and would have a heart to help them whether the patient can afford the procedure or not. For those who do pro bono work, I pray their generosity would be returned to them two-fold. Father, I pray You would touch their eyes and keep them healthy so that they can continue to work for as long as You will. In the name of Jesus, Amen.

DAY 287

FOR YOUR LOCAL COMMUNITY

Today I pray for my local community. I pray for this area where I live, for the corners of it that I haven't been to, driven through, or walked in. I pray for every home and the people who live in it. I pray for their provision and their safety. I pray their home would be filled with peace and joy. I pray it would be a refuge for the people who live inside; a place where they can rest and relax and feel rejuvenated for the next time they step outside their front door. I pray for all the children, that they would feel safe to play outside and enjoy all that this community has to offer. I pray for all the businesses in my local community. I pray that they would be of service to our neighborhood and offer the goods and services that we need. I pray they would be patronized and supported by the community so that they can be financially successful. I pray that the cars that drive through our streets would move with caution and that this community would not experience any major accidents or collisions. I pray that we would have access to the public transportation that we need so that our community members can travel to and from their homes with ease. I pray for the overall safety and wellbeing of my community. I pray that everyone would be healthy, that our air would be clean and our water would always be safe to drink and to use for our daily necessities. I pray for the local fire department and police stations that you would be with them as they protect us and serve this community. I pray that everyone in my local community would be welcoming and hospitable to each other. I pray that this would be a place that every resident would feel included and cared for. I lift up my local community to You today. In the name of Jesus, I pray, Amen.

DAY 288

FOR THOSE WHO ARE WAITING FOR JUSTICE

Oh, how hard it is to wait. It is hard to wait for a lot of things Lord, but today I pray specifically for those who are waiting for justice. Those who have experienced a crime against them, their friend, a family member or their community. For those who have been hurt, traumatized, victimized and are waiting for justice. I pray that they know You or come to know You during this waiting process. I hope You will help them to let go of any anger, pain, trauma, bitterness or unforgiveness that is eating at their ability to feel joy, find peace and move forward in their lives. I pray that You will help them to not dwell on their experience while also helping them to fight for the justice that they deserve. I pray You will help them to find contentment in the waiting. Give them strength and perseverance especially through times when it seems like justice may be denied or take a very long time. Encourage their spirit and help them see that You are at work and in control of every aspect of the situation. Please bring people alongside them to support them while they wait. Father, You know every detail of their experience and the reasons why justice in their case is being delayed. Please help them never lose hope that it will come. Give them glimpses of the victory You have planned for them and prevent them from sinking into depression, bitterness or deep discouragement. Father, I pray they will put their trust in You, no matter how things seem, knowing that You care for them and that Your Plan is always for our good. In the name of Jesus, I pray. Amen.

DAY 289

FOR NURSES

Thank You for nurses! Father, I thank You today for those who are currently nurses and those who are in the process of becoming nurses. Thank You for their desire to help and care for people. Give them the knowledge they need to manage all their responsibilities well. Give them physical strength and energy to do their jobs even in the most exhausting of days. Protect their mental and emotional well-being from being negatively impacted by all that they see, hear, and experience as they care for their patients. Help them to have insight into their patient's needs and develop plans of care that address the symptoms and conditions they are experiencing. Give them the ability to understand and monitor their patient's vitals accurately and discernment to administer the right medications and the right amounts of medications for each patient in their care. Give them clearness of communication as they record the medical history of each patient and relay important information to all the healthcare professionals who collaborate with them. I pray that nurses around the world have access to the medical equipment and tools they need to do their jobs with excellence. Please continue to help them gain more and more knowledge during their career that will help them become better and better at their job. Father, please protect all nurses who work in every environment. I pray for those who work in hospitals, nursing homes, mental health facilities, urgent care locations, on ships, in schools, in homes, in rehabilitation centers, and those who travel to provide care. Please protect them from illness and disease. Please protect them from physical harm and danger. Please encourage them in special ways that show them how important their work is and how they are positively affecting the lives of every patient they interact with. Show them they are appreciated, and let them never be taken for granted. In the name of Jesus, I pray, Amen.

DAY 290

FOR THOSE WHO HAVE NO SAVINGS

Lord, in this world, we all need money to survive. The amount of money we need may be debatable, yet we need money to live. Even those who live in areas that barter need to store up something of value to barter with. This is just a reality of life. Today, I pray for those who have no savings. Father, I don't judge the why. Whether they haven't considered that they need to save, whether they don't make enough money to save, or whether they choose to spend all their income and not save is not my concern. I just want to pray for everyone who has no savings. I pray that You would guide them and show them ways that they can save so that they are better prepared for the unexpected expenses that You will inevitably allow to come up. I pray that You will help them to identify what they can do to save for those rainy days and their future. I pray that You would provide a way for them to make or have access to the money they need when unexpected expenses come up. I hope that they would not have to take on debt but instead that they would be able to find another way to cover the cost. I pray that they will be or become good stewards of their finances and possessions, understanding the impact of the decisions they make about how to spend, invest, and save the money that they have and receive in the future. For those who need more financial literacy, I pray that they would be open to and receive the education they need. For those who need more income, I pray You would guide them in how to achieve this. For those who spend all that they make or spend beyond their means, I pray You would give them wisdom and guide them to save as You see fit. I pray that all those who don't have any form of savings will be able to create enough savings to support their needs for the future. In the name of Jesus, Amen.

DAY 291

FOR THE UNITY OF THE CHURCH

Father God, I pray fervently for the unity of the Church. I pray for all those who profess to love the Lord and Savior Jesus Christ. I pray for every Christian around the world, regardless of denomination, age, race, or ethnicity. I pray that every individual Christian would see themselves as a part of one body. I pray that every Christian would have a personal relationship with You as Father, Son, and Holy Spirit, three in one. I pray that every Christian would submit themselves to Your Word, the Holy Bible, and understand that its message is love. I pray for unity in the global Church, that we would not be divided by what is different about the way we worship or practice our faith. I pray that we will not stand in judgment of each other over things that are not biblical. I pray that we would not allow the pomp and circumstance of how we each practice our faith to get in the way of the understanding that we are all praising the same God. I pray that we would never believe that God loves one part of His Church more than another. God does not play favorites; we all have the opportunity to have a relationship with Him. Please help us not to be stumbling blocks to each other in the deepening of our faith and understanding of the truth of Your Word. I pray especially for those who believe in You yet have allowed things like politics or cultural differences to use our faith as a tool to divide Your people. I pray that all the enemy's attempts to separate the parts of the body of Christ will be thwarted. I pray that the beliefs Believers hold that stand in the way of our unity would be torn down. I pray that the Church would come together as one, loving You, our God, and loving our fellow Christians as we love ourselves. I pray that Christians around the world would speak to each other with love, truth, and understanding. I pray that the unity of the Church will be restored to a place where it can never be broken. In the name of the Father, the Son, and the Holy Spirit. Amen.

DAY 292

FOR THOSE WHO WORK RETAIL

Jesus, today I pray for those who work in retail stores. I pray for salespeople, customer service teams, store managers, store security, visual merchandisers, cashiers, and the stockroom team. I pray for those whose roles I am not aware of that help the store to run. I pray that they like the role they are in and that You would help them to do it well. Whether they are working retail temporarily or as their long-term career, I pray that they will enjoy their job. I pray that their interactions with customers will be positive. For all those who work in the store and those who handle customer service, I ask that even when they have to deal with uncomfortable conversations or complicated situations, that You give them the right words to say to navigate it well and resolve every situation in a way that is right for the customer and the store. I pray for their energy each day. I pray that they will physically be able to perform their duties. Give those who stand all day strength. Give those who lift heavy boxes or operate heavy equipment strength. Touch the bodies of those who work in the stockroom so that they would not hurt themselves or experience strain. Give those who ensure the security of the store, the employees, and the merchandise alertness to see any nefarious behavior or danger. Provide them with the tools they need to de-escalate any tense situations. Provide them with the support and backup they need from law enforcement when needed. Help those who perform checkout or cashier duties to process each purchase properly and may their registers always balance correctly when the store closes each night. Help the salespeople to make sales without stress. Bring them customers who want their assistance and appreciate their knowledge and help. Inspire the creativity of the visual merchandising staff. Give store managers insight into how to encourage and motivate the team. I pray for all retail workers' job security and that their job pays enough to meet their financial needs. In the name of Jesus, Amen.

DAY 293

FOR THOSE RIDING PUBLIC TRANSIT TODAY

Father, I pray for those who are riding public transit today. I ask that their bus, train, subway, ferry, shuttle, or tram would arrive on time. I pray no delays will negatively affect their schedule. I ask that they have the money they need to cover the cost of their journey. Please let them find a comfortable seat or plenty of space if they prefer to stand. I pray that whatever form of transit they ride on will be in good working condition and operated safely and responsibly by the driver, conductor, or captain. Give those riding public transit today peace during their trips. May they enjoy their ride, reading, working, studying, listening to a book or podcast, enjoying some other form of entertainment, or just taking in the world around them without interruption or disruption from other passengers or traffic conditions. Please give them traveling mercies and protect them physically from any danger from other passengers or transit accidents. For those whose mode of transit will not take them all the way to their destination today, please be with them as they walk, bike, or take a taxi or ride share to get where they need to go. Father, please watch over all those who are making use of public transit today and meet the needs that You know they have. I thank You for providing a way for them to get to where they need to go. In the name of Jesus, Amen.

DAY 294

FOR WOMEN WHO HAVE HAD A MISCARRIAGE

Father of All Comfort, I pray for women who have experienced a miscarriage. For the women who have or will experience one today, I pray urgently that You would not allow them to experience any complications. I pray that You would speak to their minds and help them to process all the emotions they are feeling. I pray that they are not alone and have the support they need from someone who loves and cares for them. I pray for their comfort as they grieve. I pray for all women who have had a miscarriage and also the men who have lost a child to miscarriage. I pray that the men are also able to express their disappointment and process how they feel. For the women, I pray that they will have access to the medical care that they need to recover physically. And if they need support mentally, I pray they will find a professional that can help them recover emotionally. I pray that all women who have experienced a miscarriage and still want to conceive will not lose hope. I pray their road to physical and emotional recovery will be swift so that they can try again when they are ready. Father, I pray that You would bless them to conceive, have a healthy pregnancy, and give birth to a happy child. I pray that they will not experience shame or blame themselves in any way. I pray You would bring comfort to women who have lost a child to miscarriage and give them peace that even after this, things will be okay. You know what each woman needs to hear from You, Lord. Please speak to their hearts and uplift their spirits today. In the name of Jesus, Amen.

DAY 295

FOR THOSE WHO OTHERS ARE LYING ABOUT

Your Word tells us not to lie, not to be deceitful, and not to deal falsely with one another, yet there are those who are currently the target of a lie. Today, I pray for those who others are lying about. I pray that the truth will come to light. I pray that those who are lying will be found out or convicted to retract their lie and admit the truth. I pray that those who are being lied about will not do anything that makes the situation worse. I pray they will not retaliate but instead take actions that will reveal the truth. Give them patience and wisdom in how to respond to and handle the allegations. Give others who hear the lies the ability to discern the truth. May people rally around the person who is being lied about so that they feel supported and not alone. I pray that the truth will be revealed quickly and not have any negative impact short-term or long-term on the innocent person. I pray that every lie about them will be revealed in a way that reaches every person who needs to know the truth. Expose the truth online, on social media, at their workplace, at their church, in their community, in their family, within their group of friends, in a court of law, wherever this lie has been communicated, may the truth be communicated in the same places. I pray that those who have experienced a negative impact on their life from these lies will be able to process any hurt, betrayal, disappointment, or anger they feel so that it doesn't have a lasting impact on the rest of their life. As this situation is resolved, may their hope and joy grow. May this experience draw them into a deeper relationship with You and strengthen their understanding of Your faithfulness. Amen.

DAY 296

PRAYER PROMPT
FOR SOMETHING YOU KNOW SOMEONE ELSE NEEDS

Think of a need that someone has shared with you recently. Not a want. Focus on something that someone truly needs. Use this space to pray that God would provide.

DAY 297

FOR THOSE WHO DON'T HAVE FRIENDS

Jesus, I come before You today to pray for those who don't have friends. Specifically, I am praying for adults who don't currently have any true friendships. For those who may have acquaintances, but not people that they can really talk to and share the joys and challenges of life with. I pray for all adults who desire friendships. I pray that You would schedule divine appointments for them to meet people who will bring love and value to their life. I pray these are people they can connect with and show love and support to also. Give them courage to pursue these friendships. Please remove any anxiety or worry they have about making new friends as an adult. Encourage them to reach out and make an effort to connect with the people that cross their path. Help them discern who You intend to be their forever friends. Protect them from anyone who would not have good intentions or take advantage of their loneliness. For those who want to make new friends, but are not able to physically go out and meet new people, please allow them to find other avenues, like online communities, to connect with likeminded people who they can develop genuine fellowship with. Please help all those adults who don't have friends to connect with other people who share similar hobbies or interests. Help them to connect with people who can relate to an empathize with their life experiences. I pray that all those who currently don't have a friend, would soon find themselves in a new, true friendship that will last a lifetime. Jesus, thank You for being my friend and I pray that while they wait for their earthly friend to be revealed, that You will be their friend too. Amen.

DAY 298

FOR SECURITY GUARDS

Father of all, today I pray for security guards around the world. I pray for guards that secure all places. I pray for their physical protection from harm and danger while they protect people and property. I pray that wherever they work, they will have the experience, tools and support they need to secure the location and keep the peace. I pray that you would keep them alert, with open eyes and ears to identify any potential disruptions or threats and discernment to know how to react in each unique situation. Give them excellent vision and hearing. I pray that they are respected by the people who spend time in or pass by the location that they work at. I pray that they are acknowledged with a "hello" so that they feel seen and appreciated for the work that they do. I pray You would fill them with courage and kindness. I pray that You would give them strength and empathy. I pray that You would relieve any anxiety or fear that they may feel. I pray that every interaction they have would have a positive and just outcome. I pray that You would keep them healthy and give them relief for any bodily discomfort they feel from whatever physical activity is required in their role. For those who have to stand for long periods of time, I pray their feet and backs would not experience any negative effects. I pray that their job provides them with health insurance, sick days and vacation benefits. I pray that they are being paid a living wage that is commensurate with their experience and the value of the job that they do. Father, I pray for all security guards today. I pray that You would give them security in their lives and meet all their needs. In the name of Jesus, I pray, Amen.

DAY 299

FOR CHILDREN WHOSE PARENTS ARE GOING THROUGH A SEPARATION OR DIVORCE

Father, I pray today for children whose parents are going through a separation or divorce. I pray that if it is Your Will, there would be reconciliation between their parents. I pray that You would make a way for their family to stay together and move forward as a healthy family unit. But if that is not Your Will Lord, I pray that the children would not be adversely affected by their parents' breakup. I pray that the children would not think it is their fault in any way. I pray that the children would know that both of their parents love them. I pray that the parents would shield the children from any anger that they feel for each other. I pray that You would help them to put the best interest of the children first in their decisions of how to handle the separation or divorce. I pray that the children's routine would not be drastically disrupted. I pray that the family is able to work out a way to not make the children have to choose which parent to live with. Please Lord, protect the children from feeling like they have to take a side. Please help them to understand what is going on in a way that is appropriate with their age and level of maturity. I pray that the breakup of their parents will not have a negative impact on their view of marriage and the purpose You designed it for I pray this experience would not leave baggage that they take into their future relationships. I pray that during the separation and after the divorce that there is peace in this family. I pray that their parents can be cordial to each other and model love and forgiveness no matter what the reasons for the divorce were. Father, every child has different emotional needs, I pray that You would speak to their heart during this experience and help them to maintain their mental well-being. In the name of Jesus, Amen.

DAY 300

FOR THOSE WHO STUDY THE BIBLE

Father, thank You for Your Word. Thank You for giving us the Bible. I can't imagine going through this life without the instruction, wisdom and encouragement it provides. Today, I pray for all those who study it. I pray for the Christians who study it for a deeper understanding of You. I pray You would make it plain to them and help them apply its truths to their lives. For those who have not accepted Your Son, Jesus, as their savior, but who seek to know more, I pray that You would touch and convict their hearts and minds as they study it. I pray that You would bring Believers alongside them to help them when they have questions and that Your Holy Spirit would guide them into accepting Christ into their life. For those who are studying the Bible for educational, historical, philosophical or anthropological reasons, I pray that they would be guided by truth. I pray that regardless of their spiritual or religious beliefs, they would not misunderstand Your Word. I pray they would respect the Bible and not treat it as fiction. Father, for all those who study the Bible for whatever reason, I pray that they would come to understand Your character, Your love and Your design for human life. I pray that as they study, they would come to know You on a deeper, more intimate and personal level. I pray that through their study, they would not be able to doubt or deny You as the One True God, Creator of All. I pray they recognize Jesus as the Author of our salvation. I pray they become more in tune with Your Holy Spirit. Amen.

DAY 301

FOR ANIMALS IN THE WILD

Lord, I pray today for all the animals in the wild. You designed them for nature and to roam the earth freely. I pray that their environment is conducive to the specific needs of their species. I pray that they have the space they need to live and that it is protected from destruction by human beings and from natural disasters. pray that their habitats are safe from predators. I pray they are able to procreated and protected from endangerment. I pray for their health and that the air they breathe and what they eat has not been contaminated in any way. I pray that they are able to find food to eat that will nourish their bodies. I pray that You give strength and traveling mercies to those who migrate from place to place. Thank You for the diversity of the animals in the wild Father and all that You have allowed us to learn about them. Thank You for the wonder that is experienced in seeing them in their natural habitat. May each animal in the wild fulfill its role in the complex ecosystem as You designed. In the name of Jesus, Amen.

DAY 302

PRAYER PROMPT
FOR A PLACE THAT EXPERIENCED A HURRICANE IN THE LAST YEAR

Think about or search online to learn about a place that recently experienced a hurricane. Use this space to make notes about their ongoing needs and pray for them.

DAY 303

FOR SPIRITUAL GROWTH

Oh, how You designed us to grow and learn and thrive! Being a follower of Christ is a lifelong process. We accept Him, and then we spend the rest of our days trying our best to live by His teachings and Your Word so that we can produce the Fruit of The Spirit through our lives. Today, Father, I come before You, praying for the spiritual growth of all Christians. I pray that Believers around the world would not take for granted their relationship with You. I pray that we will be motivated to continuously study the Bible and apply what we learn to the way we live our lives and interact with others. I pray that we will never become complacent, thinking that we know it all or have already learned lessons that are more complex than we can ever fully understand. I pray that we prioritize spending time with You and that we listen for Your voice. I pray that we come before You humbly confessing our sins, knowing that You already know them all. That we would hold nothing back that would get in the way of our ability to grow as Christians. I pray that we search the scriptures with the guidance of the Holy Spirit so we can focus on what You want us to learn and understand. I pray that our Bible study time will not be so self-focused that we only search for confirmation of our prayer requests and desires. I pray that our time spent studying Your Word will result in a deeper understanding of who You are and how You want us to navigate our lives to fulfill Your plans. That we would be convicted to live out the words of Micah 6:8 by acting justly, loving mercy, and walking humbly with You. I pray that Christians would support each other in their spiritual growth and not be stumbling blocks to each other in any way. May none of us think that we know it all or understand everything completely because only You are all-knowing. May we respect Your teachings and not use them against others, casting stones when we are all sinners and fall short of Your Glory. Help those who are hurting, Lord, and have resentment or are experiencing disappointment over something You have allowed to happen in their life that has caused them to stop seeking You. Draw them back to You, Lord, and give them victory over the spiritual warfare that is stunting their growth. Help Christians all over the world to not have a narrow, biased, or clouded understanding of the Bible based on where we live or our worldview. Help us to see the universal truths of scripture and understand how it applies to everyone. Help us to understand each verse in context and not misunderstand its meaning. Please help each Christian to understand where we are on our own spiritual growth journey and not compare ourselves to others. Please, Father, Son, and Holy Spirit, abide with each Christian and guide them in the way that You see fit so that we can grow and mature in Christ. Amen.

DAY 304

FOR TEENAGERS

Today, I pray for teenagers, Lord. I pray they will have joy and much happiness in this season of their life. I pray that You would help them to find their way in this period between childhood and adulthood, where they will form opinions, have experiences, and make decisions that can have a big impact on their future. I pray You would be with each teenager and guide their minds in Your Truth. May they be protected from all spiritual attacks on their minds. Protect them mentally from the enemy, from the dangers of social media, and bullying. Protect them physically from harm, especially from violence at school. I pray that they have a peaceful, healthy, and supportive home life. I pray they feel loved by their family and that they have a good group of friends. I hope they are able to dream about their future and excited for what is to come. The world changes so fast. The challenges of being a teenager today are already different than they were yesterday, so I pray that You would help them navigate the world around them. I ask that You give each teenager adults in their life that they can rely on and trust. Adults that they feel comfortable sharing their hopes, dreams, fears, and concerns with. I pray You would give those adults wisdom and compassion to support the teens in whatever way they need. Father, each teenager is unique and different, so I don't know how to pray for them specifically, so I ask today that You will meet their needs, make a way, and shower them with Your love and grace as they grow into the adults You have created them to become. In the name of Jesus, Amen.

DAY 305

FOR PEOPLE TO BE PRODUCTIVE IN THEIR WORK THIS WEEK

Today, Lord, I pray that You would be with all those who work for a living around the world. Thank You for the jobs and businesses You have provided and the ability to earn money to live, to save, and to enjoy. There are so many things that can distract people from being productive, so I ask You to help each person work efficiently and accomplish all that You have planned for them to do this week. Help each person to focus and block out anything that would deter them from checking off the things on their to-do list. Give them wisdom so that they can prioritize and make a realistic plan for what they need to get done. Please remove any barriers, like equipment issues, technology challenges, office politics, miscommunication, and missing information that might get in their way. Help them to get into a flow where they are able to manage their time efficiently and utilize their resources well. Please give them access to everything that they need. If necessary, please bring others alongside them to collaborate and provide resources or support. May their workspace be whatever is most conducive to their productivity and workstyle. I pray that their personal life will be peaceful and not distract them from what they need to get done this week. Please help them to stay on the path that You have created for them this week and help them avoid any detours that will not benefit the work You have assigned them to do. Please give energy and mental clarity to each person, and may they be open to hearing Your Holy Spirit guide them in the work of their hands so that all they accomplish will be for Your ultimate glory. In the name of Jesus, Amen.

DAY 306

FOR SCHOOL SAFETY OFFICERS AND SECURITY GUARDS

Today, Lord, I pray for those whose job it is to keep schools safe. I ask You to cover and bless all school safety officers and security guards around the world. First, I thank You for the work that they do and their willingness to serve the students, teachers, and staff of the school they work at. I ask that You would provide them with the training and continuing education they need to stay up-to-date on the best practices of their profession. I pray that the school that they work at is able to provide them with the equipment they need to do their job well. I pray that they have a positive relationship with the school community and feel seen and appreciated for what they do. I pray that You would give them compassion for the people they protect and a sense of pride for the campus. May they be paid well and have health insurance and other benefits that meet their needs. Help them to rest soundly each night and awake, ready to be alert and focused on ensuring safety all day. Give them the courage to step into difficult or dangerous situations. Touch their bodies and give them the physical strength to patrol the campus. Please protect them from being hurt or harmed in any way. May they monitor the campus and detect any suspicious activities. Give them wisdom in all the situations they encounter. Guide them on how to react to disruptive behavior by students, how to deter bullying, and how to prevent or break up any fighting. Help them to resolve conflicts and build trust. Help them respond quickly to any emergency situations and give them immediate lines of communication with law enforcement so that a resolution is reached quickly. May they be well respected and have a good working relationship with the school community, the administration, and the local law enforcement and emergency response agencies. May they be appreciated and treated as an important part of the school and the community. In the name of Jesus, Amen.

DAY 307

FOR CHILDREN BATTLING SUBSTANCE ABUSE

Oh, Father, I come before You today on behalf of children who are battling substance abuse and addictions. I ask that You would break the hold that these things have on them. I pray that You would give these children the clarity to recognize that they need help and the desire to pursue it. I pray You would perform miracles and immediately take away their desire for whatever substance has them shackled. Yet, I know that is not Your plan of escape for all children. So, for those who will struggle to get free, I pray that they have someone in their life who cares about them enough to help them. I pray You would give these children the strength to ask for help. I pray that whoever they go to will be compassionate and knowledgeable about what to do next. I thank You for the mothers and fathers who love them while leading them to a life free of drugs and alcohol. I ask You to give parents the courage to show their children tough love as needed to help them stay on a path toward recovery. Give whoever is helping these children faith that You will take away the child's desire for the substance or give them strength to resist it in the future. In the place of the substance, I pray that You would place a desire for them to draw closer to You. That they would come to rely on You for all their needs. Father, You know what led to this battle in each child's life. I ask You to address each situation in a unique way that will help each child get free and have victory in their life. I pray that You would make a way for them to be healthy physically and mentally so that they can fulfill the beautiful plans You have for their future. Give them access to the resources and bless them with the support they need. I pray they would not give up on themselves and that others in their life would not give up on them. In the name of Jesus, Amen.

DAY 308

FOR PEOPLE TO BE GOOD STEWARDS OF THEIR FINANCES

Father, thank You for being Our Provider. Thank You for the monetary wealth that You allow each person to accumulate. I pray that You would help everyone be a good steward of what they have. Some in this world have little money, and others have an abundance of it. We can do a lot with a little. We can also do nothing with a lot. So, I ask that You would help each person by giving them wisdom in what to do with the money they have. Give them guidance on what to spend and what to invest. Help them budget with consideration for their current circumstances and their future. Help them balance and weigh how they will spend money on what they need versus what they want. Give those who struggle with self-control the ability to exercise it in their daily financial decisions. Especially for those who spend in order to meet an emotional need or fill a void in their life, I ask that You send them reminders that buying more things will not meet their need. Encourage them to seek You and resist the temptation to make bad financial choices. Show everyone how and where to invest that will best benefit the plans You have for their lives. Give each person an understanding of the impact of their financial decisions. May they always choose what is best in Your eyes. Please protect everyone from getting involved in schemes that will end up being detrimental to them and result in a loss of the money they have. Help each person to be a cheerful giver, willing to set aside some of what they have to help others. May we all be grateful for the money we have and use it wisely and intentionally, not becoming lovers of it but rather using it to fulfill the plans You have for our lives and to have a positive impact on the lives of others. In the name of Jesus, I pray, Amen.

DAY 309

FOR CHILDREN YET TO BE BORN INTO THE WORLD

Today, God, I pray for all the children who are yet to be born into this world. I pray for all the unborn children who are in their mother's womb and for those who are not conceived yet but that You have planned to be born. I pray for these children before they take their first breath that they will live happy and healthy lives. I pray for their delivery into this world to be safe. I pray they will not experience any complications. I pray that even those who You do allow to experience complications will have the medical care they need. You have a plan for the life of every baby that will be born. You already know the babies that will be born to people who haven't even met yet. Father, how beyond our imagination it is, the plans You have for all of them. I pray now that they would come to know You and accept Your Son, Jesus, as their Savior during their life here on Earth. I pray that You will walk with them and give them victory over the hardships that You will allow them to face. I pray that You would fill their life with joys and celebrations and happiness. I pray that they will be loved by friends and family. I pray that they will never feel alone. I pray that they will be born into a world at peace and have hope for their future. I pray blessings on all the children not yet born into this world. Father, I thank You in advance for their lives and the part they will play in Your plans. In the name of Jesus, Amen.

DAY 310

FOR THOSE WHO ABUSE OTHERS

Father, You tell us to pray for everyone, so here goes. I pray today for those who abuse others. I ask that You would touch their minds and arrest their spirit to bring them peace and release them from whatever is causing them to inflict pain on others. Convict their hearts to stop their behavior immediately and prevent them from ever physically or mentally abusing anyone ever again. Help them to identify why they have done this and to seek professional help to heal the root cause. With the help of Your Holy Spirit, I ask that they are able to identify the unhealthy thoughts or traumatic experiences that have impacted their view of others and decisions about how to treat them. I pray that You would restrain their hands, feet and tongue from being able to hurt anyone else and give them understanding of the impact they have had on those they have abused. Give them the desire, strength, and self-control to remove themselves from relationships and living situations where they are abusing others. Give them access to treatment where they can permanently change their behavior and unhealthy thoughts. Father, today I ask You as the all-powerful God that I know You are, to stop all abusers from abusing others right now. May they repent, seek forgiveness from You and those they have hurt. May they turn their lives around and become peacemakers for the rest of their days. In the mighty name of Jesus, Amen.

DAY 311

FOR THOSE WHO HAVE EXPERIENCED RACISM

Father today I pray for every person who has experienced prejudice and discrimination because of their race or ethnicity. I lift up to You individuals and groups of people whose lives, opportunities, view of themselves and of others has been affected by racism. I pray that You would help them to see themselves the way that You see them, no matter what they have experienced or heard someone say. I pray that they know that they are worthy and loved. I pray that they know that You designed them perfectly and that no one is superior to them because of their race or ethnicity. I pray that You would give them courage to address incidents of racism that they experience and stand up for others as well. Give them discernment in how to respond and what actions to take. Protect them from those who wish to hurt or harm them because of racist hate. I pray that they would never feel ashamed of how You designed them and that because of their pride they would also celebrate the diversity of others. May they be peacemakers and champions of Your command to love others as ourselves. I pray that You would give them victory even in the face of people and situations that try to discount or oppress them. May they overcome any obstacles put in their way and may their success and joy filled life inspire and encourage others who are battling the evils of racism in their life. Father, I pray for a day when racism does not exist. A day when every person around the world can see and celebrate the beauty in each other and live by Jesus' words spoken in Matthew 22:37-40. Amen.

DAY 312

FOR WIDOWS AND WIDOWERS

Jesus, today I pray for those whose spouse has passed away. I pray for widows and widowers. Please comfort those who are grieving and bring them joy as good memories of their loved one come to mind. May their grief not overwhelm them. Be with them please Jesus, so that they do not feel alone. I pray that their spouse knew You and is now at peace by Your side. I pray that You would help those who recently lost their spouse to find their new normal as they figure out what their life looks like without their husband or wife. I hope that they would not be alone in this, but would have support from friends and family that encourage them to believe that everything will be okay. Help them as they navigate any paperwork or legal things related to their spouse's death. Guide them and give them discernment in each decision they make. I pray that they are not negatively affected financially so that that is not a worry they have to deal with. Please help them as they eventually start to go through their spouse's belongings and determine what to do with them. And for those widows and widowers whose spouse passed away a long time ago, I pray that they feel Your comfort and are at peace. I hope that there are no unresolved issues that they are still dealing with, but if there are, please bring them to a resolution soon. I pray that every widow and widower gets to a place where their joy is renewed and they live a happy and fulfilled life. May they have hope for their own future and the good life You still have planned for them to experience. In Your name Jesus, I pray, Amen.

DAY 313

FOR SOMEONE ELSE'S CHILD

Bless someone else's child by lifting them up in prayer. Use this space to write a prayer for a child of a friend, neighbor or co-worker.

DAY 314

FOR THOSE WHO ARE DEPLOYED

Father, first I thank You for all those who protect and serve our country. I pray for those who serve in the army, marines, national guard or any other branch of the armed forces. Today, I pray for those who are currently deployed. I include in this prayer those who have been sent anywhere in the world, whether they have been deployed to a place where there is peace or into a combat zone. I pray for those who have been deployed domestically or around the world. I pray that those who made the decision to send them did so with right motives, clear understanding of the situation, truth and integrity. I pray that those who are deployed have been provided a clear and honest explanation of their mission and the situations they will face. I pray they have access to the intelligence information that they need to make good decisions in the field. Please give them the weapons, technological tools and support they need. I pray for their safety and success in whatever they have been assigned to do. I pray that You would give them the physical and mental strength and courage to be victorious. I pray that You would protect their bodies from harm and their minds from mental illness like post-traumatic stress disorder, depression and anxiety. I pray that their loved ones back home would be well cared for, so that they don't have to worry and can focus on their mission. I pray that You would cover them for the length of their deployment and bring them back home safely. For those who endure a long deployment and are not able to communicate with their support systems back home, I pray that You would be their companion so that they can endure and persevere. Father, You know the personal situation of every person who is deployed, please give them what they need to do their jobs with honor and in ways that ultimately bring about Your Will in this world. In the name of Jesus, Amen.

DAY 315

FOR NEGLECTED AND ABUSED CHILDREN

A special prayer I say today for all neglected and abused children. Father, I pray that they would be rescued from the situation they are in and placed in a safe and loving environment. I pray this would happen right away! I ask that they would not experience any more pain and that they would be able to heal from their physical and emotional wounds. I pray they would be protected from their neglector or abuser and never have to be in their presence again. If they need food or water or nourishment of any kind Lord, please let it rain down like Your manna so that their physical bodies gain strength. If they need education or access to knowledge that is being withheld from them, please do not allow this to have a long-term negative impact on their life. If they are being emotionally neglected and not show the care and affection they need in their home, I pray that You would bring them godly connection and support with others in their community or at their school or place of worship that would help them understand that they are worthy of love. I pray for children who are being physically abused, that they would not be hurt anymore. I pray for children who are being mentally abused, that they would no longer be affected by the negative words, insults and lies that are spoken. I speak peace and love over them right now. In the name of Jesus, right now Lord, please stop their abuser from being able to hurt them ever again. Rescue these children from their situation and provide them with the medical care they need to fully heal. May they have support from mental health professionals to help them process the trauma and feelings that result from abuse. Father, please make a way of escape for all neglected and abused children. In the name of Jesus, Amen.

DAY 316

FOR THOSE WHO WANT A PERSONAL RELATIONSHIP WITH GOD

Father, there are those who desperately want a relationship with You. I pray that they will respond to that desire and draw closer to You. May Your Holy Spirit rise up in them and guide them in how to nurture their desire. I pray they spend more time in Your Word and that You will illuminate their understanding of who You are. Give them insight into Your character. Give them the wisdom to understand the relationship You want to have not only with Your people but also with them as an individual. Please protect them from discouragement from others who don't understand or support their relationship with You. I rebuke, in the name of Jesus, any attacks of the enemy that intend to keep them from deepening their relationship with You and Your Son Jesus Christ. Help them to sense and respond to the Holy Spirit that dwells in them. Guide them to the personal connections and communities that will support them in their journey to getting to know You on a more personal level. Please protect them from false teachers or distorted teachings that would get in the way of them accepting Your Truth. I pray blessings over all those who want a deeper relationship with You and praise You for the positive impact that Your relationship will have on their lives and the fruit they will bear because of it. In the name of You, Father, Your Son, and the Holy Spirit. Amen and Amen.

DAY 317

FOR THOSE WHO HAVE BEEN THE VICTIM OF A CRIME

For all those who have been a victim of a crime, Father, I pray they would have justice. I pray that whatever happened to them, it would ultimately not have any long-term negative effect on them personally or the plans You have for their life. I pray that if they were physically hurt during this incident, they would be completely healed. Give them strength and hope during the recovery process. I pray that if they experienced any loss of money or material possessions or opportunity, they would be made whole. As they wait for this to happen, I pray that You will provide for all their needs. I pray that whoever committed the crime would be caught and brought to justice in whatever way You see fit. I pray that the victim would not feel fear or anxiety about the person who perpetrated the crime against them. I pray that they will feel safe and secure. I pray that they will be healed of any trauma or mental anguish related to the incident. For their mental well-being, I ask that You help them to forgive and let go of any anger or bitterness that the experience has caused. I pray that their heart and mind will be at peace. No matter how horrible the crime was that they experienced, please make a way for springs of eternal hope to flow through them. Please don't allow this crime to steal their ability to live the rest of their life with joy. In the name of Jesus, Amen.

DAY 318

FOR THOSE WHO ARE CONSIDERING MARRIAGE

Father, today I pray for those who are considering marriage. For those who are reflecting on their current relationship and daydreaming about where it will lead. For those who are preparing to propose and those who are hoping a proposal will soon come. I pray that You would give each one clearness of mind to examine their relationship and the true commitment that marriage is. I pray that You would help them not to think of it lightly but to gain a deep understanding of what, for better or for worse, could look like. Help them to examine themselves and be honest about if they are ready to take vows for life. Help them to see beyond the superficial or material things and get to know the person they are considering marrying. May they not feel rushed or pressured into making a decision. Give them clear eyes to see themselves and the other person. May they be able to discuss their hopes, dreams, and fears for the future with each other. May they be able to successfully navigate difficult conversations about what their family together will look like, how they will handle their finances, their religious beliefs, and what the core values are that they live by. Give them opportunities before making this commitment to experience how each other handles stressful situations. May they experience a disagreement so that they can prove to themselves that they both have the ability to navigate conflict with each other in a healthy way. Help them to understand how their family backgrounds or relationships may impact their marriage. Help them to know with full confidence if You have designed them to be wed. Father, may Your Holy Spirit be with those who are considering marriage and guide them to make the right decision. In the name of Jesus, Amen.

DAY 319

FOR ONLY CHILDREN

Father, I pray a special prayer for only children. The experiences of only children can be different from those of those who have siblings. No one can say that having siblings is better than not having them because You design the family that is right for each child. There are pros and cons either way. So, without any judgment or personal bias, I lift up only children to You. I ask You to meet all their needs. I pray that they will not feel lonely and have long-lasting friendships so deep that they feel like siblings. I pray that they have opportunities for positive social interaction with other children at school or in their community. I pray that they are showered with the undivided love and attention of their family. I pray that they have adults in their lives that they can trust and talk to about whatever is on their minds or in their hearts. I pray You would make the time they might spend alone be to their benefit, cultivating their ability to be creative and daydream about all the possibilities in life. May they benefit from not having disruptions by siblings during their homework or study time, allowing them to learn and gain knowledge that will help them in their life and chosen careers. Father, please watch over only children and protect them in situations where others might have a sibling to defend or look out for them. I thank You for the benefits that only children experience and ask You to not let any of the challenges discourage them or negatively affect their lives in any way. In the name of Jesus, I pray, Amen.

DAY 320

FOR WOMEN WHO ARE PREGNANT BUT DON'T KNOW IT YET

Father God, for women around the world who are pregnant right now but don't know it yet, I first say thank You! Thank You for the life growing inside of them that You allowed to be conceived. I pray that whether this pregnancy was planned or unplanned, You would prepare their heart and mind to find out the news. I pray that even now, You are protecting the baby from any harm that could be unintentionally caused by strenuous physical activity, substances like alcohol, drugs, or medications that the mother may be taking. I thank You in advance for the women who have been trying to conceive and will be happy to hear the news. Thank You for this blessing. I praise You in advance for the women who have been struggling to conceive and will soon find out this miraculous news! May they give all glory and honor to You. I pray in advance for those whose pregnancy is unplanned. Please prepare them mentally and emotionally to hear the news and give them an understanding of Your Will. May they have a support system around them to walk with them as they navigate this unexpected moment. Father, for all women who don't yet know they are pregnant, I pray You will protect them and the babies in their wombs. In the name of Jesus, Amen.

DAY 321

FOR THOSE HEALING FROM A BREAKUP

Jesus, please be a friend to those who are currently in the process of healing from the breakup of a romantic relationship. First, I ask that You would shower them with an overwhelming sense of peace with the situation. Quickly bring them to a place of accepting that this relationship isn't the one that You ultimately have planned for them. Give them eyes to see why this relationship didn't work out and help them objectively understand the roles that each person played in whatever led to the breakup. Please help them gain a clear perspective on the situation. I pray You would help them release any anger or bitterness they carry so that it does not eat away at their soul. I hope that in time, there will be no hard feelings between them and they can appreciate their time spent together and what they learned from the experience. Please renew their joy even while they grieve the end of this relationship. Even if they are feeling discouraged, may they know deep down that there is someone that is not perfect but more perfectly suited for them. Please repair any damage this relationship did to their self-esteem. Give them confidence in who they are, their value, and their worth. Please guide them in how much time they need to fully heal so that they are in a healthy mental and emotional state before pursuing another relationship. I pray that they would draw closer to You, Jesus, during their healing process and truly regard You as a friend. Give them clarity on what they need in a romantic relationship. Help them discern what behavior is acceptable and not acceptable to them in a relationship. May Your Holy Spirit give them discernment as they decide to get into a relationship in the future. Please help them make smart decisions that are for their good and will lead them to the person You have designed to be their lifelong companion. In Your name, Jesus, I pray for those in the midst of healing from a breakup today. Amen.

DAY 322

FOR THOSE WHO ARE EMPLOYED

Father, I know we can sometimes take for granted the jobs You have provided for us, especially if it is a job that we don't enjoy. So today, I want to thank You on behalf of everyone who is currently employed. For people around the world who have employment of any kind, thank You. I pray that You would help each person have a thankful heart. For those who love their work and find purpose and fulfillment in it, I pray that You will allow them to continue it. Keep them inspired and motivated to do it with excellence. For those who are content with their job but are also hoping for a change, I pray You would give them the strength to keep going. Please give them guidance on how to pursue a new opportunity that is more aligned with their career and financial goals. For those who dislike their current job and are feeling desperate for a change, Father, I pray You would help them make it through each day. Help them feel grateful for the employment You have provided while they apply for jobs that they desire. Please keep their spirits uplifted so that they do not feel discouraged. Remind them of their talent and value and give them hope that You will provide a better job for them at just the right time. Father, for all those who are employed, thank You for what they are learning in their current job, for the skills they are developing, for the people they have met, and for the ways this current job is preparing them for things You have planned for their career in the future. In the name of Jesus, I pray, Amen.

DAY 323

FOR CHILDREN WITH SPECIAL NEEDS

Lord, today I pray for all children who have special needs because of a learning, medical, or emotional challenge. I pray they feel loved. I pray they have the support of family, friends, educators, and their community. I pray that they have access to the resources, equipment, tools, and medical care they need to live their life to the fullest. I pray that they always have people in their lives who understand them well so that they can communicate their feelings and needs. I ask You to help them always feel heard. I ask You to help them always feel seen and never ignored or discounted because they are different. I ask that You give them self-confidence and protect them from discrimination. May their diversity be celebrated so that they feel encouraged to pursue their dreams and fulfill the purpose that You designed them for. Father, help those who do not have special needs to become more educated about these children so that we are not stumbling blocks to their development. Give those who interact with them patience and a willingness to adjust to the needs of the child. Give others understanding and empathy so that these children are treated with respect and don't make assumptions about what they can and can't do or achieve. Father, Your Holy Spirit knows how to communicate with every heart and mind. You know the physical ability of every child's body. I pray that You would allow each child to reach their full potential. I pray that You would speak to each child's heart and mind so that they come to know You and have a personal relationship with You. I pray that their childhood will be wonderful so that they grow into high-functioning adults. I pray that they love their life and have a childhood and adulthood filled with joy. In the name of Jesus, Amen.

DAY 324

FOR THOSE WHO ARE WEARY

For those who are weary, Lord, I pray You would renew their spirit. There are so many things in this life that can wear a person down. Each person's response to what they experience is different. Some of us become weary quickly, and others have more endurance. We all have different responsibilities that change during different seasons of our lives. Some are physically weary, and some are mentally weary. Some are both! The good news is that Your Word says we can come to You if we are weary and burdened and that You will give us rest. (Matthew 11:28-30) Your Word encourages us not to become weary of doing good. (Galatians 6:9) Your Word instructs us to humbly come before You and give You our burdens because You care about us and don't want the enemy to take advantage of how we are feeling. (1 Peter 5:6-8) So for those who are weary, Lord, I pray that You would give them insight into what is causing it. I pray that they would humble themselves before You and talk to You in prayer. I pray that they will leave those burdens at Your feet and sincerely trust that You will make things better at the right time. While they wait on You, I pray that they will not pick up those burdens again. I pray that in the meantime, You will help them through and give them strength each morning. Please lift their spirit out of weariness and give them the ability to live each day with joy, knowing that You are with them. Please refresh their body, mind, and spirit in the name of Jesus, Amen.

DAY 325

PRAYER PROMPT
FOR HOW GOD SHOWED UP IN SOMEONE ELSE'S LIFE

Think about someone who has recently experienced a miracle, a blessing, or an answer to their prayers. Use this space to thank God for showing up in such a mighty way!

DAY 326

FOR SINGLE PEOPLE WHO HAVE LOST HOPE IN FINDING LOVE

You designed us to love. You command us to love You and others. Not every person desires romantic love, but for those who are single and want to find love, Father, I pray You would bless them with someone special. Especially for those who have lost hope. If it is because of their age, I pray that You would remove their assumption that they are "too old" to find love or be loved. I pray You would remind them that You control the length of our days and that You still have good things planned for their future. Please help them find opportunities to connect with others who are looking for love and lead them to the person You have been preparing for just the right time in their life. If they are feeling hopeless because of their past relationship experiences, I pray that You would heal their heartbreak and any bitterness or resentment they may be holding onto. I pray that You would give them a new perspective and show them that there is someone out there that is a great match for them. Please remove any unhealthy barriers they have erected that are getting in the way of them connecting with the person You want them to give a chance to. Please protect them from further heartbreak or disappointment. For all those around the world who have lost hope in finding love for whatever reason, I pray that You would protect them from the lies the enemy whispers that attempt to make them believe they are unworthy or not loveable. Give them confidence in their value and protect them from making a rash decision about who to give their love to out of desperation. May Your love for them suffice until the appointed time that You will bring the right person into their life. In the name of Jesus, Amen.

DAY 327

FOR MOMS OF YOUNG CHILDREN

For the mothers of young children, Father I pray that You would bless them today. Every mom is unique and has their own needs, I pray that You would meet each one. Please encourage them when they struggle or feel alone. May they have friends they can relate to and talk to about their experience as a mom. Give them unwavering love for their children that helps them make right decisions about how to raise them. Help them understand their children so that they build trusting relationships and great communication that last into their adulthood. May their children express their love to their mom in ways that make them feel appreciated. Give them energy physically to juggle parenting and all the other responsibilities they have. Please help them find ways to maintain their own mental wellbeing so that they are always at their best not just for their children, but also for themselves. Relieve their stress and anxieties. Please guide them in how to handle seasons of stress related to situations in their children's lives. Give them wisdom in what to say and do. Give them confidence as they navigate being the mom of young children. I pray they have a solid relationship with You, so that they can cast their cares and know that You will help them through every situation. I pray they know You and are constantly covering their children in prayer. Please help them manage their time efficiently and give them the support they need to take time for self-care and to renew their spirit. May they feel seen as more than only a mom, but as the woman You created them to be. In the name of Jesus, Amen.

DAY 328

FOR COUPLES WHO ARE IN MARRIAGE COUNSELING

Father, I come before You now on behalf of couples who are in marriage counseling. I thank You for their willingness to seek help to improve their relationship and address any challenges they are facing. I pray that both spouses have an open heart that sincerely wants to do the work necessary to make things better for one another. I ask that You would convict their hearts of any selfish motives that could get in the way of making progress in counseling. If individual therapy is needed, I pray You would convict their heart and direct them to seek out someone who can work with them on the things they need to work through on their own. I pray that the marriage counselor the couple is getting guidance from is well educated and skilled at working with couples who have their specific challenges. Give them wisdom on how to handle each session so that every couple they work with will have a positive result. I pray that the counselor is able to make their sessions a safe space for both spouses to share their hearts, hurts, dreams and needs. In pray that before every session, Your Holy Spirit would enter the space and cover it with Your Peace so that it is protected from the enemy's attempts to disrupt any progress or healing. I pray You would protect these couples from ungodly or unhelpful advice and opinions of those outside their marriage. May their decisions and actions regarding their relationship be guided by what You know is best for them, because You know all the details that others don't know. You know both sides. You know the hurts that can be healed. You know the lies that need to be confessed. You know the forgiveness that needs to be given. You know if Your Will is that this marriage will be restored or if there are things going on so deep and dark that it needs to end. Please I pray that every couple who is in counseling would have clarity on what the challenges are they are trying to resolve and be guided in realistic ways of addressing each one. In between sessions, I pray that each spouse is able to recall what they learned and put tools and healthy habits into practice. Father, I pray that Your Holy Spirit is in the midst of the counseling and helps each couple to address their problems, increase their love for each other and if it's Your Will, renew their commit to their marriage. I pray that each marriage would be filled with joy and each spouses' needs would be met. I pray they would better understand and be sensitive to each other's desires. I pray that every couple who is in counseling will have a healthy marriage. That they would reach a place of unconditional love, joy and trust with their spouse. No marriage is without its challenges, but I pray that You would give each couple the tools to have a healthy relationship, so that their commitment to each other brings You glory. In the name of Jesus, I pray, Amen.

DAY 329

FOR THOSE WHO ARE REBUILDING DUE TO DESTRUCTION CAUSED BY A NATURAL DISASTER

Father, the devastation after a natural disaster can change the course of a person's life. For those who are currently rebuilding their home or business due to the destruction that has been caused, I first thank You that they are okay. If they did experience any physical injury, I pray that it has been or will be fully healed and that have the medical coverage or financial means to get the care they need. If the experience of losing their home or other properties has caused them mental anguish, I pray that You would comfort them and help them work through any emotional trauma that they are experiencing. I hope and pray that their home or other buildings were insured and that the insurance company is handling their claims in an ethical and just way. I pray that they are able to also receive support and financial relief from government agencies that can help them rebuild. I ask You to give them wisdom and discernment on if they should rebuild, where they should rebuild and how they should build their new home or structure. If Your Will is for them to rebuild in the same place, I pray that You would help them to build a structure that will withstand future weather and climate events. I pray that the structure they build will keep them and their loved ones safe and never be destroyed again. If Your Will is for them to build in a new or different place, I pray You would remove any obstacles and make the process of buying land or moving smooth. Guide them to re-establish themselves in the place that You have determined will be the best benefit to their future. For all those who are rebuilding, I pray that You would lift any feelings of discouragement or depression. Give them relief from any anger over what they have lost. Like Job, I pray that You will give them twice as much as they had before and bless their latter days more than the days that came before. (Job 42:10-12) In the name of Jesus, Amen.

DAY 330

FOR CHILDREN WHO ARE NERVOUS ABOUT AN UPCOMING EXAM

Lord Jesus, I pray You would be with every child who is nervous about an upcoming exam. I ask that You would calm their nerves so that they can focus on preparation. I hope that they know You and pray to You about their anxieties and fears. I pray that You will respond to their prayers with a sense of peace. I pray that they channel their nervousness into positive actions, like studying and asking for help from teachers, teaching assistants, tutors, parents, or their peers who are well-versed in the subject matter. I ask that You don't allow their nervousness to overwhelm them into inaction or a spirit of defeat. If they are struggling to understand the material, I pray that You will give them access to resources that can help them. I pray they would feel no shame in asking for help and seeking out the resources that they need. I pray that they will have uninterrupted study time and a place to study that is most conducive to how they learn. Please give them clearness of mind so that they can focus and increase the strength of their memory so that they retain more information. On the day of the exam, may they be well rested and wake up with energy and a positive attitude. Give them a sense of peace and calm. I pray they have confidence that they have done all they can to prepare for this exam. During the exam, please help them recall what they have studied and show what they have learned. I pray that because of their diligence, they will be rewarded with a good grade. In Your name, Jesus, I pray, Amen.

DAY 331

PRAYER PROMPT
FOR A FRIEND YOU KNOW IS WORRYING ABOUT SOMETHING

Father, for my friend...

I know they are worrying about...

I pray...

DAY 332

FOR PARENTS WHO ARE STRUGGLING TO GET THEIR CHILDREN THE HELP THAT THEY NEED

Father God, You have all power, so I come before You right now, praying You would make a way for any parent who is currently struggling to get their child the help that they need. Whatever the situation is, I know You are able. I pray that they know You already or come to know You soon so that they pray and ask You for help. But today, I will pray a prayer of intercession for all parents who find themselves unable to financially provide something their child needs, get access to something their child needs, or are fighting as an advocate on behalf of their child. If finances are getting in the way of the help their child needs, I pray that You would make a way for them to earn, receive, or be gifted the money. If it is special education, tutoring, medical care, or anything else, please make a way. If the parent is struggling because of their work schedule, I pray that You would resolve the conflict and make a way. If the parent is struggling because what their child needs isn't provided by the schools, hospitals, or available in the community where they live, I pray You would make a way for them to gain access to the service that their child needs. If what their child needs is available but obstacles are blocking them from gaining access, I pray that You would be on their side as they fight to advocate on behalf of their child. Please make a way. If their child is being bullied or mistreated at school or in an extra-curricular activity they participate in, please give the parents victory in working with those in charge to provide a safe place for their child to learn and participate. Father, You know the struggles that each parent faces to make sure that their child has everything that they need. I pray You would be in the midst of every situation and give the parents resilience, strength, and courage as You help them do the best that they can for their child. Thank You for being the WayMaker. Amen.

DAY 333

FOR SIBLINGS

Having siblings can be a blessing, yet stories throughout the Bible show us that sibling relationships can also be complicated. Father, only You truly know why some sibling relationships are positive and some are filled with turmoil. So today, I pray for all siblings. I pray that they will have healthy relationships filled with love, mutual respect, two-way support, and unbreakable bonds. I pray that those who have siblings will never feel alone and will always be able to call upon their brother or sister in times of need. I pray that siblings would not be pitted against each other or made to feel like they have to compete for their parent's love. I pray for young siblings who are separated and living in different households that they can still maintain a connection regardless of the reasons they don't live under the same roof. I pray for adult siblings that they also stay connected no matter where their individual lives take them. For those siblings who have an unhealthy relationship, I pray for healing. For those siblings who have a contentious relationship, I pray for forgiveness. For those siblings who have no relationship at all by choice, I pray for reconciliation. For those siblings who have no relationship, because they have never met or don't know each other exist, I pray that they would come to know each other and have a positive relationship if that is Your Will. Father, there is a reason You create siblings, and I pray that each one comes to understand Your purpose for their sibling in their life and Your purpose for them in their sibling's life. I pray that that purpose is fulfilled in a way that brings them joy. In the name of Jesus, Amen.

DAY 334

FOR THOSE WHO ARE IN DESPAIR

Oh, Father, I pray for those who are right now in a valley of despair. For those who are hopeless, distressed, afflicted, and in anguish. I pray for those who are in a place so deep that they can't climb out on their own. Show them that they are not alone and that they can climb out with You. Please protect them from sinking so deep that they hurt themselves or make choices that will have bad consequences. Please rescue them from the pit and help them see the light of hope. Send them people who will not speak in platitudes but will listen to their pain, have empathy, and be willing to speak life to them in a way that genuinely acknowledges what they are going through. May those who are struggling be encouraged to try to restore their hope. With each moment of each day, please stand alongside them and help them combat the negative thoughts, lies, and temptations of the enemy and demolish every argument that stands against Your Truth. You promise to be close to the brokenhearted, and I pray that in this valley season, they call out to You and accept Your care for them. I pray that by doing this, they will have the strength to take captive every thought and make it obedient to Christ. (2 Corinthians 10:5) I ask on their behalf that You will make their despair brief; yet, I know You have a good purpose even for the long seasons of despair You allow us to experience. So, please be with those who are struggling, and at Your right appointed time, give them victory over despair. Renew their joy and help them rejoice always. I thank You in advance for the better days and happier seasons of their life that are to come. Thank You, Lord. I praise You! Amen.

DAY 335

FOR THOSE WHO ARE STRUGGLING TO LOVE THE WAY THEY LOOK

We have such a distorted way of understanding true beauty, Father. The standards of beauty we humans have established vary around the world. It is fickle, changing with the seasons, cultural trends, and marketing strategies of businesses. In many circumstances, those standards are unhealthy, unrealistic, and unattainable or sustainable, causing many to struggle to love the way they look. Father, today I pray that You will help every person to see themselves the way You see them. Help men and women to love the way they look. May they love the way they look now and in every season of their life. Help them to accept and appreciate how You designed their face, their hair, and their form. Give them the ability to stop thoughts of comparison and appreciate the attractiveness they see in others without it negatively affecting how they see themselves. Give everyone a global perspective on different races and ethnicities so that they see Your creativity and are not biased in their opinion of what is physically attractive. Increase our knowledge of and compassion for different medical diagnoses or physical disabilities that affect our bodies so that we are less judgmental about how people "should" look. For those who have experienced a significant change in their appearance due to an illness, accident, or any other event, I pray that You would not allow it to have a negative effect on how they view themselves. Help them to work through accepting the changes and to fall in love with the way they now look. Guard our hearts and minds from entertainment, marketing, and social media that promote an unhealthy view of the human form and warp our ability to love ourselves as we are. Please help those who are struggling with their appearance to not struggle with it anymore. In the name of Jesus, Amen.

DAY 336

FOR THOSE WHO ARE SEPARATED FROM THEIR SPOUSE

Father, for spouses who are separated, I come before You today. You know the history of their relationship and if Your Will is for them to remain married or not. I know Your Word says that when a man and woman get married, the two become one flesh. (Matthew 19:6) You designed marriage as a lifelong commitment, yet the Bible also talks about divorce in certain circumstances being allowed. Only You know what the right outcome is for the couples who are currently separated. I won't assume that I know best. Right now, I want to pray for the spouses for whom Your Will is restoration. I pray that this separation is temporary and they will remain married. I pray for reconciliation. That whatever caused them to decide to separate can be worked through and healed. I pray for peace. That Your Holy Spirit would be in the midst of all their conversations and interactions and help them navigate back to a place where they desire to be together. I pray that during this time apart, they will each address the things that they need to work on as individuals. I hope that they will both examine themselves and humbly submit to one another out of reverence for Christ. (Ephesians 5:21) If they don't have a personal relationship with You, I pray that this separation period would be a time that they feel a desire to seek You and spend time pouring their heart out to You as they listen for Your guidance in how to find their way back to their spouse. I pray that they will reunite at Your appointed time and that their marriage will be stronger going forward. In the name of Jesus, Amen.

DAY 337

FOR PREGNANT WOMEN

Today, I say a prayer for all pregnant women. For women in my country and around the world. For every woman who is at any stage of pregnancy, I pray that their body will be strong and healthy. I pray that their minds will be joy-filled and at peace. I pray that they have comfortable living conditions, clean water, and healthy food that will nourish their body as well as the child or children in their wombs. I pray that they have a support system of people in their life that will help them in whatever ways they need. Please allow them to access the medical care that they need throughout their pregnancy to make sure that everything is okay. If they work, I pray that they have support from their employer to adjust their responsibilities if necessary. For those with pregnancies that are considered high-risk, I pray that You would protect them and their babies from any complications or problems. For pregnant women who are on bed rest, I pray that You will give them patience and peace. Please help all pregnant women to stay in a positive state of mind. Remove any worries that any pregnant women have about the health of their child, and help them to release them to You. Give each woman wisdom as they think about their birth plans. Help them discern the location, type of delivery, and the right doctor, midwife, or doula that they want to be involved. Educate them on their options and what is best for them and their baby. Give them the courage to advocate for themselves to ensure that their decisions are respected. I pray in advance that whatever medical professionals are involved in the birth are highly skilled and provide compassionate care. I pray that every pregnant woman has a safe delivery and brings healthy children into this world. In the name of Jesus, Amen.

DAY 338

PRAYER PROMPT

FOR THE HEALTH OF THE PETS IN YOUR HOME OR OF FAMILY, FRIENDS AND NEIGHBORS

Father God, today I pray for the health of...

DAY 339

FOR THOSE WITH DEMENTIA OR ALZHEIMER'S

Father God, Creator of our intricate minds, today I pray for those experiencing dementia or Alzheimer's. I don't understand why You allow some to be afflicted with the loss of their cognitive abilities and memory. I pray that someday, You would allow a cure to be found. For those who are experiencing dementia symptoms or Alzheimer's disease, I pray that they have been properly diagnosed. How scary and frustrating it must feel to start experiencing symptoms and be unsure of what is going on. I ask that You don't let the symptoms go on too long before they are identified. I pray that they are not ignored and that their symptoms are not written off by loved ones. I ask that those who are suffering are treated with compassion, patience and understanding. I pray that there are people in their life who will advocate for and encourage them when they are feeling vulnerable and helpless to stop the decline in their mental abilities. I ask that Your Holy Spirit would help them to maintain their sense of identity and self-worth. I ask You to provide care givers that are skilled or are willing to become skilled in how to best care for someone with cognitive decline. I pray that even in moments of confusion or frustration, they would recognize the voice of Your Holy Spirit within them and feel Your Peace. Please don't let them feel lonely or alone. Please protect them from hurting themselves or others out of confusion or frustration with what they are experiencing. Please help them to hold onto special memories that will still bring them joy, even as some memories fade away. Father, I ask that You would slow the decline of those experiencing dementia or Alzheimer's disease, so that they and their loved ones can enjoy as much time with each other as possible. In the name of Jesus, Amen.

DAY 340

FOR THOSE DEALING WITH TRAUMA

Father, You are the God of all comfort, You are the God of peace. I come before You, asking You to alleviate the feelings of distress or grief of those dealing with a traumatic experience. Help those who are trying to process something that happened in the past and those who are in the midst of a traumatic event right now. Urgently I ask that the trauma would end. Please protect them from being re-traumatized in any way. Give them the care that they need to heal. Father, please heal their mind and spirit. Touch their thoughts with Your loving words and give them hope that they will be okay. Bring them to a support group or therapist that is specifically tailored to help people who have gone through similar things. Through fellowship and counseling may they overcome the trauma and find strength to move forward, knowing that they are not alone. Please prevent their experience from becoming something that negatively defines who they are or how they see themselves. Please help them to see that their true identity is in You. Give them confidence as they overcome any fears or anxieties related to what happened. Show them that they are strong and courageous and loved. Turn any feelings for victimization into victory. Turn any feelings of shame into dignity. Turn any feelings of powerlessness into courage. You know what each person has experienced and what they need to heal. I pray that You would walk beside each person and shower them with what they need. Thank You Father. Amen.

DAY 341

FOR THOSE WHO ARE ENGAGED

Thank You Jesus for those who are engaged to be married! I pray that the desires of their hearts are aligned with Your Will for their life. I ask that You guide them in determining how long their engagement should be. Protect them from the pressures of other people's expectations, so that they take the time that You know they need to prepare their hearts and minds for the commitment they will make to each other. I pray that they both know You and have a relationship with You. If not, and they don't recognize Your hand in their life, I pray that they will still be guided by Your still small voice to make decisions that will benefit their union. I pray that engaged couples would develop healthy communication; learning how to share their hopes and dreams, learning how to resolve conflicts and developing a foundation of trust. I pray that every couple would have the opportunity to experience good and hard times during their engagement, so that they have a realistic understanding of how their fiancé reacts to different situations. I hope they take the time to talk about their spiritual beliefs, what they want their family to look like, how they want to handle finances and all the areas that are important to them as individuals. Expose their imperfections and differences and help them have empathy for each other and find common ground. Please help them to go deep in their conversations so that they are confident that they will be on one accord after they say "I do". Please help them start to become one even before their wedding day, so that they have no doubt that the person they are marrying is perfectly suited for them. Father, may they go into their wedding day full of joy and hope for the future. Please prepare them for the joys and challenges they will inevitably experience in their life together. Thank You for bringing them together and I pray that nothing will break them apart. In the name of Jesus, Amen.

DAY 342

FOR HIGH SCHOOL STUDENTS

Oh, the joys and challenges of high school! Christ Jesus, I come before You today asking that You would be a friend to all high school students. The high school experience is different for each generation. It can be different depending on the country where the school is located. It can be different depending on the community the school is in. One student's experience can be totally different from another's based on the type of school they attend. High school students have the added layer of not just getting a good education, but also navigating the social climate on campus and online. They face different opportunities and challenges, depending on their family dynamics, socio-economic status, age, gender, hobbies and interests, race, ethnicity, religion and so much more. This prayer can't cover every situation that high school students face, but I know You can. Jesus, You can walk with each student in this season of their life. I pray that overall their high school years would be positive. I pray that they would learn and grow in their understanding academically and socially. I pray that they would feel that their school is a safe place for them to explore who they are and who they want to become in the future. I pray it is a safe place for them physically. That no harm, hurt or danger would touch them. Protect their school from all violence. Protect them from bullying. Protect them from other students or adults who mean them harm. Please protect them mentally from anxiety or worry about the safety of their school. I pray that all high schoolers would have friends and none of them would feel alone. I know it's normal that they will have positive and negative friendship experiences during this season in their life. Lord, I pray that the good will outweigh the bad and that any bad experiences will not become emotional baggage that they carry into adulthood. May their school be a peaceful place for them to learn. Help them study and gain understanding that will be a strong foundation for whatever Your Will is for their future. I pray that they have talented teachers that support their development and inspire them to dream big. If they need tutoring or special help, I pray that it would be made available to them and that they will take advantage of it. I pray an extra special blessing on those who are juggling additional responsibilities like caring for a family member or working while also going to high school. Give them strength so they can persevere and make good decisions on how to manage their time and responsibilities. I pray that nothing gets in the way of them being able to graduate. For those who are dating, I pray that You would help them discern who they get involved with and the boundaries to set. Help them keep a right perspective on any romantic relationships they have. For those who are struggling with self-esteem, please help them see their value. Open their eyes to see why The Father designed them the way He did. Help them to understand their strengths and accept the areas where they need to mature. May they give themselves grace and have trustworthy and god-fearing people in their life who encourage and uplift them. Jesus, be a friend to any high school students who are struggling with their mental health. I pray that You would not let them suffer in silence. Give them the courage to seek help, to talk to their parents, or a teacher or school counselor. Help others to recognize that they are struggling and be proactive about getting them the care and support they need. Jesus, being a high schooler can be complicated, but You can make things simple. You make paths straight. So, I pray that You would walk with and guide each high school student on the right path so that their life is a testimony of Your faithfulness and love. I pray that if they don't know You right now, they come to know You soon. In the name of Jesus, Amen.

DAY 343

PRAYER PROMPT
FOR THE PEOPLE OF A COUNTRY YOU HAVE NEVER VISITED

Identify a country you have never visited and pray for the people, the government, their resources, and their future. Make notes about what you want to pray for or write your prayer in this space.

DAY 344

FOR THOSE STRUGGLING TO PAY THEIR SCHOOL TUITION

Father, You are The Provider. Thank You for all those who are in school or preparing to attend school all over the world. Thank You for their desire to learn and gain knowledge. I pray that the education they receive will prepare them for the work that You have ordained the to do here on Earth. I pray today for those who are struggling to pay for their school tuition. I ask that You would make a way for it to be covered. Whatever they are studying, I pray they have the financial resources to not only attend school, but also to purchase or get access to books, supplies, tools, technology equipment, and other materials that they need. I ask that You would make a way for them to be able to pay their tuition without going into debt or having a negative impact on their long-term finances. Give them opportunities for tuition aid through scholarships, grants and gifts. If it is Your Will that they need to apply for loans or use credit cards or other means to cover the cost of their education, I pray that You would protect them from being taken advantage of. I pray that You would give them wisdom and discernment on the interest and repayment terms that they agree to. I ask that the debt they accrue would not be overwhelming and that the income from their employment now or in the future would more than cover what they owe. I pray that You would make a way for them to pay off any student debt within a reasonable amount of time and that it would not negatively impact their financial future. I thank You for the generosity of family and friends who might help them to pay for things along the way. I thank You for jobs that they have that will reimburse them for educational costs. I pray You would give an extra dose of strength and energy to those who work their way through school so that they can cover the cost of tuition. Father, I ask for Your financial provision on all those who are struggling to pay their tuition. Please give them hope and help them so that their burdens are lifted, and they do not have this added stress. In the name of Jesus, Amen.

DAY 345

FOR THOSE WHO LONG FOR MORE EMOTIONAL INTIMACY IN THEIR MARRIAGE

Thank You for marriage and the way that it reflects Your desire for intimacy with us. Father, thank You for those who have committed to love one another and gotten married. Marriage is a beautiful gift, yet it can experience seasons when the emotional intimacy wanes. For those who are in a season where they do not feel close and connected, I pray that You would help them to hold onto hope. May they know that it is possible for them to reconnect. Please help husbands and wives who long for more emotional intimacy in their marriage communicate their needs to each other. Please help them to listen to one another and respond with compassion. Help them to seek to understand each other's feelings and not ignore or discount each other's emotions. Give them clarity of each other's point of view and protect them from the enemy's attempts to keep them apart. The foundation of intimacy needs trust. I ask that You help them to trust each other more deeply so that they are willing to be vulnerable with each other. Even when they don't fully understand how each other feels, may they feel safe to express their true feelings. Father, for those who are struggling to trust their spouse, I hope they trust in You. I hope they know Your character and Your promises and that they hold on to those while You work in their marriage. I pray that You are the bond that holds them together in the times that they struggle to connect with each other. If they need support from a counselor, I pray that You would open both their hearts and give them the desire to seek the guidance they need to break down any barriers that are getting in the way of their emotional intimacy. I ask that You draw them closer together so that they can experience a level of intimacy that reflects Your love for them and the intimacy You desire to have with them. In the name of Jesus, Amen.

DAY 346

FOR SINGLE PARENTS

Christ Jesus, I pray for all single parents. Please bless them with a double dose of strength and energy. Please shower them with love and support that helps them navigate the challenges of raising children alone. I pray that they don't ever feel alone or unseen for all that they do. When they need parenting advice or just want to talk through situations they are facing, may they have a sincere and caring friend they can connect with. I hope they also have a community they can rely on in whatever ways they need. If they are working, I pray that their job or employer is flexible in allowing them to be there for their children. I pray that they are able to attend events, be involved in their activities, and take the time off from work to care for all their children's needs. Please help them to find time not only for the responsibilities of parenthood but also to take care of their own mental and physical well-being so that they can be healthy for themselves and their family. I ask that You would surround their home with a hedge of protection and fill it with peace, laughter, and love. Every single parent's situation is unique. Some are unmarried, some are divorced and not remarried, and some are widowed. Some are raising one child, and some have more. Both women and men can be single parents. So, with all this in mind, I ask that You meet the needs of every situation. I ask You to supply all their needs. Please watch over them and help them to be amazing parents who raise amazing children. In the name of Jesus, Amen.

DAY 347

PRAYER PROMPT
FOR YOUR FAVORITE SINGER, MUSICIAN, OR GROUP

Father, today I pray for...

Thank You for the talent You have blessed them with and for the effect that their music has had on my life. I pray for their health. I pray for their mental well-being. I pray for their financial stability so that they can continue to create music for a living. I ask You to give them traveling mercies when they go places to perform. I pray that You would inspire them as they create music so that everything they do makes You proud. I hope that they know You and have a relationship with You so that they are convicted to use their talent, influence, or testimony to give You glory in some way. I also ask that...

DAY 348

PRAYER PROMPT
FOR SOMEONE YOU HAVE NEVER PRAYED FOR

Think of someone you have never prayed for. It can be someone you know or someone you've never met. Use this space to pray for them.

DAY 349

FOR NEWBORNS

Father, there are babies being born today! There are probably babies being born all over the world as I say this prayer. I lift up all newborn babies to You right now. May they be blessed by the prayers of their parents but also by the prayers of strangers like me, welcoming them into this world. I thank You for whatever You have designed their purpose to be. I thank You for their birth and pray that they are healthy and loved. I pray that whatever road You have planned for them, that they will walk it with You, knowing that they are not alone. I pray that they will have victory over every struggle and relief from every pain. I pray that they will have comfort in seasons of grief or sorrow. I pray that all the days of their life will be overwhelmingly filled with joy. My hope for them is that they will live a life that is happy, fulfilling, and full of love. I pray that they will feel love and give love. I pray that they will take advantage of all the experiences that this life has to offer. I pray You would protect them from physical harm. I pray that You would protect them from psychological danger. I pray that You will teach them to be strong and courageous. I pray that they would hear Your still, small voice and desire to respond. I pray that they will come to know their Creator, love Him, and love others. Father, for every newborn, I pray a blessing over them right now, as their lives are just beginning, that at the end, You will say to them, "Well done." Amen.

DAY 350

FOR THOSE WHO FEEL STUCK AND CAN'T MOVE FORWARD

Father, in the name of Jesus, I rebuke the chains that are making some people feel stuck. I ask You to break them right now so that they can move forward. For those who feel like they are stuck in a place or season and for those who feel like they are stuck in a situation that can't change, I pray that You would kindle in them the belief that anything is possible. If they are tired, give them renewed energy. If they are overwhelmed, please relieve the pressure. If they are in a cycle of anxiety, obsessing, or rumination, please help them channel that into action that helps them break the unhealthy patterns that are holding them in place. If they are so discouraged that they are accepting defeat, please encourage them by renewing their hope. Show them that You are at work in their situation even when they don't know how or when things will change. Give them a vision of the good things You have planned for their future and help them to be patient while also actively participating in preparing themselves for Your plans. Help them to challenge any feelings of being stuck that are not true and give them a right perspective of what is actually going on. Help them to accept the things they can't change and surrender those to You. Help them to address the things they can change, and as they move forward, please remind them that You are with them every step of the way. Encourage them to stay aligned with You and move at Your right pace, never running ahead or falling behind You. May they find contentment in knowing what matters is their willingness to keep moving forward, regardless of whether they are running, walking, or crawling. Please send them little signs along the way that You are proud of them. I pray that all those who feel stuck will feel unstuck very soon. In the name of Jesus, Amen.

DAY 351

FOR THOSE GOING THROUGH A DIVORCE

Father, today I pray for those couples who are going through a divorce. I don't know the reasons, but You know every event, choice, hurt and circumstance that led them to this place. I pray that You are with them in this season and directing them in the decisions they will make. I pray every decision is aligned with Your Will. If divorce is not part of the journey You have planned for them, please make a way for them to reconcile and stay married. Help them to work through whatever brought them to the brink of divorce and heal their relationship. But if divorce is what You allow in their situation, I pray that You would be with each of them. Help them to heal emotionally from whatever has happened so that they leave this marriage mentally healthy and strong. Help them to remember the love they had for each other in the beginning and understand the truth of whatever led to where they are now. Help them to forgive each other and themselves for anything they did to contribute to the breakdown of their union. Please help them to learn and grow from this in a way that will prepare them for the future. I pray that they would be fair and respectful to each other as they make decisions on how to separate the money and material possessions they accumulated during their marriage. I pray that Your Holy Spirit would be the mediator in their conversations so that the fruit of their communication with each other is peace. If there are children involved, I pray that You would help this couple to protected from being negatively affected. I pray they would guard their tongues when talking about each other, so the children are not put in a position of having to take sides. I pray that You would give them guidance in what to say, how to say it and when to say it. I pray that even though the marriage will end, their bond as a family will continue on. The reasons for a divorce can be complicated Lord, so I know that this prayer cannot cover every aspect of every couple's situation, so I end this prayer by asking You to address every nuance that this couple faces. Give them clarity of understanding and wisdom as they negotiate and make plans. Guide them and please prevent them from doing anything that will increase tension or conflict in their situation. If it is Your Will to allow them to divorce, please help them to do it in a way that produces peace, kindness, grace and love for one another. Even if that love isn't romantic anymore, I pray that they can love each other as people who they once were willing to spend their life with. Please use even their divorce as a n example of the power of Your Love. In the name of Jesus, Amen.

DAY 352

FOR THOSE WHO ARE RECOVERING FROM BEING BURNED

God of Mercy, I lift up to You today those who are recovering from being badly burned. I pray that You would give them access to all the medical care they need throughout the entire time it takes them to heal. I pray the healing of their skin and bodies would be quick; yet I know in some circumstances it may take weeks, months or years. During their rehabilitation, I ask that You grant them relief from this affliction. For those who need pain medications, I pray that they would give them relief and that You would guard them from becoming addicted to them. Please touch the dressings on their wounds, keep them clean and protect them from infection. I pray their scarring would be minimal. But for those who have a lot of scarring, I pray that You would help them make the right decision on what to do. For those who decide to have plastic surgery, I ask that the procedure would go well and that their recovery would be swift. For those who decide to accept the scarring, I pray that You would give them confidence in their appearance. I pray that others would not stare or ostracize them because of how they look. I pray that every person who has experienced severe burns would be able to live a full and happy life. I pray that not only their bodies, but also their minds would be healed from any trauma related to what they experienced. Father, please show Your care for those who are recovering from being burned in special ways that give them joy and hope that this experience cannot take away. In the name of Jesus, Amen.

DAY 353

FOR THOSE WHO ARE DEBILITATED BY THEIR EMOTIONS

Thank You for the complexity of human emotions Lord. Emotions are a part of how You designed us, so we know that they have a purpose; yet we can be overwhelmed by them and have a hard time managing them in a way that honors You. So, today I pray for those who are debilitated by their emotions. I lift up to You those whose emotions impair their ability to be who You have called them to be. I pray that whatever they feel, whether it's sadness, anger, fear, disappointment, confusion, anxiety, embarrassment, or shame, that You would touch their mind and help them to arrest every thought that has them stuck, going in circles, or is holding them back. Clear their minds Lord and help them to see past what they are feeling. Help them recognize the unhealthy or negative thoughts and give them the mental strength to fight them. Give them a right estimation of their situation and shine a light on the way forward. For those who may need a friend or a professional to help them process their emotions, I pray that You would bring them someone who will give them godly wisdom and speak truth to them in love. I pray that all those who are currently debilitated by their emotions would break free of what is holding them captive and learn healthy habits and coping skills so that they can keep moving forward and never find themselves in this situation again. In the name of Jesus, Amen.

DAY 354

FOR THOSE WHO HAVE EXPERIENCED VIOLENCE

For those who have experienced violence of any kind, I pray healing. Lord, You know exactly what happened and the effect it has had on them physically, mentally, emotionally. You know if they are still holding onto fear, anger, or pain. You know if the experience is something they will be able to move past quickly or if it is something that has changed the course of their life. I pray that You, our all-knowing Father, would be with each individual and bless them with what they need. If the violence was perpetrated upon them, You know what they need. If the violence was something they witnessed, You know what they need. Please bring healing to them in the places that are obvious to us and in the places within them that no one else can see. I wish that they never had to be exposed to this; yet You allowed it. I know You are God, so I will not question why. I will just ask You to bring some good out of what they have gone through and beg You to protect them from ever experiencing violence again. In the name of Jesus, Amen.

DAY 355

FOR YOUNG ADULTS

Today, Jesus, I pray for those who are transitioning from childhood to young adulthood. I pray for young adults all over the world as they take on new responsibilities and enter a new season of life. This experience is different depending on where they live, but I pray that as they are able to make decisions about their future, You would give them wisdom. I pray that they are able to gain the knowledge they need to make good decisions. Give them the self-awareness to identify what they don't know and seek out the advice or information they need. May the sources of information that they go to be truthful and trustworthy. Please guide them as they gain more independence and start living on their own, managing their own finances, and making their own decisions. Help them recognize when they make mistakes and show them how to move forward. I pray that every young adult grows into the adult that You designed them to be. I pray that they know You and draw closer into a personal relationship with You during this time of their life. I pray that they never feel that they are facing the challenges of life alone. I pray that they know You, Jesus, as their friend in times of joy and need. I pray they also have a strong support system of friends and family to help them along their journey. Amen.

DAY 356

FOR THOSE WHO ARE HAVING SURGERY OR A MEDICAL PROCEDURE

You God are The Great Physician. Even with all the medical advancements, knowledge and talented professionals here on Earth, we still need You. I pray for all those who are having a surgery or medical procedure today. I pray You would give them a sense of peace and relieve any worry or fear. I pray that they are well prepared and any arrangements for their recovery or aftercare have been taken care of. I pray they have a support system that they can rely on. I pray for the medical team who will be involved in this procedure. I pray that they are well rested and focused. I pray that they have a clear and correct understanding of what needs to be done and the best way to do it. I pray for the surgeons, nurses, anesthesiologists all other healthcare professionals that will be involved. Guide their hands and their minds so that they perform their role with excellence and care. I pray that everything goes smoothly and that there are no complications; yet if there are, I pray that You would guide their reactions and help them to still perform the surgery successfully. I pray that the patient feels a sense of calm during the procedure and that Your Holy Spirit would be with them in the room. For everyone who is having a surgery or medical procedure today, I pray that all would go well and that they would know You Father are with them through it all. In the name of Jesus, I pray, Amen.

DAY 357

PRAYER PROMPT
FOR YOUR SPOUSE OR SOMEONE ELSE'S

Father, today I pray for…

DAY 358

FOR MENTAL WELLNESS

Father God, for those who are struggling with their mental health, please be their strength. I pray that You would give them immediate and complete healing from this affliction; yet I know that this is not Your Will in all circumstances. For some, this is a temporary situational struggle that will end. For some, this is the thorn You have allowed to be placed in their side or the cross they must carry throughout their life. I wish this wasn't true, but Your Ways are above ours and I have to accept that You have Your reasons why. For those whose struggle is temporary, I pray that You would help them to overcome and work through what they are experiencing with the help of Your Holy Spirit, friends, family and therapy if necessary. I pray that You would touch their mind and make it well. And for those who You allow to experience a long-term mental health condition, I pray that You would give them the ability to live a full and healthy life in spite of it. May they receive the therapy, psychiatric care, or medication they need. Father, I lift up to You the mental health of our entire world. There are so many who are struggling because of so many different things. I pray that they would never feel alone or hopeless. I pray that they would not feel ashamed to seek help. I pray that You would fight their battles in the spiritual realm and give them relief. I pray for healthy minds, sound minds and minds that know Your Word and Your Truth, so that no matter the mental affliction, they are able to fight their way to a place of joy and hope that never fails. In the name of Jesus, Amen.

DAY 359

PRAYER PROMPT

FOR SOMEONE WHO HAS BEEN AN EXAMPLE OF CHRIST'S LOVE IN YOUR LIFE

Who has been a role model of the unconditional love of Jesus Christ in your life? No human is perfect, but there are those special people who have, through their words, behavior, or actions, been an example of Christ's love. Pick someone and praise God for them today. Use this space to journal about why you chose them or to write your prayer.

DAY 360

FOR THOSE WHO HAVE TO MAKE A CRITICAL DECISION TODAY TO HAVE WISDOM

Please, Lord, give wisdom to those who have to make a critical decision today. I pray that they know You and seek You in this process. I ask that You have given them openness and clearness of mind so that they can consider all perspectives, gain knowledge, and seek good counsel for advice. I pray that You give them a vision of the effects of their decision and the possible outcomes or consequences. Help them to weigh the pros and cons accurately and without bias. Remove any selfish desire from their heart so that the decision they make is what is best in Your eyes. Give them confidence in the right decision and help them remain steadfast in the face of any opposition that would attempt to push them to any path You have not laid out for them. If this decision is one that they have to make without answers to their key concerns, then I pray You would give them faith to trust the direction You are leading them in and an overwhelming sense of peace as they move in it. For all those who have to make a critical decision today, please give them wisdom that leads to the right decision. In the name of Jesus, Amen.

DAY 361

PRAYER PROMPT
FOR SOMEONE ELSE'S DREAMS AND GOALS

Father, I pray for…

DAY 362

FOR THOSE WHO WON'T LISTEN TO GOD

Thank You for free will. Thank You for allowing us to choose to love You, to choose to listen to You. I thank You for this freedom, yet today, I pray for all those who won't listen to You. I include myself in this prayer because I know that I don't always listen to You. So, I don't want to come before You as a hypocrite and not acknowledge my own disobedience. Please forgive me and hear my prayer. Please help all of us who don't listen to You, those who know You and choose at times not to listen, and those who don't know You as Lord who You are talking to but can't hear. I pray that all our ears would be opened to hear You clearly. I pray that our minds will not be so cluttered with the noise of this world that we are distracted from Your voice. I pray that our hearts will not be so hardened that we think we don't need to respond to what You say with our actions. I ask Your forgiveness on behalf of all of us who ignore You. I thank You for the grace You show us that is undeserved. I pray for those whose hearts are so hardened towards You that they can't hear You speaking or that they think it is something else and give credit to idols or themselves. Breakthrough to us all, Father. We need to hear You. Give courage to those who try to listen, to help others recognize Your voice for themselves. When we do listen, may we give You the glory and be a shining example that inspires others to listen for Your voice as well. Father, I ask all this in the name of Your Son, Jesus, Amen.

DAY 363

FOR PEOPLE TO GROW IN THE SPIRIT

Oh, Holy Spirit, thank You for dwelling in us. Thank You for working through us and showing us the way to live life. I pray that everyone would come to know You and feel You in their spirit. For those who know You now, I pray that they would never take You for granted, instead challenging themselves to grow and produce more of the fruit described in Galatians 5:22-23. I pray that all people will develop the practice of self-control. That we would all be better at controlling our behavior, our habits, our actions, and our tongues. I pray that all people would develop more empathy and thoughtfulness that results in gentleness toward each other. I pray that all people would be compassionate and intentional about not causing others harm so that we interact with gentleness even in times of conflict. I pray that all people would rid themselves of evil and hate so that we produce goodness and can recognize the goodness of each other. I pray that all people would cultivate the ability to bear with one another in love so that we can give each other the gift of patience. I pray that all people would feel a spring of hope deep down inside that would help them navigate life with joy, even when they are not happy. I pray that every person will know Jesus and His Peace. Not only for themselves but so that they are inspired to be peacemakers in this world. And I pray that all people would develop trust in You, God, that leads to an understanding of Your love and faithfulness towards them, resulting in their sharing that love and faith with others. Amen.

DAY 364

FOR THOSE GOING THROUGH PHYSICAL THERAPY

Father, thank You for the physical therapists who provide care to those who desire to restore or maintain their mobility or find relief from pain. I pray today for all those who are currently going through physical therapy. Father, please give the therapists wisdom and insight into what each person needs. Please help them to develop a good repour with their patients, so that they work as a team to accomplish the goals of their care. Please give the patients the mental strength and courage to overcome the health obstacles they face. Give them determination and prevent them from becoming discouraged. Give them discernment about what they are able to do and help them communicate any pain, stiffness, or discomfort to their therapist. Help them to trust their therapist and safely push through any discomfort when appropriate. I pray that through the process of physical therapy, they are able to maximize their mobility, improve their physical function, and find ways to manage any chronic pain. May physical therapy improve their overall health and be a benefit to their quality of life. In the name of Jesus, Amen.

DAY 365

PRAYER PROMPT
FOR 365 DAYS YOU HAVE PRAYED FOR OTHERS

Now, take a moment to reflect on your journey of intercessory prayer. Use this space to record how prioritizing praying for others has impacted you, and write a prayer to thank God for the power of and ability to intercede on behalf of others.

TOPIC INDEX

ADDICTIONS

Food	22
Shopping	44
Smoking	161
Substance Abuse	51

CHILDREN

Adopted	269
Being Bullied	176
Computer Access	45
Daughters	48
Foster Children	296
High School Students	385
Homelessness	3
Incarcerated Parents	94
Juvenile Detention	68
Knowing Christ	55
Making Friends	225
Neglected	354
Newborns	397
Only Children	358
Orphans	123
Separation or Divorce	335

Social Media	111
Someone Else's Child	351
Sons	65
Special Needs	362
Substance Abuse	345
Teenagers	342
Trying Out for a Team	301
Unborn	347
Upcoming Exam	371
Young Adults	404

CHURCH

A Pastor	297
Foreign	112
Missionaries	213
Open Hearted Believers	12
Pastors Preaching	211
Prayer Warriors	2
Unity	326
Your Church	69

EARTH

Birds	271
Earthquakes	119
Environment	299
Floods	209
Hurricane	338

National Parks	46
Natural Disasters	370
Natural Resources	71
Sea Animals	121
Shelter Animals	294
Storms	33
Stray Animals	144
Tornado	272
Wild Animals	337

EDUCATION

Adult Students	124
Applying to School	136
Bible Teachers	270
GED	200
Graduating	183
Learning a Language	31
PhD	173
Schools	72
Starting College	5
Struggling in School	275
Students in Your Area	152

FAITH

Atheists	73
Bible Study	336
Blind to The Truth	232

Christ's Love	409
Don't Know Jesus	276
Intimacy with God	184
Friend Who Doesn't Know Christ	168
God-confidence	105
God's Assignment	235
God Showed Up	364
Growth	96
Growing in the Spirit	415
Hard Time Praying	6
Hardened Hearts	126
Hunger for God's Word	122
Idolatry	74
Listening to God	414
Mad at God	98
Miracle	198
Opened Heart	300
Personal Relationship with God	355
Salvation	181
Searching for God	47
Seeing God in Creation	179
Spiritual Growth	340
Spiritual Warfare	129
Struggling with Faith	236

FAMILY

Caring for Parents	75
Estranged Family	13
Estranged Siblings	233
Grandparents	170
Hard Decisions	185
Not Treated Well	191
Peace Inside Homes	292
Pets	214
Quality Time	7
Raising a Family Member's Child	118
Siblings	375
Unity	97

FINANCES

Artists	278
Car Payments	49
Debt	99
Dreams	76
Great Wealth	217
No Savings	325
School Tuition	389
Rent or Mortgage	186
Retirement	240
Security	66
Stewardship	346
Stolen Identity	8

Taxes   234

GRIEF

Death of a Father   77

Death of a Mother   9

Death of a Child   100

Died in War   279

Family   237

Mass Shooting   43

Mourning   50

Police Violence   187

Senseless Tragedies   16

HEALTH + WELLNESS

Abortion   222

Appearance   377

ADHD   101

Back Surgery   24

Bipolar   78

Bitterness   247

Burned   401

Cancer   302

Chronic Illness or Pain   241

Clean Water   246

Crushed in Spirit   190

Dementia or Alzheimer's   382

Depression   218

Despair	376
Distractions	83
Emotions	402
Endometriosis Pain	280
Eyesight	84
Feeling Stuck	398
Gaining Weight	295
Giving Up	79
Health Insurance	11
Health of Pets	380
Hearing	91
Heavy Situations	103
Hospice	82
Hospital	219
In Treatment Program	268
Lonely	193
Mastectomy	159
Menopause	137
Mental Wellness	408
No Diagnosis	67
Physical Therapy	416
Police Officers who have been shot	26
Politicians Protection	261
PTSD	160
Recent Diagnosis	239

Schizophrenia	194
Self-worth	163
Sexual Assault	281
Struggling with a Decision	1
Suicidal Thoughts	115
Surgery	405
Tired	162
Trauma	383
Uncertainty	81
Violent Thoughts	196
Weariness	363
Weight Loss	102
Work Life Harmony	164
Worrying Friend	372

MARRIAGE

A Couple	220
Cheating Spouses	145
Considering Divorce	285
Considering Marriage	357
Divorcing	399
Divorced	243
Emotional Intimacy	391
Engaged	384
Husbands	86
Jealous of Marriage	288

Lonely Spouses	195
Marriages	54
Marriage Counseling	368
Separated	378
Sexual Intimacy	303
Spouses	406
Widows and Widowers	350
Wives	104
Wives of Pastors	274

PARENTHOOD

Adopting	34
Adoptive Parents	197
Adult Children	166
Advocating for Children	374
Fathers of Young Children	283
Infertility	140
Miscarriage	329
Mothers of Young Children	367
New Parents	138
Parent Child Relationships	146
Pregnant Women	379
Single Parents	392
Surrogates	57
Trying to Conceive	88

PEOPLE + LIFE

Abusers	348
Being Lied About	330
Breakthrough	277
Buying a New Home	252
Car Accident	23
Car Trouble	250
Caregivers	63
Celebrity	60
Committing a Crime	202
Court Battle	258
Decisions	411
Deployed	353
Dreams and Goals	412
Electricity	312
Ethnic Heritage	41
Evil	259
Falsely Imprisoned	245
Hard to Love	286
Hate Groups	30
Heating and Air Conditioning	201
Human Trafficking	208
Homelessness	290
Internet Access	21
Last Person You Saw	254
Learning Disabilities	188

Liars	17
Moving	206
Natural Disaster, Electricity Loss	95
Needs	331
Prison	32
Public Transit	328
Purpose	125
Racism	349
Refugees	128
Resisting Temptation	177
Scared to Go After Dreams	228
Scripture Over Someone	230
Season of Change	25
Seeking Direction	182
Single and Happy	139
Social Media	253
Someone New	395
Support System	256
Traveling	311
Unexpected Responsibilities	151
Unjustly Accused	320
Unknowingly Pregnant	359
Victim of a Crime	356
Violence	403
Waiting for Justice	323

| Without Food | 29 |

RELATIONSHIPS

Abusive Relationships	80
Childhood Friend	106
Co-Workers in Conflict	58
Dating	165
Encourager	317
Forgiveness	85
Friend	35
Friendship Betrayal	157
Friendship Broken	304
Friendships Growing Apart	56
Hurt Feelings	89
Lost Hope Finding Love	366
No Friends	333
Romantic Breakup	360
Someone Who Prayed for You	142

WORK

Actors	28
Airline Industry	27
Armed Forces	14
Artists	108
Athletes	158
Closing a Business	59
Coast Guard	64

Construction Workers	15
Creatives	244
Daycare Service Providers	127
Delivery	305
Dentists	282
Doctors	147
Employed	361
Entertainment Industry	37
Entrepreneurs	167
Factory Workers	38
Farmers	141
Fire Fighters	109
Fired	135
Firing Someone	110
For God's Glory	189
Freight Logistics	242
Gardeners	227
Government Guards	229
Grocery Store	226
Health Care Workers	155
Homemakers	172
Human Resources Professionals	192
IRS	156
Job Interviews	148
Journalists and Reporters	92

Judges	207
Lawyers	178
Managing Others	267
Marriage Counselors	216
Medical Researchers	262
Mechanics	215
Mental Health Professionals	224
Multiple Jobs	223
Musicians	319
Non-Profit	284
Nurses	324
Nursing Home	260
Ophthalmologists	321
Payroll	117
Police Officers	180
Politicians	20
Post Office	251
Productivity	343
Public Utilities	307
Retail	327
Sanitation Workers	116
School Safety Officers	344
Security Guards	334
Shelters	266
Singer or Group	393

Social Workers	174
Space Program	315
Starting a Business	248
Taxi Drivers	10
Teachers	249
Technology	310
Truck Drivers	257
Underemployed or Unappreciated	175
Unemployed	130
Valet and Parking	289
Veterans	263
Veterinarians	293
Wedding Coordinators	131
Writers	18

WORLD

City	308
Fires	4
Famine	154
Food Insecurity	133
Generosity	265
Kindness	132
Local Community	322
Love	205
Pandemics	52
Peace	19

Peacemakers	264
People of Another Country	387
Political Party	313
Presidents	150
Technology	203
Terrorism	40
USA	134
War	149

ABOUT THE AUTHOR

Jamila Jackson, the Chief Encouragement Officer of loved+blessed®, combines her diverse expertise to empower individuals in both their personal and professional lives. Holding a psychology degree from the University of Southern California and manufacturing management credentials from the Fashion Institute of Design & Merchandising, she draws from over 30 years of experience in product development and people management. Her roles have spanned from being a Vice President of Culture and Talent Development to buyer, sourcing manager, director of client services, and designer to a creative director for renowned fashion, homeware, travel, entertainment, and beauty brands.

Jamila's journey took an unexpected turn when she transformed her longing for motherhood, despite infertility challenges, into founding lovedandblessed.com. This platform harnesses her talents, offering care packages and fostering community.

Her message of encouragement resonates as a beacon of hope, inspiring others to embrace life's joys and navigate challenges. Residing in Southern California, her favorite place to be is anywhere with her husband, cherished fur child, and a large order of fries.

www.lovedandblessed.com

www.ingramcontent.com/pod-product-compliance
Lightning Source LLC
Chambersburg PA
CBHW060546080526
44585CB00013B/458